东亚峰会框架下的高等教育合作

HIGHER EDUCATION COOPERATION WITHIN THE EAST ASIA SUMMIT FRAMEWORK

主　编　张秀琴　何天淳

Editors-in-Chief: Zhang Xiuqin & He Tianchun

云南大学出版社

YUNNAN UNIVERSITY PRESS

图书在版编目 (CIP) 数据

东亚峰会框架下的高等教育合作 / 张秀琴，何天淳主编. — 昆明 ：云南大学出版社，2010
ISBN 978-7-5482-0331-5

Ⅰ. ①东… Ⅱ. ①张… ②何… Ⅲ. ①高等教育 — 国际合作 — 研究 —东亚 Ⅳ. ①G649.31

中国版本图书馆CIP数据核字（2010）第260183号

东亚峰会框架下的高等教育合作

主编 张秀琴 何天淳

责任编辑： 蔡红华 刘 焰
装帧设计： 丁群亚
出版发行： 云南大学出版社
印　　装： 昆明市五华区教育委员会印刷厂
开　　本： 787mm×1092mm 1/16
印　　张： 21.25
字　　数： 317
印　　数： 2000
版　　次： 2011年4月第1版
印　　次： 2011年4月第1次印刷
书　　号： ISBN 978-7-5482-0331-5
定　　价： 55.00元
地　　址： 昆明市翠湖北路2号云南大学英华园内（650091）
电　　话：（0871）5031070/5033244
网　　址： http//www.ynup.com.
E-mail: market@ynup.com

中华人民共和国国务院

贺信

值此“东亚峰会高等教育合作论坛”在春城昆明开幕之际，我谨代表中华人民共和国政府向本次论坛的举办致以热烈祝贺！对莅临论坛的各国教育官员、大学校长和朋友们表示诚挚欢迎！

东亚是世界经济发展最具活力和潜力的地区之一，随着东亚地区经济一体化进程的加速发展，东亚各国的联系进一步得到加强，教育交流已成为成员国之间最活跃的合作领域之一。

我相信，借助“东亚峰会高等教育合作论坛”这个平台，共同探讨东亚峰会框架下在高等教育领域的合作前景和有效途径，必将能够增进东亚各国相互了解和友谊，推动区域间的教育交流和合作。希望各位朋友充分利用本次论坛，广泛沟通交流，深化合作内涵，努力开创携手共进、互利共赢的新局面。

预祝本次“东亚峰会高等教育合作论坛”取得圆满成功！

中华人民共和国国务委员

刘延东

二〇一〇年九月

On the occasion of the opening of "the East Asia Summit Higher Education Cooperation Forum" in Kunming, the City of Eternal Spring, I would like to, on behalf of the Chinese government, offer my warm congratulations on the successful convening of the Forum and extend my heartfelt welcome to the education officials, university rectors and friends from East Asian countries to attend the Forum.

East Asia is one of the regions with the greatest vitality and potential in the world economy. As economic integration in East Asia speeds up, ties among East Asian countries are further strengthened, and education has become one of the most vibrant areas in regional exchanges and cooperation.

I am sure that, with "the East Asia Summit Higher Education Cooperation Forum" as a platform, discussions on the prospects and effective methods of cooperation in higher education within the East Asia Summit framework will surely enhance understanding and friendship among East Asian countries, and will practically promote regional exchanges and cooperation in education. It is hoped that all the friends make the best use of this platform to fully exchange views and further our cooperation, and then work hard to open up a new phase by developing hand in hand for our mutual benefits and win-win results.

I wish the "the East Asia Summit Higher Education Cooperation Forum" a complete success!

Liu Yandong
State Councilor,PRC
September 2010

中国教育部副部长王立英在开幕式上宣读国务委员刘延东贺信
Mme. Wang Liying, Vice Minister, Ministry of Education of PRC, reading State Councilor Mme. Liu Yandong's Letter of Congratulations

云南省副省长李江致辞
Mme. Li Jiang, Vice Governor of Yunnan Province, delivering a speech

澳大利亚教育、就业和劳资关系部副部长凯瑟琳·坎贝尔致辞

Mme. Kathryn Campbell, Deputy Secretary, Department of Education, Employment and Workplace Relations, Australia, delivering a speech

中国教育部国际合作与交流司司长张秀琴主持“东亚峰会高等教育合作论坛”开幕式

Ms. Zhang Xiuqin, Director General, Department of International Cooperation and Exchanges, Ministry of Education of PRC, chairing the Opening Ceremony

“东亚峰会高等教育合作论坛”会场

Plenary Venue

中国教育部副部长王立英、云南省人民政府副省长李江、云南省政协副主席罗黎辉与部分参会代表合影

Mme. Wang Liying, Vice Minister, Ministry of Education of PRC, Mme. Li Jiang, Vice Governor of the People’s Government of Yunnan, Mr. Luo Lihui, Vice Chairman of Yunnan People’s Consultative Congress, and other participants

开幕式暖场演出

Opening Show

“东亚峰会高等教育合作论坛”全体参会代表合影

Group Photo of Participants

序　言

为落实温家宝总理在第四届东亚峰会上的倡议，中国教育部和云南省政府于2010年10月14日至15日在昆明成功举办了“东亚峰会高等教育合作论坛”。东亚峰会15个成员国的教育官员、大学校长等150余人参加了论坛。中央政治局委员、国务委员刘延东亲自发来贺信，盛赞论坛的开创之举，祝贺论坛的成功召开。

高等教育是人才培养的高地，是科研创新的摇篮，是科技进步的孵化器。高等教育承担着培养高级专门人才、发展科学技术文化、促进现代化建设的重大任务。高等教育事业的发展，在某种程度上决定着一个国家、一个地区的经济增长方式和经济结构调整。东亚是世界经济发展最具活力和潜力的地区之一，近年来，东亚各国经贸往来的日益密切，人文交流的日益紧密，既为各国在高等教育领域开展交流与合作创造了有利条件，又提出了迫切需求。

中国和东亚峰会各成员国都高度认识到高等教育的重要性。中国首倡各成员国应加强在高等教育领域的交流与合作，提出举办“东亚峰会高等教育合作论坛”，论坛上各国代表充分交流，畅所欲言，就如何加强东亚各国高等教育的交流与合作，相互取长补短，最终实现互利共赢的目标发表了深刻的见解，提出了切实可行的行动建议，各方受益匪浅。在论坛顺利闭幕之际，我们将与会代表的演讲稿和部分论文集结出版，以记录各位代表的精彩发言，定格论坛的精彩瞬间，延续论坛的积极影响。

让我们以本论坛为起点，以这本文集为见证，共同努力，携手共进，努力提高东亚各国的高等教育水平，促进东亚区域高等教育交流与合作，实现东亚区域的高水平发展。

中华人民共和国教育部副部长

2011年1月

Foreword

In an active response to a proposal made by Premier Wen Jiabao at the 4th East Asia Summit, the Ministry of Education and the People's Government of Yunnan Province jointly hosted the "East Asia Summit Higher Education Cooperation Forum" on October 14~15th, 2010. More than 150 education officials and university presidents from 15 EAS countries attended the forum.Mme. Liu Yandong, CPC Central Committee Polibureau member and State Councilor, commended the forum as a ground-breaking event in her letter to the hosts and congratulated on the successful opening of the Forum.

Higher education provides a vantage point for human resource training; it is the cradle for scientific innovations and an incubator for scientific advances. Higher education is committed to producing top-notch professionals, enhancing science and culture, and promoting modern development. Higher education development impacts the economic growth model and economic structure adjustment of a country or region. East Asia is one of the regions that abound in business development momentum and potentials. Closer economic and cultural relations have been forged among East Asian countries in the past few years. This has created advantages as well as imperative needs for higher education cooperation among these countries.

China and other EAS countries are fully aware of the importance of higher education cooperation. China proactively advocates higher education cooperation and took initiative to host the "East Asia Summit Higher Education Cooperation Forum" where the participants shared their ideas and insights and proposed practical actions on how to promote higher education cooperation among East Asian countries, how to benefit from one another' s advantages in a complementary way, and how to achieve common goals in a win-win manner. As the forum closed successfully, we have decided to publish a selection of the papers presented at or submitted to the Forum to share ideas of the authorsand speakers record the inspiring moments of the Forum, and promote the impacts of the Forum.

With this Forum being a starting point and this collection being an evidence of our efforts, let us work together to promote East Asian countries' higher education cause, promote higher education cooperation in East Asia, and promote rapid progresses in East Asia.

Hao Ping
Vice Minister, Ministry of Education, PRC
January 2011

目 录

第一部分 开幕式致辞

第二部分 教育官员发言

第三部分　大学校长发言

第四部分　专题论文

第五部分　论坛成果

第六部分　媒体报道

Contents

Section Ⅰ: Opening Speeches

Section Ⅱ: Speeches by Education Officials

Section Ⅲ: Speeches by University Administrators

Section Ⅳ: Papers

Section Ⅴ: Achievements of the Forum

Section Ⅵ: Media Coverage of the Forum

第一部分　开幕式致辞

Section I: Opening Speeches

积极务实推进东亚峰会
成员国间高等教育交流与合作

中华人民共和国教育部副部长　王立英

尊敬的云南省委常委、副省长李江女士，

各位中外嘉宾，

女士们、先生们：

在这繁花似锦的金秋十月，我们相聚春城昆明，共商东亚高等教育合作大计，我谨代表中国教育部，对莅临本次论坛的东亚峰会各成员国教育官员、大学校长和朋友们表示热烈的欢迎！

“东亚峰会高等教育合作论坛”是由温家宝总理2009年10月在“第四届东亚峰会”倡议召开的，主要目的是沟通交流各国在东亚峰会框架下开展教育交流与合作的政策性倾向与计划。中国政府高度重视本届论坛，国务委员刘延东女士特地发来贺信，下面，请允许我宣读她的贺信。

值此“东亚峰会高等教育合作论坛”在春城昆明开幕之际，我谨代表中华人民共和国政府向本次论坛的举办致以热烈祝贺！对莅临论坛的各国教育官员、大学校长和朋友们表示诚挚欢迎！

东亚是世界经济发展最具活力和潜力的地区之一，随着东亚地区经济一体化进程的加速发展，东亚各国的联系进一步得到加强，教育交流已成为成员国之间最活跃的合作领域之一。

我相信，借助“东亚峰会高等教育合作论坛”这个平台，共同探讨东亚峰会框架下在高等教育领域的合作前景和有效途径，必将能够增进东亚各国相互了解和友谊，推动区域间的教育交流和合作。希望各位朋友充分利用本次论坛，广泛沟通交流，深化合作内涵，努力开创携手共进、互利共赢的新局面。

预祝本次“东亚峰会高等教育合作论坛”取得圆满成功！

女士们，先生们：教育交流作为人文交流的重要组成部分，是东亚峰会成员国之间互联互通、携手合作的重要载体，将发挥着基础性、先导性、广泛性和持久性作用，对于增进成员国之间的相互信任至关重要。东亚峰会成员国由于国情不同，文化不同，高等教育也各有所长，在很多方面可以相互学习、交流、借鉴。同样，各国在高等教育领域也面临着共同的问题和挑战。

新中国成立特别是改革开放以来，中国政府始终把教育放在优先发展的战略位置。近期，中国政府对外公布了《国家中长期教育改革发展规划纲要（2010—2020 年）》（以下简称《纲要》），这是中国进入 21 世纪以来第一个中长期规划纲要。对未来 10 年中国的教育发展提出了宏伟目标，加快从教育大国向教育强国迈进、从人力资源大国向人力资源强国迈进。《纲要》制定了规划目标，到 2020 年，中国要进一步提高高等教育大众化水平，毛入学率由目前的 24.2% 提高到 40%；主要劳动年龄人口中受过高等教育的比例达到 20%，具有高等教育文化程度的人数比 2009 年翻一番。《纲要》还就中国如何提高高等教育的质量、提高人才培养质量、提升科学研究水平、增强社会服务能力和促进高校办出特色等方面提出了具体要求和改革目标。

女士们，先生们：21 世纪是一个开放性、竞争性和高效性的新世纪，中国与东亚峰会其他成员国面临着同样的机遇和挑战。中国政府已将全方位、高层次地进行教育国际合作与交流，扩大教育对外开放、加强国际合作与交流作为国家教育战略的关键环节。中国政府愿意与东亚峰会其他成员国在高等教育领域共同开创新理念，迎接新挑战，探索合作共赢之路。为此，我提出以下几点倡议：

一是进一步拓展东亚峰会成员国之间开展多边合作对话的有效平台，完善交流与合作机制，加强教育高层对话，共同研究和推动中国与东亚峰会其他成员国教育的战略性合作。

二是进一步扩大东亚峰会成员国之间互派留学生规模，希望大家共同努力，从长远角度和战略高度对计划进行规划和设计，重点进行高端人才交流和培养。

三是进一步推进东亚峰会成员国高校之间的学分转移和互认，增进学术交流与科研合作，鼓励中国与东亚峰会其他成员国大学建立全面、务实的教育合作关系。

四是进一步加强青年学生之间的语言、文化和体育交流，以增强相互理解，发展人民的友谊，促进睦邻友好关系，为本地区乃至世界的和平与发展作出贡献。

女士们，先生们：本次“东亚峰会高等教育论坛”是东亚峰会成员国开展多边教育合作对话的有效平台，希望各国教育官员和大学校长能够围绕“东亚峰会框架下的高等教育合作与发展”的主题，以更加积极的姿态和更加务实的行动推进彼此间的友好交流与合作。相信本次论坛将对东亚峰会成员国教育的改革与发展产生积极的影响，为本区域经济建设和社会发展作出积极的贡献。

预祝“东亚峰会高等教育论坛”取得圆满成功！预祝东亚峰会成员国之间的教育合作有更加广阔的前景！

王立英简历

1971—1974 年，云南生产建设兵团西双版纳景洪农场知青、团支部书记。

1974—1978 年，云南合成树脂厂团支部书记、车间党支部书记。

1978—1979 年，参加共青团“十大”组织组筹备工作。

1979—1984 年，团中央组织部组织处干部。

1984—1986 年，中国青年政治学院大专班学生。

1986—1991 年，团中央组织部干部一处主任科员、副处长。

1991—1993 年，团中央组织部干部一处处长。

1993—1998 年，团中央组织部副部长。

1998—1999 年，团中央机关党委常务副书记兼组织部副部长。

1999—2001 年，中宣部干部局副局长。

2001—2005 年，中宣部干部局局长。

2005—2008 年，中纪委、监察部驻新闻出版总署纪检组长、党组成员。

2008 年至今，中纪委、监察部驻教育部纪检组长、党组成员。

发挥优势　共赢合作

云南省省委常委、副省长　李　江

尊敬的教育部副部长王立英女士，

尊敬的各位来宾，

女士们、先生们：

大家早上好！

金秋十月，欢迎大家来到美丽的云南，聚集昆明，共同探讨东亚峰会各成员国之间高等教育的前景和未来。在此我代表中共云南省委、云南省人民政府，对东亚峰会高等教育合作论坛的成功开幕，表示热烈的祝贺！也向远道而来的各位嘉宾表示诚挚的欢迎和良好的祝愿！

教育，是一个国家和民族发展振兴的基石，加强国际间教育的交流与合作，是增进理解、提升认同、合作共赢的重要基础。通过圆桌会议、教育论坛、学术研讨等活动，探讨教育交流合作的新方式、新途径，必将对丰富教育合作的内涵、提升合作的层次与质量，推进人文交流产生重要的影响。

云南是中国西南的一个边疆省份，国土面积有 39 万平方公里，与缅甸、老挝、越南三国接壤。加强与东南亚、南亚的交流与合作，不断地拓展对外开放的广度和深度，是我们云南的一项长期的任务。

近年来，云南成功举办了“中国昆明出口商品交易会”、“国际南亚国家商品展”、“大湄公河次区域经济合作走廊活动周”、“南亚商务论坛”等重大经贸活动，极大地推进了云南省与东南亚、南亚地区的经贸合作。随着昆明通达缅甸、老挝和越南的高等级国际公路和起于新加坡止于云南的泛亚铁路的建成，将使中国与东盟各国从交通运输上紧密地联为一体，为双方深化交流与合作奠定更好的基础。优越的地理位置使云南省与东亚峰会各国的交流与合作具备了得天独厚的便利条件。

2009 年 7 月，胡锦涛总书记视察云南时提出，要把云南建设成为中国面向西南开放的重要桥头堡。2009 年 12 月，中共云南省委八届八次会议提出了建设经济强省、民族文化强省和中国面向西南开放的桥头堡的战略目标，基本扫除青壮年文盲的历史性任务开辟了更广阔的空间。未来发展，关键靠人才，基础在教育。当前，云南省正积极地实施“科教兴滇”和“人才强省”战略，现在已经完成了普及九年义务教育，高中教育的毛入学率已经达到了 58.6%。普通高中和中等职业学校的学生比例达到了 1∶0.29，高等教育毛入学率达到了 17.57%。云南省历来高度重视高等教育的改革和发展。教育的发展为解决保持快速增长和社会的全面进步提供了有利云南省的支撑。

2008 年以来，我们实施积极的教育基础设施建设、重点学科建设、科研平台建设、高水平教师队伍的建设，深化办学体制改革、管理体制改革、教育教学改革、后勤社会化改革，加快推进国际化发展的步伐。目前，全省高校已经与 50 个国家、地区和国际组织建立了教育的合作关系，赴滇的留学人数已经达到了 1.5 万人。留学生中 60% 以上来自东盟国家。云南省已成为中国吸纳东盟国家留学生最多的一个地区。同时，云南省在国外已经建立了 7 所孔子学院，省内高校普遍开设有东南亚语种专业教育，在学人数突破了 1 万人。

此次“东亚峰会高等教育合作论坛”在云南成功举办，既是落实东亚领导人峰会的一项重要举措，也是促进东亚峰会成员国之间教育、合作、交流的重要途径。必将在更广阔的区域范围内促进教育互补协作、资源共享，推动教育事业不断向前发展。衷心地希望各位嘉宾对云南的教育发展提出宝贵的意见和建议。

女士们，先生们，深化教育交流是推动东亚峰会成员国友好事业持续发展，增进人民友谊的纽带。云南省非常愿意在互惠互利的前提下，进一步加强与东亚峰会各国、各地区在教育、文化、经贸等方面的交流与合作，建立更加密切的关系，促进共同发展。

最后，预祝会议圆满成功，祝各位嘉宾在昆明度过一段愉快而美好的时光！

谢谢大家！

李江简历

1973 年 12 月—1976 年 1 月，云南省会泽县待补公社知青。

1976 年 6 月—1978 年 2 月，云南省会泽县铅锌矿一车间工作。

1978 年 2 月—1982 年 2 月，昆明工学院冶金系炼钢专业学习。

1982 年 2 月—1983 年 2 月，湖南中南工业大学进修。

1983 年 2 月—1986 年 1 月，昆明工学院团委干事、副书记。

1986 年 1 月—1990 年 7 月，昆明工学院团委书记。

1990 年 7 月—1996 年 4 月，共青团云南省委副书记。

1996 年 4 月—1999 年 10 月，共青团云南省委书记。

1999 年 10 月—2000 年 2 月，云南省玉溪市委副书记、副市长。

2000 年 2 月—2001 年 2 月，云南省玉溪市委副书记、市长。

2001 年 2 月—2003 年 2 月，云南省玉溪市委书记。

2003 年 2 月—2008 年 1 月，云南省委常委、组织部部长。

2008 年 1 月—2008 年 3 月，云南省委常委、副省长，省委组织部部长，省政府党组成员。

2008 年 3 月至今，云南省委常委、副省长，省政府党组成员。

加强区域教育合作，推动区域发展

澳大利亚教育、就业和劳资关系部副部长　凯瑟琳·坎贝尔

中华人民共和国教育部王立英副部长，
云南省李江副省长，
云南大学何天淳校长，
各位尊敬的来宾，
女士们、先生们：

今天能在这里与大家齐聚一堂，我感到无比荣幸。

在此，允许我对“东亚峰会高等教育合作论坛”的主办方表示热烈的祝贺！

中华人民共和国教育部和云南省政府主办这样一次论坛非常好，也非常及时。

这次论坛是东亚区域高等教育合作的一次盛会。东亚区域人口占全球总人口的50%，是全球经济最具活力的一个区域，也是很多领域在全球极具优势的一个区域。

我认为这次论坛在中国举办非常合适，因为中国是一个正在崛起的教育大国，而昆明是中国西南部重要的教育城市，这里有12所高校和300余所科研机构。

中国成功地树立了从派出学生赴外留学大国转变为接收外国学生大国的典范。这不仅展示了中国教育交流的成功和教育质量的提高，同时也说明，中国的教育在应对世界市场发展和需要方面做得很成功。

教育的交流与合作能够提高我们的应变和反应能力，有助于我们这

个区域的经济与社会发展，有助于我们应对突如其来的挑战。

一、亚太区域影响力增强

在过去的10年中，全球教育和研究活动的重心已逐步转移到亚太区域。

1999年世界拥有高等教育学生人数最多的区域是西欧和北美——这两个区域共有2600万名高校学生，而当时的亚太区域只有2100万名高校学生。

到2007年，这种形势就发生了根本的转变：亚太区域高校学生人数迅速增加至6400万，一跃成为世界最大的高等教育区域。相比之下西欧和北美的高校学生人数仅增至3000万。

同时，亚太地区在学术研究方面也扮演着越来越重要的角色。例如，亚太区域在世界领先的学术期刊上发表的论文数量大幅度增长。

近年来，大多数发达国家在学术期刊上发表论文的增长率每年约为2%，而中国却以16.5%的速度增长，韩国的增长率是14.1%，新加坡的增长率是10.5%。

二、结　论

日益增长的教育供给、研究与创新产出都是为社会带来极大效用的公共物品。

教育与创新对国家及区域的发展至关重要。

教育可以改善人力资源，推动技术进步，提升管理技术。

作为一个服务产业占据很大比重的经济体，澳大利亚有实例表明，全国总增长的44%来自教育。

国际教育交流不仅使直接参与的学生和教育机构获益，也使教育输出和输入国的教育体系受益。教育交流可以改进教育输出国和输入国的教育质量、管理规则以及学历互认。

教育交流可以促进技术传输、扩大贸易和投资。学术联系与知识联系是增进人与人之间文化交流、相互理解的桥梁。

这次论坛将进一步加强高等教育合作的对话。我看到在座的各位很多都是和我们一样从很远的地方来的。我感谢你们不辞辛劳前来参加论坛，希望在接下来的两天中能与各位充分地交流思想和经验。

我预祝本次论坛取得丰硕的成果，谢谢各位！

（郑蔚　译）

凯瑟琳·坎贝尔英文发言稿

Cooperation and Development of Higher Education Under the East Asia Summit (10+6) Framework

Kathryn Campbell

Deputy Secretary, Department of Education, Employment and Workplace Relations, Australia

Ms. Wang Liying, Vice-Minister of Education, People's Republic of China,
Ms. Li Jiang, Vice Governor of Yunnan Province,
Mr. He Tianchun, Yunnan University,
Delegates and observers,
ladies and gentlemen,

It gives me great pleasure to have the opportunity to welcome you here today.

I would like to congratulate the organizers on hosting the East Asia Summit Higher Education Cooperation Forum.

This Forum is an excellent and timely initiative on the part of China's Ministry of Education and the Department of Education of Yunnan Province.

The East Asia Summit, or EAS, is a fantastic forum for education cooperation. The EAS grouping is home to almost 50 per cent of the world's population and contains many dynamic and robust economies with complementary areas of strength and expertise.

It is fitting that these discussions take place in China—an emerging education powerhouse—and moreover, in Kunming, the major centre for education in China's south-west and home to 12 universities and colleges and over 300 scientific research institutions.

China is an excellent example of how countries that have a history of sending students offshore for education can transform themselves into major destinations for international students in their own right. This demonstrates not only the success of education exchange in building capacity, but also that education is highly dynamic and responsive to emerging needs and developments.

Fostering that flexibility and responsiveness through exchange and cooperation will enhance the economic and social development of our region and our ability to meet unforeseen challenges.

The growing role of the Asia Pacific

During the last decade, the balance of global educational and research activity has moved steadily to the Asia Pacific region.

In 1999, the world's largest tertiary student population base was 26 million in Western Europe and North America, compared to 21 and a half million in Asia and the Pacific.

By 2007 the balance had shifted and grown, with Asia and the Pacific now home to the largest student population base with 64 million students, outstripping Western Europe and North America's 30 million.

Likewise, Asia is playing an ever greater role in academic research with, to give one example, a large increase in the number of science papers appearing in peer-reviewed academic journals.

While the number of papers by developed countries increased by on average 2% annually over the same period, in the 12-year period to 2007 the number of published science papers increased by 16. 5 per cent from China, by 14. 1 per cent from Korea and by 10. 5 per cent from Singapore.

Conclusion

Increased education offerings, and increases in research and innovation output, are public goods of clear, far-reaching and enduring benefit.

Education and innovation are crucial to national and regional development.

Education improves human capital, drives technological improvements and enables the effective combination of growth factors by enhancing management skills.

As an example from my country, it has been shown that up to 44 per cent of overall growth in Australia—an economy with a large services sector—may be education derived.

International education exchange brings benefits not only for those students and institutions directly involved, but to the host and home education systems as well. Education exchange can drive improved regulation, qualifications recognition and quality of provision in both recipient and providing countries.

Education exchange transfers skills and technologies and promotes trade and investment. Academic connections, intellectual connections are a bridgehead for people to people links and improving cultural and personal understanding.

This Forum will add to the ongoing dialogue of international cooperation in higher education. I see many delegates who have travelled a long way to be with us. I thank you for your commitment to the objectives of this Forum and I look forward to exchanging ideas and experiences with you all over the next two days.

I wish you a successful and productive Forum.

Thank you.

凯瑟琳·坎贝尔简历

2010年5月至今担任澳大利亚教育、就业和劳资关系部副部长。此前在澳大利亚财政部、国防部任职。获应用科学（应用数学）学士、信息科学硕士及工商管理硕士学位，并于2008年参加哈佛大学商学院的高级管理课程。

加强高等教育国际合作，为区域社会经济发展作出贡献

云南大学校长　何天淳

尊敬的中国教育部副部长王立英阁下，
尊敬的云南省副省长李江阁下，
尊敬的澳大利亚教育、就业与劳资关系部副部长凯瑟琳·坎贝尔阁下，
尊敬的各位与会代表，
女士们、先生们：

早上好！

今天我们在这里隆重集会，共同出席“东亚峰会高等教育合作论坛”。本次论坛由中国教育部和云南省人民政府共同主办，由云南省教育厅和云南大学承办。在此，我代表云南大学，向出席本次会议的所有代表表示热烈的欢迎！这次论坛将为我们提供一个相互交流、互通有无、取长补短的平台，让我们共同分享东盟各国在高等教育合作与区域经济发展过程中所取得的成就和经验，并就“东亚峰会框架下的高等教育合作与发展”这个题目展开具体的讨论。

云南大学作为本次论坛的承办者之一，我们感到十分荣幸。云南大学地处云南省省会昆明市，创建于1922年。经过近九十年的发展，现已成为一所以民族学、生态学为特色，文、史、哲、经、管、工、理、法、农、教育等学科门类较为齐全、人才密集的全国重点综合性大学，并且是云南唯一的一所实施国家“211工程”的地方综合性大学、国家西部重点支持高校和省部共建高校。为了配合西部大开发和“桥头堡”建设

的战略，我校提出了学校未来十年的发展和建设的总目标，即“经过五年的努力，主要发展指标进入全国高校50强，再经过五年的努力，综合实力进入全国高校50强，把云南大学办成区域性高水平研究型综合大学”。

作为云南省成立最早的高等学府之一和云南唯一的重点高校，云南大学历来重视国际教育交流与合作。早在建校之初，首任校长董泽先生就提出：“东陆大学非一人之所有，更非云南的，中国的，实世界的也。”近20年来，云南大学充分发挥“211工程”大学多学科、高层次的综合办学优势，和毗邻南亚、东南亚的独特区位优势，以“辐射两亚”为教育国际化的基础，积极推进国际交流与合作，“走出去”、“引进来”，汉语国际推广、招收留学生、引进智力、合作办学等工作成效明显，学校教育国际化进程不断加快，师生国际化视野进一步拓展，为区域经济社会发展提供了人才和智力支持。

目前，云南大学与世界23个国家和地区的100余所院校和教育机构建立了合作关系；吸引了五大洲23个国家的众多留学生到云南大学学习，并可自主招收面向东盟各国的政府奖学金学生；新拓展了一批国际合作项目，在伊朗德黑兰大学、孟加拉南北大学和缅甸福庆学校共建了孔子学院。尤其重要的是，在东亚峰会框架下的高等教育合作中，我们与东南亚、南亚、东北亚各国乃至整个亚太地区的众多高校的合作也得到不断的加强。

我们认为，当今，以民族或国家为基本单位的高等教育体系正在跨越民族文化和国家的边界，各国高等教育间的相互交流与合作越来越成为一个国家高等教育健康发展所必不可少的条件，积极推动并参与国际交流与合作，已成为一种新的办学理念。这其中，区域化的高等教育合作与交流既是一个双向互动的过程，也是一个多向联动的过程。因此，为了给东盟各国和来自中国、日本、韩国、澳大利亚、新西兰、印度等国家的高校提供一个稳定的交流、合作平台，我们建议把“东亚峰会高等教育合作论坛”确立为一种制度化的机制，以便各高校和其他利益相关体定期会晤、彼此借鉴、互通有无，开展广泛、深入的教育合作与交流。

女士们，先生们，作为教育界的同行，我们是一个区域性的社群，虽然我们具有相似的目标和使命，但是社群内部的交流与沟通仍然是必不可少的。我们需要不断更新对各自的了解，从而在“东亚峰会高等教育合作论坛”这一平台上实现互利共赢的合作。我诚挚地希望各位与会代表能够充分借助这次难得的机遇，分享我们彼此的经验和洞见，共同构建东亚峰会框架下的区域性高等教育合作与交流的平台。云南大学也诚挚希望与更多东亚地区高校建立良好的交流关系，开展广泛而深入的合作，共同为区域经济、社会和政治发展作出应有的贡献。

最后，祝各位代表身体健康，事事如意！祝本次论坛取得圆满成功！

谢谢大家！

何天淳发言英文稿

Promote Higher Education Cooperation and Contribute to Regional Socio-economic Development

He Tianchun
President of Yunnan University

Respected Mme. Wang Liying, Vice Minister of the Chinese Ministry of Education,

Respected Mr. Li Jiang, Vice Governor of Yunnan Province,

Respected Mme. Kathryn Campbell, Deputy Secretary of the Australian Department of Education, Employment and Workplace Relations,

Dear participants,

Ladies and Gentlemen,

Good morning!

Today, it is my great pleasure to join you here in launching the East Asia Higher Education Cooperation Forum. Co-hosted by the Chinese Ministry of Education and the People's Government of Yunnan Province, the Forum is jointly organized by Yunnan Provincial Department of Education and Yunnan University. First, I would like to, on behalf of Yunnan University, extend my warm welcome to all the attendees present here. The Forum, a platform for dialogue, communication and learning, will offer us access to sharing achievements and experience in higher education cooperation and regional economic development by the ASEAN member states. We will also have productive discussions on the topic of "Higher Education Cooperation and Development within the EAS Framework".

It is our great honor to be an organizer of the Forum. Founded in 1922,

Yunnan University is situated in Kunming, capital of Yunnan Province. Over the past nearly 90 years, Yunnan University has developed into a national key comprehensive university with an excellent faculty, highlighting ethnology and ecology and offering a complete collection of disciplines like literature, history, philosophy, economics, management, engineering, science, law, agriculture and education. More importantly, all over Yunnan Province, Yunnan University boasts itself as the only one university that has won the membership of "the Project 211", and the only one that is listed among the key universities in the West China Development Strategy and jointly supervised by the Chinese Ministry of Education and the People's Government of Yunnan Province. Following the West China Development Strategy and the "bridgehead building" program, Yunnan University has decided its blueprint for next decade, namely ranking among the top 50 universities nationwide in terms of main development indicators within the first five years and ranking among the top 50 universities nationwide in terms of comprehensive strength during the latter half decade and finally developing into a regional comprehensive university excellent in high-level research and teaching.

As one of the oldest institutions of higher education and the only one national key university in Yunnan Province, Yunnan University always attaches great importance to exchanges and cooperation in international education. At the very beginning of the founding of Yunnan University, its first President Dong Ze had a famous saying- "Donglu University (later known as Yunnan University) is not subject to a private individual and confined to Yunnan Province, but serves the entire China and even the whole world". In recent 20 years, Yunnan University has given full play to its comprehensive educational resources as a "Project 211" university with a wide range of high-level disciplines. Thanks to its geographical contiguity to the South and Southeast Asia, Yunnan University has vigorously promoted the strategy of "going global" and "bringing in" on international exchanges and cooperation focused on the South and Southeast Asia. Significant progress has been made by us in Chinese language promotion, enrollment of international students, overseas expertise introduction and cooperative training programs. We have also quickened our internationalization of education, widened the international vision of our faculty and students and made contribution to regional socioeconomic development by offering talents and brains. At present, Yunnan University has cooperative ties with over 100 institutions of higher learning from 23 countries and regions, and sees international students from 23 countries. Especially it is authorized to independently enroll candidates for Chinese Government scholarship among the ASEAN countries. We have also launched a set of new international cooperative programs, as establishment of Confucius Institute at the University of Tehran in Iran, North South University in Bangladesh and Fuqing International Language and Computer Training Center in Myanmar. More importantly, as for the higher education cooperation within the EAS framework, we have doubled our efforts to work together with counterparts in the Southeast Asia, South Asia and Northeast Asia, and even the Asia-Pacific region at large.

We believe that the system of higher education originally confined to a single nation is now developing beyond the boundaries of national culture and state. And it is growing more important for a country to develop its own higher education in a sound way by promoting international exchanges and cooperation. We should have a fresh idea in running schools that is to improve education by facilitating international exchanges and cooperation. In this context, regional exchanges and cooperation in higher education must be conducted in an interactive manner. In order to set up a regular platform for higher education exchanges and cooperation between the ASEAN and Australia, China, India, Japan, the Republic of Korea and New Zealand, I propose making the East Asia Higher Education Cooperation Forum an institutionalized mechanism, so that relevant institutions of higher learning and interest groups can make regular contacts and learn from each other for wider and deeper education exchanges and cooperation.

Ladies and Gentlemen, We are all from the academic community in the same region and work for a common mission, but it is necessary to keep close contact among us. We should keep informed of each other and strive for a win-win solution on the East Asia Higher Education Cooperation Forum, so as to contribute to the improvement of regional economy, society and politics. It is my sincere hope that all attendees to the Forum can avail themselves of this opportunity to share experience and visions, and contribute to the establishment of a platform for higher education exchanges and cooperation within the EAS framework. Yunnan University is always open to all counterparts in the East Asia for inclusive and deep cooperation, so as to make joint efforts to facilitate the regional development of economy, society and politics.

To conclude, I wish all participants good health and every success in your life, and the Forum a complete success.

Thank you all!

何天淳简历

2008年1月至今，担任云南大学校长，教授。曾任昆明理工大学校长、云南省教育厅厅长等职。1985年9月，获昆明工学院硕士学位；1988年11月，获德国弗赖贝格矿业学院博士学位；1994年11月，在德国卡尔斯鲁厄大学从事博士后研究。承担和参加了国家级、省部级科研基金等十余项课题的研究，先后发表科研论文70余篇，著作多部。

高等教育的区域协作

印度旁遮普大学校长　琅勃·钱德尔·索博蒂

我们现在正朝着加强高等教育方面努力，我们希望在高等教育方面有较快的发展。我们要本着开放的态度，来进行交流，进行资源的互访、互换。对于各个层次的教育机构，要不断地交流各方面的工作，在这个合作过程中，首先要明确我们要加强交流的合作内容是什么？我们要对学生进行培训，我们要把新型的知识进行传播。所以我们的教学目标是培养具有前瞻性的学生和教职员工。

我们可以看到，我们学校有 2600 名师生参与了国际交流。我们这所大学，是印度最古老的学校之一，我们从 1882 年就开始了非常迅猛的发展。我们有 2 万名学生入学就读。而且我们在国际研究方面处于领先地位，还有一些泰国的学生也到我们的大学就读。旁遮普大学有各种机构、各方面的学科。我们总共有 80 个不同的部门，有 20 个不同的研究机构。在高等教育方面，我们的师资力量是非常强的。我们不断地进行研究，不断地提升研究的质量。同时，我们在研究方面的成果丰硕。对于学生而言，我们希望他们有工作的意识，使他们不仅适应印度的要求，也适应全球的要求。在过去的一年，我们开设了一个新兴的学科。在旁遮普大学，我们有很多新兴学科。不同国家的学生可以到我们的大学就读不同的学科。

我们大学非常有建树，我们的资源非常丰富。我们的政府对我们的科学研究工作也进行了奖励。我们有一个具体的项目，是由政府拨款资助的。我们是名列全世界 500 强的大学，这是印度唯一一所在理工科方面名列世界 500 强的大学。我们和英国、法国、澳大利亚、加拿大、美国、巴基斯坦以及瑞士日内瓦的大学、研究机构，有着紧密地合作。我们一同进行有关的教学和研究，涵盖了多个学科。因此，我们在有关师生互访、学位互认方面都建立起了一个非常全面的体系。我们和欧洲及美国都建立了一些互认的体系。比如说，就管理等学科我们可以进行互认。

我们也得到了许多奖励，我们的社会学研究方面得到了政府的认可，给予我们很多奖励。我们也有社会经济学科，它是针对不同的情况进行研究。我们在教育方面，在印度是非常具有权威的。对于东亚的国家而言，我们也和它们进行了合作。我们要组织一些国际性的研讨会，应对这个地区所面临的问题，提升这个区域的竞争性。我们要不断地跨越语言方面的障碍。在这些方面，我们设置了一些管理机构，它们能够提升我们的竞争力、透明度，帮助我们构建整体的构架。

我们和东亚峰会各成员国大学，都能够找到更好、更快的沟通方式，我们和他们有着更加紧密的联系，能够在各个学科进行跨学科的交流。我们也建立起了知识网络，这样的网络可以允许我们不断地进行知识分享。我们有各种机构，能够提供知识的来源，我们也结成了合作伙伴。

我们建立了一些知识中心，这些知识中心能够帮助我们提高学生的知识面和技能技巧。同时，我们也能够促使我们的学校以及师生在这方面和其他大学进行合作。所有这些都将有助于印度本身的发展。因为在一个学术机构，这些活动是能够广泛应用的。而且我们能够在知识层面进行广泛合作，改变人们的思维模式。我们也可以进行一些远程的教学。因此我们在有关基础研究方面，也进行了很多研究，也发表了很多论文。知识的分享是非常有意义的。我们可以设立一些研究机构，对政府的政策产生一定的影响。我们大学和印度的其他大学都进行了很多类似的合作。我们将使得世界成为一个和平的世界。

谢谢!

（刘飞　译）

琅勃·钱德尔·索博蒂英文发言 PPT

Higher Education Coordination and Cooperation

Ranbir Chander Sobti
Vice Chancellor, Panjab University

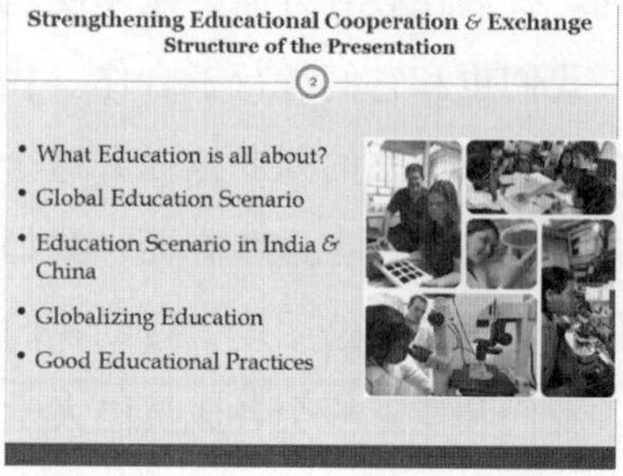

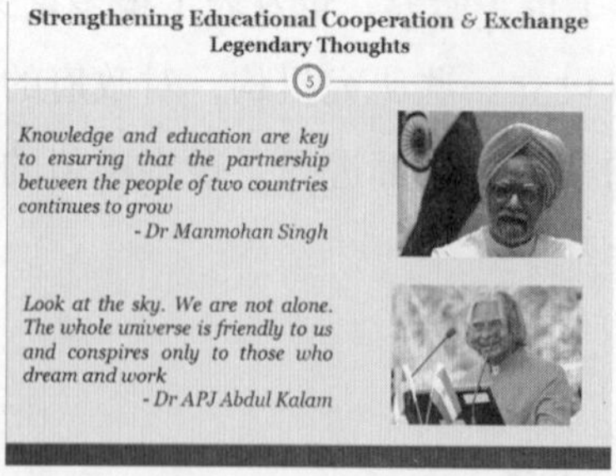

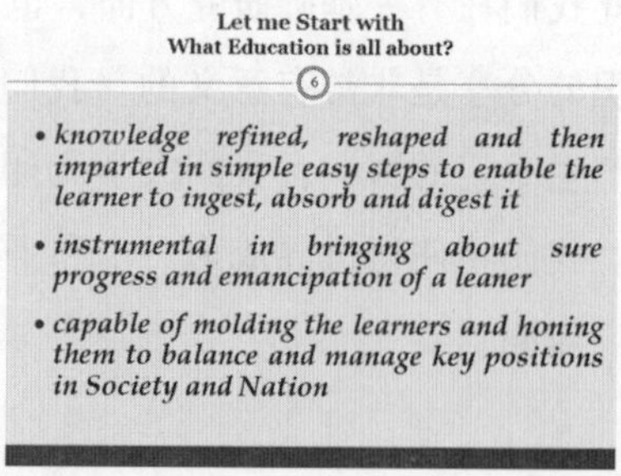

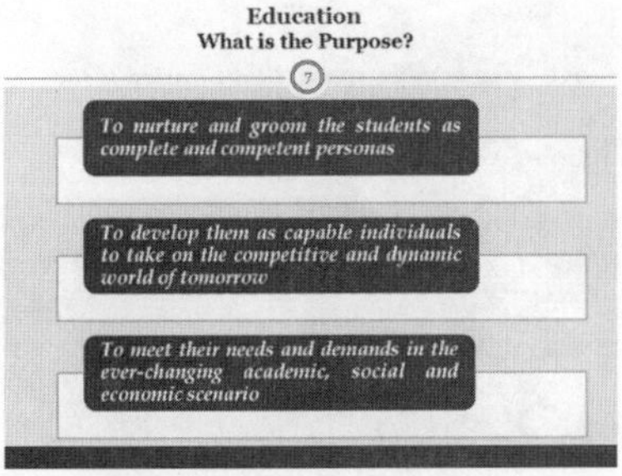
Education
What is the Purpose?
7
To nurture and groom the students as complete and competent personas
To develop them as capable individuals to take on the competitive and dynamic world of tomorrow
To meet their needs and demands in the ever-changing academic, social and economic scenario

Global Village
lized education is...
der, borderless, or transitional education
all types of modes of delivery of higher
s of sets of courses of study or educational
ch learners are located in a country different
ere the awarding institution is based"

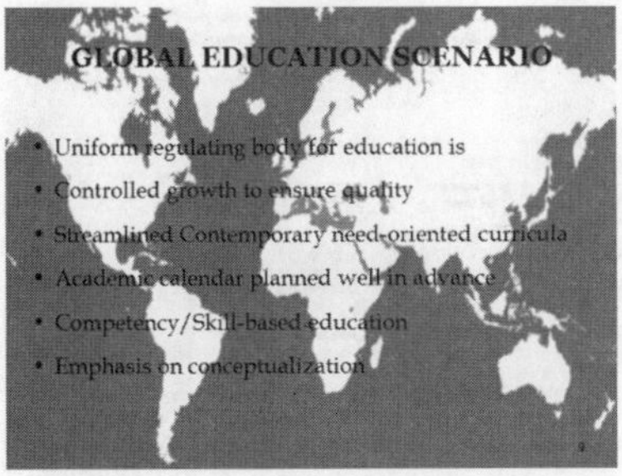
GLOBAL EDUCATION SCENARIO
Uniform regulating body for education is
Controlled growth to ensure quality
Streamlined Contemporary need-oriented curricula
Academic calendar planned well in advance
Competency/Skill-based education
Emphasis on conceptualization
9

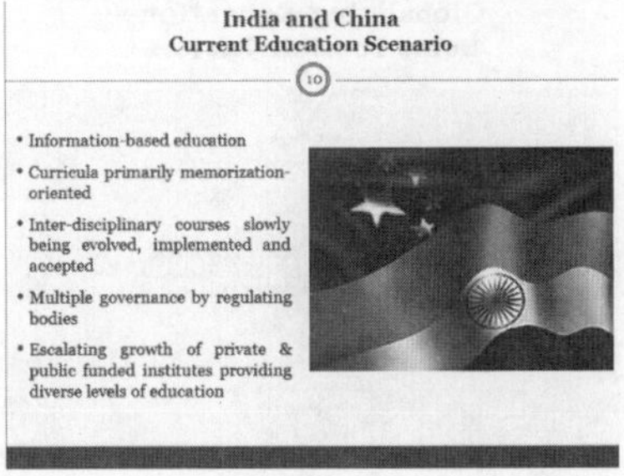
India and China
Current Education Scenario
10
Information-based education
Curricula primarily memorization-oriented
Inter-disciplinary courses slowly being evolved, implemented and accepted
Multiple governance by regulating bodies
Escalating growth of private & public funded institutes providing diverse levels of education

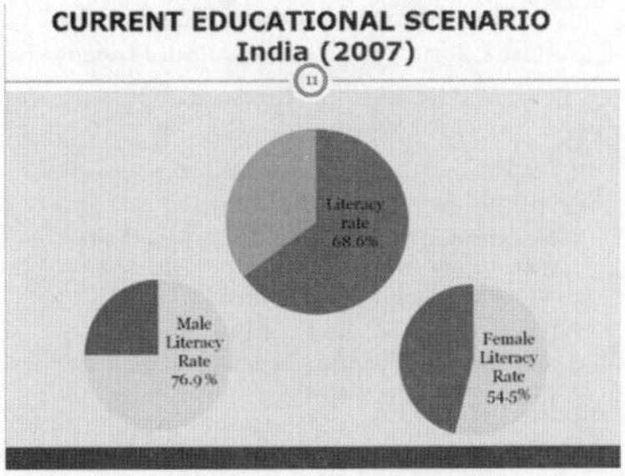
CURRENT EDUCATIONAL SCENARIO
India (2007)
11
Literacy rate 68.6%
Male Literacy Rate 76.9%
Female Literacy Rate 54.5%

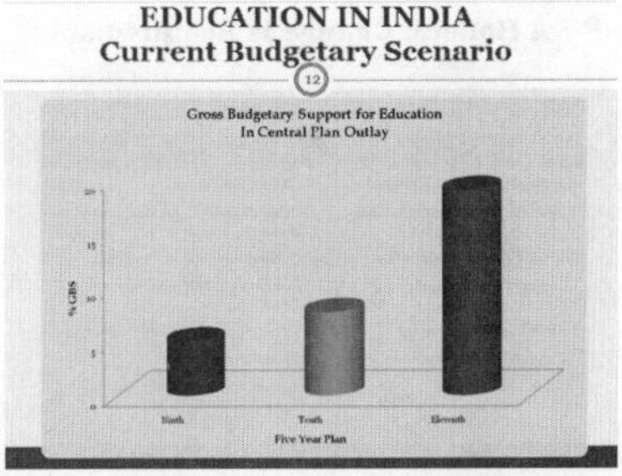
EDUCATION IN INDIA
Current Budgetary Scenario
12
Gross Budgetary Support for Education
In Central Plan Outlay
% GBS
Ninth
Tenth
Eleventh
Five Year Plan

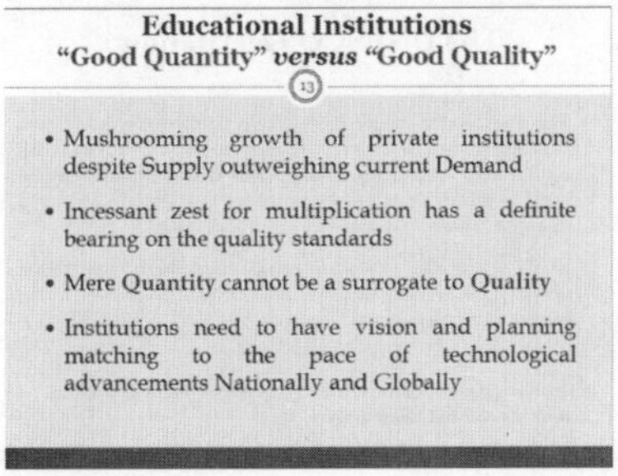
Educational Institutions
"Good Quantity" versus "Good Quality"
13
Mushrooming growth of private institutions despite Supply outweighing current Demand
Incessant zest for multiplication has a definite bearing on the quality standards
Mere Quantity cannot be a surrogate to Quality
Institutions need to have vision and planning matching to the pace of technological advancements Nationally and Globally

Education Collaboration
Global vs. Developing Countries
Significant gap tends to exist...

Globalizing Education
Some Possible Factors

17

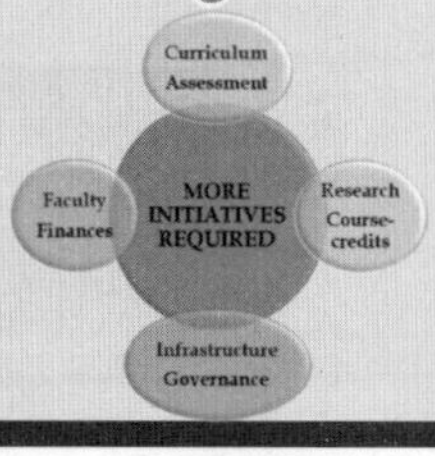

Let Education be not treated by narrow perceptions, ignoring the comprehensive scenario, analogous to the old adage of **BLIND MEN & THE ELEPHANT**

18

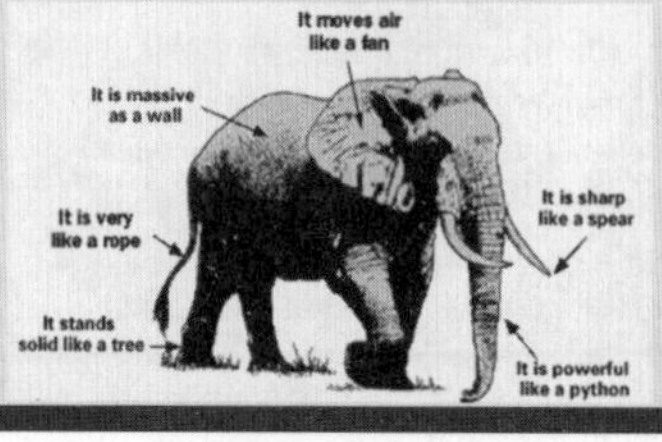

A Holistic Change is Required.....

19

FROM	TO
Individualized "ivory towers"	Globalized vision
Classroom & laboratory training	Workshops & Corporate-sponsored research projects
Information-based education	Competency-based education
Personal Development	Professional & Vocational development
Full service organizations	Disaggregated multiple campuses
Comprehensive curriculum	Specialized courses
'Just in case' process	'Just in time' approach

Flexible and Updated Curricula

Latest Topic of Today will be Outdated Tomorrow

20

Hence...

- Flexible, modular and current technology-based curricula are required.
- A curriculum designer should have the power of imagination and adequate vision to develop curricula with futuristic potential.
- There is acute need of an autonomous curriculum restructuring committee to meet and thrash updates regularly.

Globalization
Key Advantages

21

✓Encourages updated quality enhancement
✓Significantly widens the horizons
✓Inculcates a feeling of world citizenship/ universal brotherhood amongst pupils as well as in teachers
✓Enriches both the institute and the students
✓Generates cross-border goodwill
✓Generates financial resources
✓Promotes inter-national cultural exchange

The UNESCO Declaration

22

- The Declaration at the 1998 World Conference on Higher Education for the Twenty First Century and Framework for Priority Action for Change and Development may be cited as a historic reference point for the developing world to accept and prepare itself for the challenge.
- Its sequel in 2003 looked at cross border higher education on three continents and in three different countries- India, Jamaica and Sierra Leone.

The starting point of the challenge in the developing world is nothing else but demography

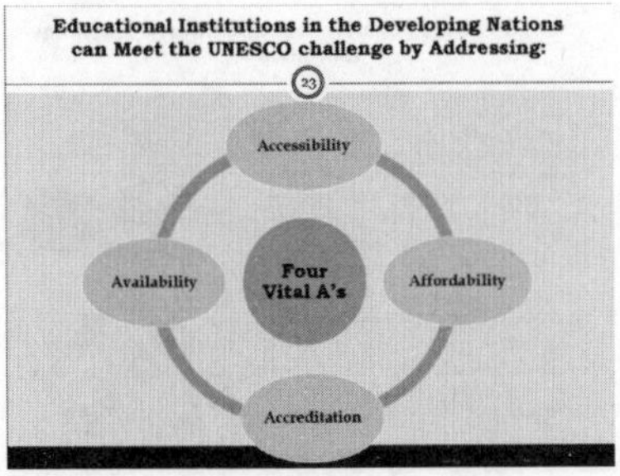
Educational Institutions in the Developing Nations
can Meet the UNESCO challenge by Addressing:
23
Accessibility
Availability
Four
Vital A's
Affordability
Accreditation

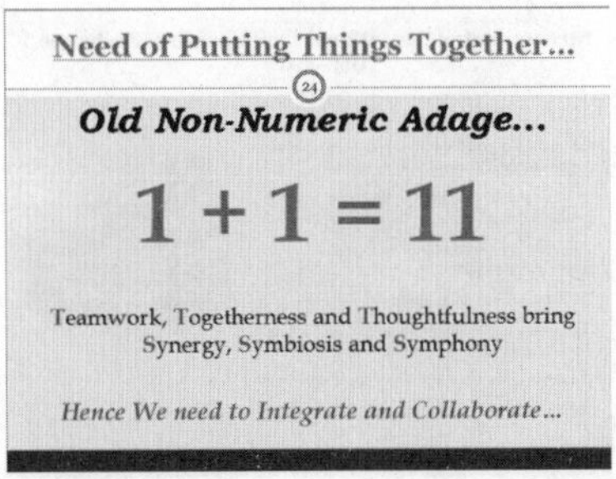
Need of Putting Things Together...
24
Old Non-Numeric Adage...
1 + 1 = 11
Teamwork, Togetherness and Thoughtfulness bring
Synergy, Symbiosis and Symphony
Hence We need to Integrate and Collaborate...

As Far As The Pace of
Economic Development is Concerned...
25
The Whole
World

As Far As The Pace of
Economic Development is Concerned...
26
The Whole World
Apprehends...

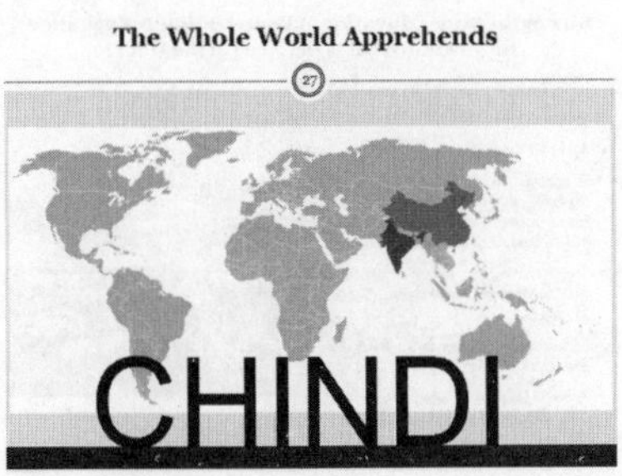
The Whole World Apprehends
27
CHINDI

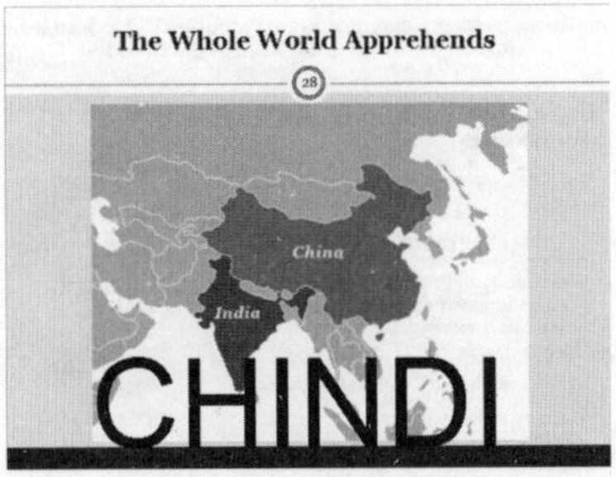
The Whole World Apprehends
28
China
India
CHINDI

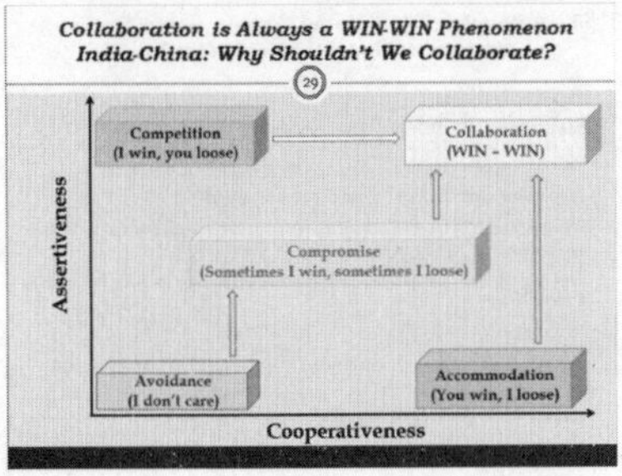
Collaboration is Always a WIN-WIN Phenomenon
India-China: Why Shouldn't We Collaborate?
29
Competition
(I win, you loose)
Collaboration
(WIN - WIN)
Compromise
(Sometimes I win, sometimes I loose)
Avoidance
(I don't care)
Accommodation
(You win, I loose)
Assertiveness
Cooperativeness

This Way We can Harvest the
BEST of Both the Crops
30
The best of both worlds

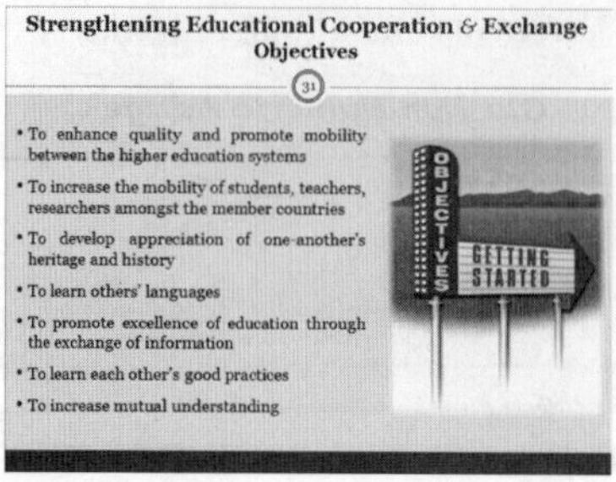
Strengthening Educational Cooperation & Exchange
Objectives
31
• To enhance quality and promote mobility between the higher education systems
• To increase the mobility of students, teachers, researchers amongst the member countries
• To develop appreciation of one-another's heritage and history
• To learn others' languages
• To promote excellence of education through the exchange of information
• To learn each other's good practices
• To increase mutual understanding
OBJECTIVES
GETTING STARTED

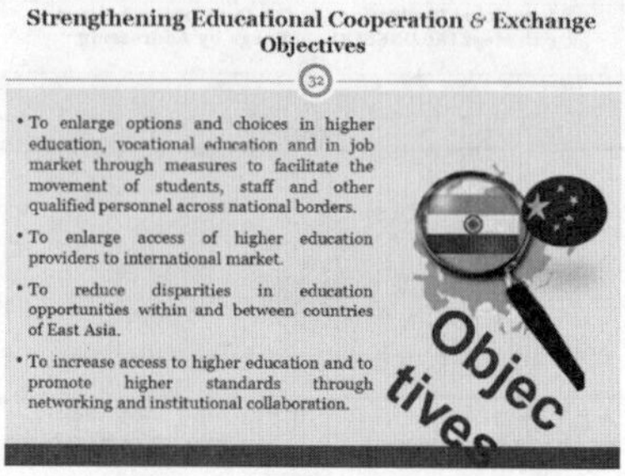
Strengthening Educational Cooperation & Exchange
Objectives
32
• To enlarge options and choices in higher education, vocational education and in job market through measures to facilitate the movement of students, staff and other qualified personnel across national borders.
• To enlarge access of higher education providers to international market.
• To reduce disparities in education opportunities within and between countries of East Asia.
• To increase access to higher education and to promote higher standards through networking and institutional collaboration.
Objec
tives

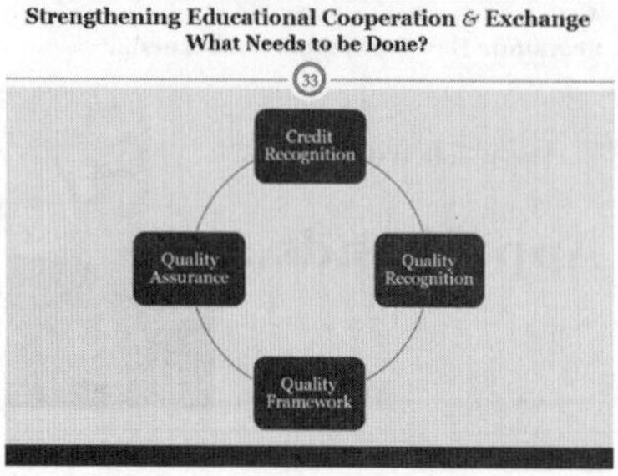
Strengthening Educational Cooperation & Exchange
What Needs to be Done?
33
Credit Recognition
Quality Assurance
Quality Recognition
Quality Framework

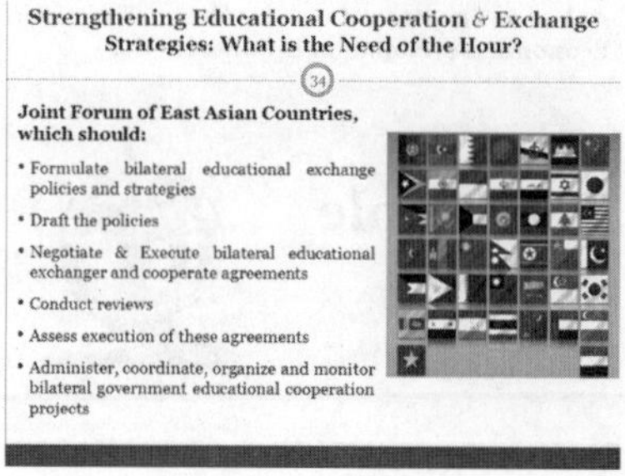
Strengthening Educational Cooperation & Exchange
Strategies: What is the Need of the Hour?
34
Joint Forum of East Asian Countries, which should:
• Formulate bilateral educational exchange policies and strategies
• Draft the policies
• Negotiate & Execute bilateral educational exchanger and cooperate agreements
• Conduct reviews
• Assess execution of these agreements
• Administer, coordinate, organize and monitor bilateral government educational cooperation projects

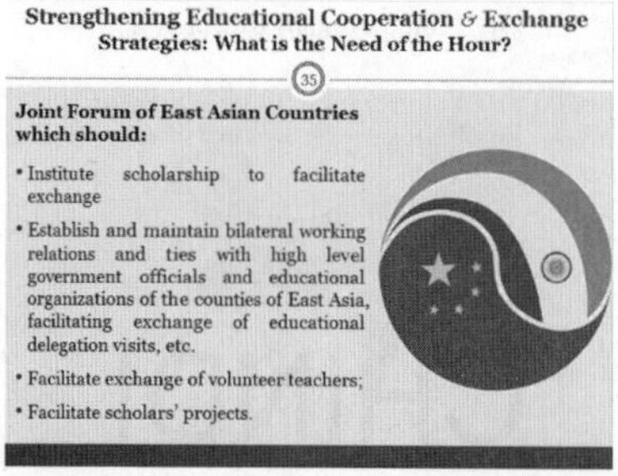
Strengthening Educational Cooperation & Exchange
Strategies: What is the Need of the Hour?
35
Joint Forum of East Asian Countries which should:
• Institute scholarship to facilitate exchange
• Establish and maintain bilateral working relations and ties with high level government officials and educational organizations of the counties of East Asia, facilitating exchange of educational delegation visits, etc.
• Facilitate exchange of volunteer teachers;
• Facilitate scholars' projects.

Strengthening Educational Cooperation & Exchange
Strategies: What is the Need of the Hour?
36
Exchanges in the field of Higher Education:
• Summer Camps
• Programs to share the information, experiences in carrying out substantial cooperation and exchanges and plan future course of action in its light.
• Conferences for educational Administrators, Planners, Teachers, Students.
• Encourage learners to go to different countries.
• Provide learners with opportunities and experience to go abroad for studies

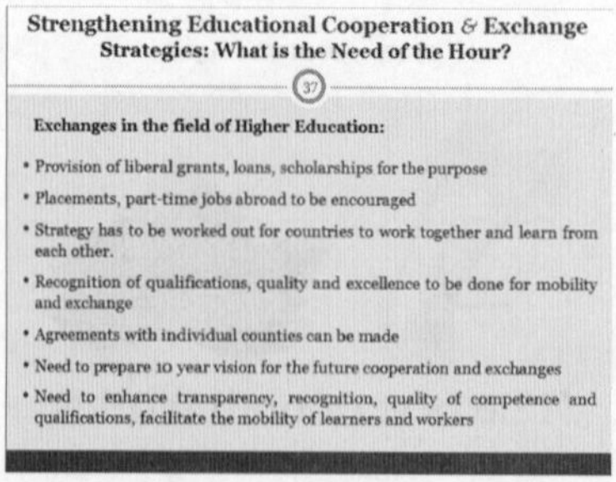
Strengthening Educational Cooperation & Exchange
Strategies: What is the Need of the Hour?
37
Exchanges in the field of Higher Education:
• Provision of liberal grants, loans, scholarships for the purpose
• Placements, part-time jobs abroad to be encouraged
• Strategy has to be worked out for countries to work together and learn from each other.
• Recognition of qualifications, quality and excellence to be done for mobility and exchange
• Agreements with individual counties can be made
• Need to prepare 10 year vision for the future cooperation and exchanges
• Need to enhance transparency, recognition, quality of competence and qualifications, facilitate the mobility of learners and workers

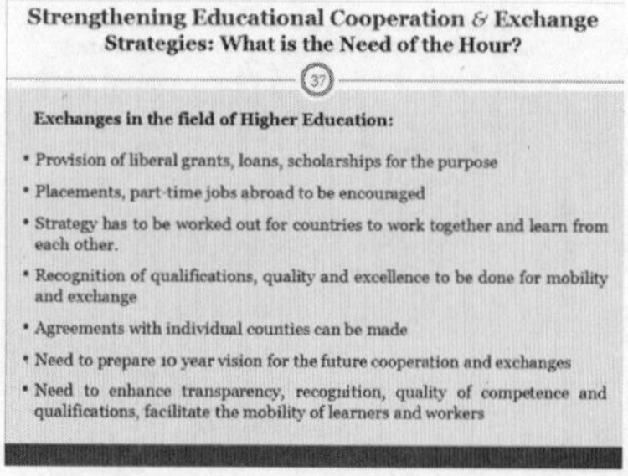
Strengthening Educational Cooperation & Exchange
Strategies: What is the Need of the Hour?
37
Exchanges in the field of Higher Education:
• Provision of liberal grants, loans, scholarships for the purpose
• Placements, part-time jobs abroad to be encouraged
• Strategy has to be worked out for countries to work together and learn from each other.
• Recognition of qualifications, quality and excellence to be done for mobility and exchange
• Agreements with individual counties can be made
• Need to prepare 10 year vision for the future cooperation and exchanges
• Need to enhance transparency, recognition, quality of competence and qualifications, facilitate the mobility of learners and workers

Strengthening Educational Cooperation & Exchange
Educational Exchange Programs in India

39

- With the expansion of education sector and internationalization of education, an International Cooperation Cell has been set up in the Ministry of HRD.
- A separate budget provision is made for international academic exchange activities of the Ministry.
- Initially, the Plan Scheme "Strengthening of External Academic Relation" was intended to facilitate exchange of Ministerial level delegations with foreign countries for furthering bilateral relations in education.
- However, the scope of the scheme has expanded considerably in recent years with new initiates in bilateral cooperation.

Strengthening Educational Cooperation & Exchange
Educational Exchange Programs in India

40

Since 2002, the Ministry has entered into exclusive Education Exchange Programs (in some cases, called as MoUs) with 32 countries including:

- Mongolia
- Armenia
- Tanzania
- Guyana
- Israel
- Australia
- Myanmar
- Hungry
- Syria
- Uzbekistan
- New Zealand
- Thailand
- Sri Lanka
- Mexico
- Brazil
- Afghanistan
- Croatia
- South Africa
- Saudi Arabia
- China
- Portugal
- France
- Ethiopia
- Vietnam
- Norway
- Chile

Strengthening Educational Cooperation & Exchange
Educational Exchange Programs in India

41

During 2009-2010, the following Joint Working Group meetings were held:

- 1st India-Oman JWG in Oman on March 29-30,2009
- 1st India-Norway JWG in Norway on August 12-13, 2009
- 1st India-Czech Republic JWG in New Delhi on December 7-10, 2009
- Sub-working groups of JWG between India and Australia on October 7, 2009.

Strengthening Educational Cooperation & Exchange
Educational Exchange Programs in India

42

The EEPs/MOUs envisage cooperation through several initiatives like:

- Exchange of scholars/ students/ researchers
- Sharing of information/ publications
- Organizing joint seminars/ workshops/ conferences etc.
- Working towards mutual recognition of qualifications
- Developing institutional linkages
- Providing scholarships to students/ researchers

Strengthening Cooperation & Exchange
Other Initiatives of Indian Government

43

- The Ministry of HRD has been playing a significant role in international organizations like Commonwealth, SAARC and UNESCO for promoting educational standards across the globe.
- Hon'ble Minister of Human Resource Development attended the 17th Commonwealth Conference of Education Ministers held in Kuala Lumpur on June 15-19, 2009.
- The Ministry is also playing a pivotal role in activities of multilateral bodies like ASEAN, East Asia Summit, Arab League, Indian Ocean RIM, OECD, EU etc.
- The Ministry, through IC Cell and HE Bureau, is actively involved in the establishment of the world-class international higher educational institution, *viz.* "South Asian University" in New Delhi under SAARC.

If We can Perform So Well in Economic Reforms...

44

Why Can't We Restructure Our Education System?

We Have to Carry Out SWOT Analysis...

The SWOT Analysis

45

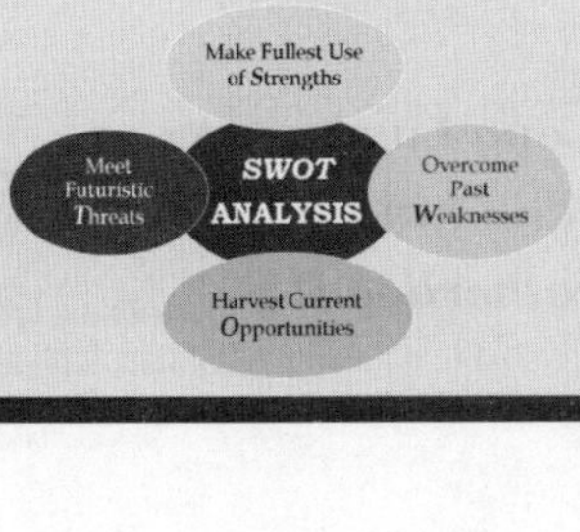

India and China
Strengths

46

- Largest literate manpower
- Commitment to cause
- Availability of resources
- High quality institutions
- Painstaking and sincere efforts
- Good research outcome
- Unity in Diversity

India and China Weaknesses

47

- Language barriers
- Unethical practices
- High dropout rate
- Individual Ivory Towers
- Uncontrolled growth of self-financed institutes
- Facilities under utilized/unutilized
- Reluctance to adopt innovative teaching methods
- Curricula less pertinent to contemporary needs
- Inadequate high-tech instrumentation
- Inadequate institutional ambience
- Escalating population

India and China Opportunities and Threats

48

Opportunities

- To impart education to 100% of local populace
- To make India and China as Global Education Hubs.

If countries like UK, US, Australia, New Zealand and Canada can do it, WHY CAN'T WE?

Threats

- Cultural hiccups
- Linguistic barriers
- Bureaucratic red-tapism
- Lack of adequate will *(to take up the onerous challenges)*

Good Educational Practices

49

These Six-Element GEP's were proposed at Vancouver in 2007 as ADVICE characteristics:

- Activity
- Diversity
- Virtuosity
- Interaction
- Cooperation
- Expectation

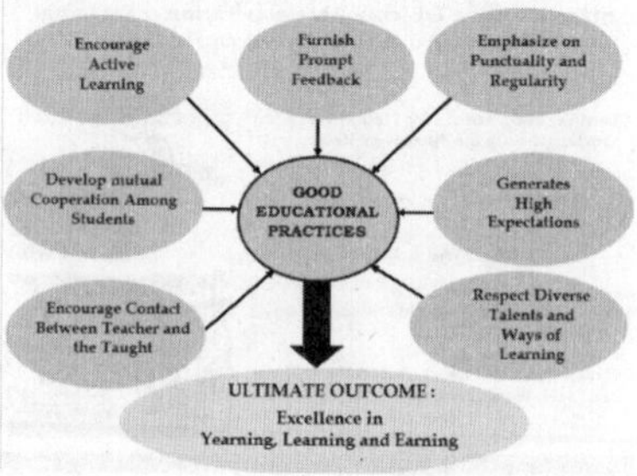

Continuing Education Distance & Open Learning

51

The Course Material Should Meet the CRISIS Criteria

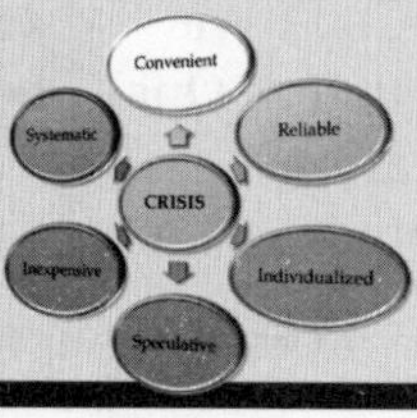

Hence, Let us....

Bring the real world into classrooms

Take the classroom to the real world

52

At Last...

This is an opportune time to reverberate and fortify the popular slogan once coined and used by our ancestors, now again...

Hindi-Chini Bhai-Bhai!

Long Live! Indo-Chinese Brotherhood!

Prime Ministers, Mr Chou-En Lai (China) and Pt Jawaharlal Nehru (India)

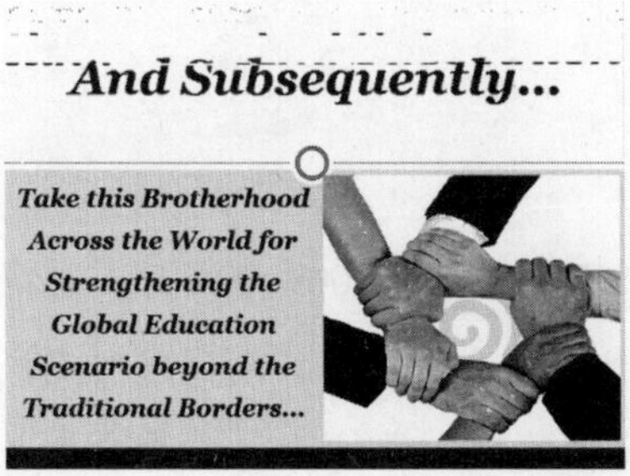
And Subsequently...
Take this Brotherhood Across the World for Strengthening the Global Education Scenario beyond the Traditional Borders...

Aiming to Strengthen...
Indo-China Educational Relations
56
THANK YOU

琅勃·钱德尔·索博蒂简历

2006年7月至今，担任印度旁遮普大学校长。2009年4月，获得由印度总统颁发的杰出贡献奖。2009年10月至今，兼任印度国家研究发展中心主任。获得美国迈阿密大学公共卫生学硕士学位，印度旁遮普大学博士学位。旁遮普大学生物科技系及生物科技中心的创建人和带头人，出版专著22部，发表学术论文140余篇。

第二部分　教育官员发言

Section II: Speeches by Education Officials

坚持教育开放，加强交流合作，促进共同发展

——在“东亚峰会高等教育合作论坛”上的主题发言

中华人民共和国教育部国际合作与交流司司长　张秀琴

尊敬的各位官员，各位校长，

女士们、先生们，朋友们：

下午好！

很高兴在中国美丽的彩云之南，在有着悠久文化历史和多彩民俗风情并素以“春城”享誉海内外的昆明相聚，与各位宾朋一道，满怀喜悦的心情，共同参加“东亚峰会高等教育合作论坛”。我谨代表中国教育部，对前来参加论坛的各国教育官员和大学校长们表示诚挚欢迎！

本次论坛是落实2009年10月温家宝总理在东亚峰会上提出的倡议的具体行动，是首次在东亚峰会框架下搭建多边教育交流合作平台的新尝试，是东亚高等教育在广阔领域进行深入合作的一个新开端。借助“东亚峰会高等教育合作论坛”这个平台，共同探讨东亚峰会框架下在高等教育领域的合作前景和有效途径，必将能够增进东亚各国的相互了解和友谊，推动区域间的教育交流与合作。

女士们、先生们，教育是沟通人与人心灵和情感的桥梁，是国与国加深理解和信任的纽带。教育交流比政治交流更久远，比经济交流更深刻。中国政府历来重视教育的国际交流与合作，在今年7月颁布的《国家中长期教育改革和发展规划纲要（2010—2020）》中对此专门作出安排，明确将教育开放作为今后一个时期推动教育改革和发展的重要战略

举措。改革开放三十多年来，中国教育国际交流与合作不断加强，交流机制逐步完善，交流成效日益凸显。截至2009年底，中国已与188个国家和地区以及国际组织建立了教育交流与合作关系，与34个国家和地区签订了学历学位互认协议，签订了190个联合培养高层次人才协议；各类出国留学人员已逾140万人，累计接收180多个国家和地区的来华留学生146万人次；在海外建立了282所孔子学院和272个孔子课堂；全国24所高等学校共设立海外分校或举办境外办学项目达到45个；批准设立的在华合作办学机构和项目多达1204个。目前在华学习的留学生已达到22.35万人，而1978年仅为1226人，增加了近180倍，几乎每五年来华留学的总人数就翻一番。

女士们、先生们，东亚是世界经济发展最具活力和潜力的地区之一，尽管东亚各国经济发展水平不同，文化传统多样，教育发展层次各异，但东亚高等教育各具特色和互为近邻的优势及经济发展上的互补性，不仅使未来东亚教育交流合作有着广阔的前景，也使其成为促进东亚和谐发展的强大动力。加强东亚教育交流，促进东亚教育合作，既为本国人民带来福祉，也是加快东亚经济繁荣与社会进步的有效途径和重要保障。我们高兴地看到：

双边多边交流增进了共识。近年来，在各种合作框架协议下，各成员国教育高层接触密切，教育团组往来频繁，双边多边交流日益活跃。中国与澳大利亚、新西兰等国家建立了副部级双边长效交流磋商机制；连续三年举办“中国—东盟教育交流周”，2010年8月还举办了首届“中国—东盟教育部长圆桌会议”，东盟十国教育部长悉数出席；与日本、韩国设立了“中日韩大学交流合作促进委员会”，共同推进和建设“亚洲校园”项目。此外，中国还充分利用联合国教科文会议、亚欧教育部长论坛、APEC教育部长论坛、亚洲教育北京论坛等多边国际会议，积极与东亚峰会各成员国进行沟通与交流。

政府间教育合作协议保障了合作。目前，中国与各成员国在教育领域内均签有教育交流合作协议，与菲律宾、泰国、越南、韩国、澳大利亚、新西兰已签署学位学历互认协议，为双边教育交流合作提供了政策上、法律上和机制上的支持和保障。

语言教学推动了交流。中国开齐了东亚峰会各成员国语言教学专业，在各成员国共建立了81所孔子学院和孔子课堂，在多所高校设立成员国的国别研究机构，进一步深化了对东亚峰会国家的了解，对加强与各成员国的交流与合作起到了积极的推动作用。

互派留学生深化了理解。中国与各成员国互为重要留学生源国和目的国，互派留学生数量持续增加。2009年，各成员国来华留学生总数达到133254人，占当年在华留学生总数的41%；在各成员国学习的中国学生总数近37万人。

校际交流拓展了空间。中国许多高校根据自身特点和优势，积极“走出去”和“引进来”，与东亚峰会各成员国高校开展了广泛的校际交流与合作，签署了大量合作协议，建立了大批合作平台，开创了多种交流模式。

青少年交流夯实了基础。中国—东盟青少年夏令营、中日高中生交流、中国—新加坡学生交流等成员国之间的双边多边青少年交流项目，极大地开阔了青少年学生的国际视野，增进了彼此间的友谊，为推动成员国之间的友好合作、持续健康发展提供了活力与保障。

我们相信，东亚峰会各成员国在上述各领域的双边、多边交流促进了彼此间的理解，沟通了各国渴望建立稳定交流机制、开展广泛合作的愿望，夯实了各国共同搭建东亚区域教育交流合作平台的基础。

女士们、先生们，在经济全球化和区域经济一体化正在向纵深发展的今天，经济上的互补和渗透既成事实，教育交流已成为各国经济社会发展的主要支柱和重要依托，在区域发展中有着鲜明的基础性、先导性、集聚性和辐射性特征。同时在东亚峰会上，教育也是各国领导人优先重视、倡导优先发展的重要领域之一。为进一步拓展各成员国教育交流的深度、广度，我对上午王立英副部长代表中国教育部提出的几点倡议，作进一步阐述。

第一，共同搭建东亚峰会框架下教育交流合作机制。各成员国应在东亚峰会框架下，不断加强各成员国教育高层对话，从长远的角度和战略的高度建立制度化的多边合作磋商机制和稳定的交流合作平台，积极推动成员国在教育领域的务实合作。

第二，继续扩大留学生互派规模。中国教育部将不断扩大中国政府奖学金名额，继续稳步落实温总理在2009年第四届东亚峰会上提出“在未来5年内向东亚发展中国家成员新增2000个中国政府奖学金名额和200个公共管理硕士（MPA）奖学金名额”的承诺，积极实施好2020年东盟来华留学生和中国到东盟的留学生都达到10万人左右的“双十万计划”。

第三，不断深化高校校际合作。各成员国应从各国重点大学开始，加强学术交流和科研合作，推动校际学分转移和互认；开展高端人才交流和联合培养，推动设立著名高校间优秀学生交流项目；共享优质教育资源，各取所长，共同发展，提高区域内高等教育在世界范围内的竞争力和影响力。

第四，重视加强人力资源培训合作。各成员国应高度重视人力资源共同发展，充分发挥各自比较优势，在人力资源培训方面充分交流，加强合作，设置相应的培训项目，促进区域人力资源素质的共同提高。

第五，积极开展青年人文交流活动。中国教育部将积极落实国务委员刘延东提出的“未来十年内邀请来自东盟国家的1万名青年来华参加语言、文化、体育、艺术等交流活动”的倡议。各成员国应积极在东亚峰会框架下开展多边青年交流活动，增进相互了解，加深彼此友谊。

女士们、先生们，东亚峰会区域是世界上人力资源最丰富、发展潜力最大的地区。教育一直是促进人力资源开发、振兴经济、推动社会进步的最基本要素。全面加强教育交流合作有助于缩小各国发展差距，提高区域整体竞争力，促进区域可持续发展和繁荣。我相信，有东亚各国政府的支持，有在座教育官员和大学校长的共同努力，东亚高等教育的交流与合作一定会获得新的发展，取得新的成就。

谢谢大家！

张秀琴简历

教育背景：

1978 年，考入天津外国语学院英语系，同年获中国政府奖学金赴英国杜伦大学留学。

1986 年，获英国文化委员会奖学金在英国利兹大学学习，获教育管理硕士学位。

工作经历：

1981 年，进入教育部工作，曾担任原国家教育委员会（现教育部）留学生司美大处副处长、外事司美大处处长，教育部国际合作与交流司副司长。

1988 年，派驻中国驻美国大使馆教育处任三秘。

1995—1998 年，任中国驻多伦多总领事馆教育参赞。

2004 年，被任命为国家留学基金委秘书长。

2008 年 1 月，出任教育部国际合作与交流司司长，现主持全司工作。

积极参与区域教育合作，推进柬埔寨教育现代化

柬埔寨教育、青年与体育部高等教育司副司长　马克·诺伊

各位尊敬的领导，

各位尊敬的来宾，

女士们、先生们：

我非常荣幸，也非常高兴能够参加这次由中华人民共和国教育部和云南省人民政府共同在云南省昆明市主办的“东亚峰会高等教育合作论坛”。我谨代表柬埔寨教育、青年与体育部向中国教育部和云南省人民政府表示衷心的感谢！感谢你们对柬埔寨代表参加此次论坛给予的支持和盛情款待！同时，我还要特别感谢云南省教育厅和云南大学共同承办与筹备了本次论坛，在你们的精心筹备之下，本次论坛一定会取得圆满的成功和丰硕的成果！

这次论坛将给我们东亚各国的高等教育部门带来一次分享经验、开展对话、探索未来教育发展道路的良好机会。我相信这将是一次非常有纪念意义的盛会，它表明我们这个区域在为本区域的经济发展而加快人力资源培养与建设的步伐。

柬埔寨国家政府已经深刻地认识到，开展区域性的、全球性的教育合作活动对于分享高等教育改革经验和教训非常有益。对于正在努力推进教育系统现代化的柬埔寨来说，积极参与这样的活动是非常重要的。

众所周知，柬埔寨是饱经战乱而导致人力资源发展近乎倒退的国家。但是为了重建国家，增进我国与区域和全球的融合，我国政府正在努力

克服困难，重新建设人力资源。在洪森首相的英明领导下，柬埔寨在1998年获得最终的和平，在接下来的2000年至2009年这段时间内，国家的发展取得了重大成就。现在柬埔寨人民生活在一个和平、稳定、统一的国家中，充分享受着自由和民主。

我想强调的是，柬埔寨政府非常重视教育和技术部门的发展，以推动柬埔寨融入区域和全球劳动力市场。因此，柬埔寨政府已经把人力资源的发展作为国家战略发展规划的重点。

在国家战略发展规划的指导下，教育、青年与体育部制定了一个五年规划和一个教育战略规划来确保教育改革的实施。我们的目标是确保所有的柬埔寨公民，不论其性别、居住地、父母经济状况如何，都能够平等享有受教育的权利。这是把柬埔寨建成一个知识型社会，保证柬埔寨在区域和全球合作中具有竞争力的关键所在。

各位尊敬的领导，女士们、先生们：

教育的质量是我们教育、青年与体育部关注的重点，因为我们生活在一个知识与信息的世界，这要求我们拥有大批具备高度的技能、知识和创造力的人才。到目前为止，柬埔寨教育部门在国内外政府和机构的大力支持下，在提高教育质量、扩大教育规划方面取得了可喜的进展。

自从1999年柬埔寨成为东盟的正式成员国以来，我们积极地参与该地区的高等教育合作。同时，柬埔寨是一个欠发达国家，它通过参与区域内合作改进教育体制，通过接受其他国家的奖学金培养了大批的人才。柬埔寨政府与东亚各国政府合作是柬埔寨的教育发展取得成就的重要原因，尤其是受到各国奖学金资助使柬埔寨学生能到国外学习。在此，我们对各国的支持表示衷心的感谢！

柬埔寨认为，东亚各国增进区域内的高等教育合作是促进各国共同发展的一个重要途径，是增强区域竞争力和发展能力的重要手段。因此，今天举办的这个论坛意义重大，也很及时。借此机会，我想提议从以下几方面采取措施来增强区域意识、区域竞争力以及区域的整体发展：

首先，应该通过学术交流、研究合作以及奖学金项目来缩小区域内差距。

其次，应该建立区域内学分转换、学历互认机制，真正建立起区域内的教育合作机制，以实现区域内的教育经验分享，提高本区域的整体教育质量。

再次，应该定期举行交流会、研讨会、研修班，以分享大家在教育方面的实践与创新经验。这对各层次的教育都很重要，对于高等教育的科研与发展方面更为重要。

最后，我相信这样的交流一定能够促进各国在合作与竞争中取得平衡发展。我相信“东亚峰会高等教育合作论坛”将对增进本区域内各国间的合作、友谊与学术交流起到深远的影响，进而为提高东亚区域高等教育质量、推进区域经济发展、技术进步与人才培养起到重要作用！

谢谢各位！

（郑蔚　译）

马克·诺伊英文发言稿

Participate in Regional Education Cooperation and Promote Education Modernization in Cambodia

Mak Ngoy

Deputy Director General, Directorate General of Higher Education, Ministry of Education, Youth and Sport, the Kingdom of Cambodia

Excellencies,

Distinguished Delegates,

Ladies and Gentlemen,

I am greatly delighted and honored to attend the East Asia Summit Higher Education Cooperation Forum held here in Kunming, Yunnan Province, the People's Republic of China, which is jointly hosted by the Ministry of Education of the People's Republic of China and the People's Government of Yunnan Province. On behalf of the Ministry of Education, Youth and Sport of the Kingdom of Cambodia, I would like to express my sincere appreciation to the Ministry of Education of the People's Republic of China and the People's Government of Yunnan Province for their kind support and warm hospitality extended to the Cambodian delegation. I would also like to express my deepest thanks to Yunnan Provincial Department of Education and Yunnan University for jointly organizing this important Forum. Their excellent arrangements for this Forum have significantly contributed to the productivity of this important event.

This Forum indeed provides all of us from higher education sub-sector in East Asia a great opportunity to share and exchange dialogues and experiences to explore development options for education sector, particularly higher education. I think this is a truly proud and memorable gathering, showing that our region is on the accelerated path of building competent and talented human resources to accelerate the pace of socio-economic development.

In this connection, the Royal Government of Cambodia recognizes that regional and global activities in education development are an important mechanism for sharing experiences and learning lessons about education reform, especially higher education. This is particularly critical for Cambodia as we try to move quickly to restore, develop and modernize our education system.

As you might already know Cambodia is a post conflict nation, having experienced great tragedy that has led to a reduced human capacity. After great hardships, the Royal Government of Cambodia is dedicated to developing its human resources in order to reconstruct the country and integrate with the regional and global community of nations. With the selfless commitment and great wisdom of Samdech Akka Moha Sena Padei Techo Hun Sen, Prime Minister of the Kingdom of Cambodia, the hard-found peace in Cambodia was finally secured in late 1998 and the impact of the subsequent capacity development between the years 2000 – 2009 has been very significant. Cambodian people currently are living in peace, stability and national unity, enjoying full rights, freedom and democracy.

In this sense, I would like to stress that the Royal Government of Cambodia has given great importance to the education and skills development sector to accommodate Cambodia into the regional and global labour market. As a result, the Royal Government has identified human resource development as one of its priorities and as an important agenda in the Rectangular Strategy and in the National Strategic Development Plan.

Guided by the mentioned national strategies, the Ministry of Education, Youth and Sport has formulated a five year plan, the Education Strategic Plan to enable the implementation of education reform. Our aim is to ensure that all Cambodian citizens have equal access to quality education regardless of their gender, where they live, or the wealth or poverty of their parents. That is the key to building a knowledge-based society that will ensure Cambodia's competitiveness in integrating herself into the region and the world.

Excellencies, Distinguished Delegates, Ladies and gentlemen, quality of education is one of the major concerns for our Ministry as we live in a world of knowledge and information technology which includes skills, know-how, innovation and creativity of human resources. Up to now, the education sector has proudly developed in terms of both quantity and quality with the support and assistance from the Royal Government and national and international communities and donors.

Since Cambodia became a full member of the Association of Southeast Asian Nations in 1999, it has actively participated in regional cooperation on higher education especially in the SEAMEO and AUN contexts. At the same time, Cambodia, as a less developed country, also benefits from regional cooperation in developing its education system as well as building its human capital through scholarship programs and other important contributions from the countries in the region. In this connection, I highly appreciate the collaboration between the Royal Government of Cambodia and the Governments of the EAS countries that have led to these important educational developments in Cambodia, particularly the support to human resource development through the provision of scholarships to Cambodian students for further study in their countries.

In this regard, Cambodia considers cooperation on higher education within EAS countries as a crucial means of cultivating awareness of one another's developments. That is a significant means of promoting regional competitiveness and development. So, the Forum today is a symbolic and timely starting point to this cooperation with many important steps to be followed before its process is completely fulfilled. On this occasion, I would like to share with all of you what we should do to further promote and strengthen regional awareness, competitiveness and development.

* Disparity within the region should be reduced through academic exchange and cooperation, research collaboration, and scholarship programs.

* Higher education quality within the region should be enhanced through creating harmonization of quality assurance and credit transfer systems, and qual ification frameworks. That way we can draw on and benefit from each other's experiences.

* Seminar, workshop or training should be regularly organized to share best practices and other initiatives on contemporary educational issues. This is important in all levels of education, but we see major opportunities at the higher education level in terms of research and development.

Lastly, I believe such exchanges will ensure a healthy balance between cooperation and competitiveness. Such exchanges will also provide a focus on cooperation that benefits the majority rather than a few. I am confident that the EAS Higher Education Cooperation Forum has further strengthened the friendships, academic linkages and networking locally and regionally. Those connections will lead directly to an improving quality of higher education in the region, and promote further regional economic development as well as talent and skills cultivation.

Thank you.

马克·诺伊简历

毕业于澳大利亚新英格兰大学。现任柬埔寨教育、青年与体育部高等教育司副司长，负责高等教育政策与发展战略制定。曾任柬埔寨认证委员会标准与认证处处长，柬埔寨教育、青年与体育部高等教育司高教处副处长。

推进高等教育的可持续、区域化发展

老挝教育部高等教育司副司长　布恩桑·法西波利奔

尊敬的王立英副部长，

尊敬的各位来宾，

女士们、先生们：

我谨代表老挝教育部高等教育司和老挝代表团向本次论坛的主办方——中国教育部和云南省人民政府表示感谢，感谢你们邀请老挝代表参加这次在美丽的云南省昆明市举办的“东亚峰会高等教育合作论坛”。

同时，我也要向中国教育部和云南省人民政府表示祝贺，祝贺你们通过主办这次论坛来增进东亚地区的高等教育合作与交流。

尊敬的来宾，女士们、先生们：

东亚区域的高等教育合作与交流对于增进区域内的师生交流和学术合作具有重要意义。高等教育的质量对于区域内的可持续发展非常关键。

众所周知，高等教育机构的传统职责是教育、科研和服务社会。现在，高等教育机构还有义务为本国居民提供常规的乃至终身的教育机会。除此之外，高等教育机构还有另一个重要的职责，那就是促进社会、文化、经济与政治的发展，成为增进社会公平、民主与和平的支柱。东亚各国通过参与全球化获得的主要利益是，包括区域内资源共享、知识与信息的交流、教师和学生交流在内的跨境合作。

目前，高等教育的跨境合作让我们有机会共同讨论高等教育发展趋势、高等教育所面临的机遇与挑战，进一步明确高等教育合作的领域。全球化使各个国家之间的联系日益紧密，而这种紧密的联系需要发展中国家之间的合作与竞争，这必将促进各国之间的高等教育合作。一个国家的发展潜力加上全球化所带来的机遇使这个国家参与区域乃至国际的合作与融合成为必然。

在高等教育合作中，教育项目的输入和输出以及远程教育非常重要。如果没有相关的法规和标准来管理，或者教育体制不能为国家之间的学位学历认证提供合理的保障，那必将影响到教育项目输入和输出的质量。目前一些国家在开展跨国教育合作时已注意到这个问题，并建立起了国家的学历认证、教育质量保证体系，但有的国家在应对跨国教育合作方面的挑战时还有待采取更加积极的策略。

通过宏观层面和机构层面的双边与多边高等教育跨境交流，依据这种精神并通过校际协议的签署而建立的国家级、区域性、国际化网络将成为一个良好的平台，让人们得以交流信息，传播知识，增进彼此对适合于各个国家的高等教育的质量的针对性理解。通过加强政策对话来增进东亚区域的教育国际合作是一种最有效的途径。

我们应该通过加强符合人类、社会、经济和文化发展需要的跨境高等教育合作来提高东亚教育质量。应该建立跨境高等教育合作的规范框架，并且在包括政府、高等教育机构、学生以及质量监督体系等在内的各群体内进行推广。

学术自由应当在高校力所能及的范围内逐步推进，与尊重学术规则、重视学术透明度并驾齐驱。

高等教育机构应通过相互之间的科研团队合作来提高质量，通过与大学、政府部门、科研机构之间的联系来谋求发展，来解决区域内面临的重大问题。大学应通过国家的、国际的网络和研究群体来进一步扩大科研范围，而不是仅仅在大学里开展科研，要通过公、私合作关系，通过参与式研究、行为研究、合作研究等形式来扩展科研范围。

尊敬的来宾，女士们、先生们：

老挝的高等教育对老挝的人力资源开发起着至关重要的作用。政府的国家开发战略强调，人力资源的开发要符合国家发展战略，要与本国的经济发展、国家结构以及全球经济发展紧密联系。更重要的是，它必需立足于发展能够支持国家工业化和现代化建设所需的科学和技术。人力资源的开发和建设将为国家社会经济发展的需要培养高技能的人才。它也将推动这个国家与东亚区域内、外的国家的融合。这需要对不同层次的教育给予支持与投资。

为了实现我们的发展战略以及政府的政策，高等教育规划应该符合劳动力市场和所有公有、私有经济部门的需求。高等教育应当培养国家的建设与发展所需的各个领域的高层次学术和科研人才。在加强老挝高等教育建设的框架下，亚洲开发银行将对老挝至2020年高等教育发展战略给予学术和财政的支持。这一战略符合政府的社会经济发展规划，为规范国家高等教育规划提供了参考。另外，这一战略也作为公立和私立高等教育机构提高办学质量的一项政策依据。这一战略包括三项行动计划：一是增进高等教育准入的平等性；二是提高教育质量和针对性；三是改进监管与管理。

这个高等教育发展战略涉及国家的相关部委、高等教育机构以及中心和南北部省区与高等教育相关的机构。2010—2020年高等教育规划包括宗旨、任务、项目、目标与目的几个方面。例如：

建设、改善和扩大高等教育；改革高等教育；高等教育机构教职人员的培养；完善高等教育质量监督体系；推动科研与科研发展；改进高等教育管理信息系统；改善高等教育的监管与管理。

高等教育的发展规划分为两个阶段：第一个阶段是2010—2015年，这一阶段的任务是规范高等教育机构的教育项目、目标与目的、活动，强调2010—2015年间高等教育发展的特殊培养和资助领域。这一阶段发展所需资金将来自政府支持、国内外基金或银行贷款。第二阶段（2016—2020）的主要任务是让高等教育为支持国家的工业化和现代化进程作好准备。

为了提高东亚区域内高等教育质量，推进区域经济发展和人才培养，增加区域内的高等教育合作与交流，履行高等教育在增进东亚区域可持续发展中的职责，我们建议区域内高等教育合作采取以下举措：

为高等教育系统设置相应标准，包括高等教育机构、课程、设备、设施等标准；推进学分转换、跨境高等教育，修订所有高等教育项目的课程与授课模式以满足劳动力市场的需要；通过双边和多边的合作促进区域内和国际知名高校之间的学术交流与流动，以分享经验，为达到国际标准而携手共进；建立一个区域性、国际性的质量监督和认证体系；通过支持透明和量化的管理来引进科学的高等教育监管和管理机制。

我希望"东亚峰会高等教育合作论坛"的举办能够有助于解决我们共同所面临的问题，并且能够加强我们在高等教育方面的合作，以便东亚地区实现可持续发展。

我预祝此次论坛取得圆满成功。

谢谢！

（郑蔚　译）

布恩桑·法西波利奔英文发言稿

Promote Sustainable and Regional Development of Higher Education

Bounthaen Phesiboriboun
Deputy Director General, Department of Higher Education,
Ministry of Education, Lao PDR

Distinguished Excellencies,
Distinguished delegates,
Ladies and Gentlemen,

On Behalf of the Department of Higher Education, Ministry of Education, Lao People's Democratic Republic and on behalf of Lao delegation and personally, I would like to express my sincere thanks to the Ministry of Education of China and the People's Government of Yunnan Province for extending the invitation to the Lao Delegation and facilitating our participation to the East Asia Higher Education Cooperation Forum in the beautiful City Kunming, Yunnan Province, People's Republic of China.

On this specious occasion I would like to congratulate the Ministry of Education of China and the People's Government of Yunnan Province to organize the Forum for the cooperation and exchanges concerning strengthening higher education in the East Asia.

Distinguished Delegates, Ladies and Gentlemen, The East Asia Higher Education cooperation and exchanges is very meaningful for enhancing the students and staff exchanges and cooperation in the academic mobility. The quality of higher education will be very critical for sustainable regional development.

As we are all aware that the higher educations institutions have the traditional mandate to provide education, undertaken research and provide services to society. At present the higher education institutions have the functions to provide education for citizenship by undertaking regularly the higher learning through lifelong learning. Besides higher education institutions have an important role to contribute to develop the culture, socio-economic and political development and is a pillar to boost the solidarity, democracy and peace. Through the globalization, the main benefits to be gained by higher education institutions across East Asian countries entering into cross border collaborations include the sharing of resources, the exchange of knowledge and information, the exchange of staffs and students based on mutual interest and solidarity.

At present cross-border higher education collaboration through the regional cooperation gives the opportunity to discuss on the trends of higher education, the issues and challenges and to identify the areas of cooperation. The cross border higher education collaboration was also able to achieve success since globalization and links between countries are now an international reality and these movements also require cooperation and competition among developing countries. The national development potential and global opportunities enable the country to participate in the regional and international integration.

The import and export of higher educational programs and the distance learning is also critical and could affect the quality of delivery if there is no regulations and standards to govern and if the educational system is not readable and comparable in terms of promotion of pathways between each education level and the recognition of higher education degrees and certification. While in some countries the national quality assurance frameworks, accreditation and the recognition of qualifications have taken into account cross-border higher education, in many countries they are still geared to addressing the challenges of cross-border provision.

Through bilateral and multilateral cross-border higher education cooperation at the macro level and institutional level, the national, the regional and international network through this spirit and the signing of agreement between universities itself will serve as a good platform to exchange information and good practice, disseminate knowledge and increase the mutual understanding on the quality and relevance of higher education which fits into each country. The promotion of ASEAN dimension and international organization cooperation through this policy dialogue would be a good platform and offers the most promising strategy for strengthen higher education across China and East Asia Countries.

The East Asia quality network should be strengthened and linked with China quality network through cross-border higher education that meets human, social, economic and cultural needs . The regulation framework for cross-border higher education should be developed, disseminated broadly for different groups including government, higher education providers, students, quality assurance bodies, etc.

The academic freedom should be undertaken step by step based on the capability and the efficiency of the university and should be parallel with the respect of regulations, the capability to demonstrate their accountability and transparency which will lead to university ranking.

Higher education institutions should be strengthened through collaboration between competent research teams within universities to address critical regional problems and through the links between universities and institutions and within government ministries and through partnership with academies of science. The university research can be broadened through the national and international networking and research cluster not only within universities but also with the public an private partnership through participatory research, action research and collaborative research. The need of expertise in Science and Technology is still a need for human resource development for East Asia countries.

Distinguished Delegates, Ladies and Gentlemen, higher education in Lao PDR plays a very significant and important role in human resources development. The Government's national development strategy highlighted that human resources development should be aligned with the national development strategy, relevant to economic components and structure of the country and linked with the global economy. Furthermore, it must facilitate and make the country's economic infrastructure strong, based on science and technology which would develop skilled manpower equipped to support the country's industrialization and modernization plans. Building capacity in human resources will produce a highly skilled manpower and respond to the socio-economic development needs of the country. It will also propel the country's integration with other countries in the region, particularly in East Asia and beyond. This requires support and investments in all levels of education.

In order to realize the development strategy and the Government's policy, planning in higher education should be relevant and meet the demands of the labor market and all economic sectors, both public and private. Higher education should produce academicians and researchers with skills and abilities in certain areas and levels of knowledge and expertise required to develop the community and the country as a whole. The strategy and master plan prepared on higher educational development by 2020 is financially and academically supported by the ADB within the framework of the strengthening higher education in Lao PDR project, which is prepared as a reference for formulating higher educational plans since it is aligned with the Government's socio-economic development plans. In addition, it is used as a strategic and policy documentation referred to by the public and private higher educational institutions as they implement academic training as part of quality improvement in higher education. This is in line with the three action plans as:

(i) increasing equity access to higher education; (ii) improve quality and relevance; (iii) improve governance and management.

Strategy and master plan on higher educational development involved the parties from line-ministries, higher education providers, actors and stakeholders across the sectors concerned in higher education through the means of survey and data collection conducted in the central and some provinces in the southern and northern regions. The higher education master plan 2010 – 2020, is composed of the vision, mission, programs, targets and goals pertaining to strategic options such as:

* Building, improving and expanding higher education;
* Reforming higher education;
* Development of teachers and administrators in higher education;
* Improving quality assurance in higher education;
* Promoting research and research development;
* Improving higher education management information system (HEMIS);
* Improving governance and management in higher education.

The master plan on higher educational development is divided into two phases: 1st phase by 2015 is to formulate programs, targets and goals, and activities taken by higher educational institutions emphasizing on the specific areas of training and financing plans used for implementation during 2010 – 2015, and proposed to the Government for funding, and that may be proposed for the grants or loans allocated from domestic and external sources. 2nd phase (2016 – 2020) is to identify for the major preparation of higher education to support the country in the process of industrialization and modernization.

The actions suggested towards regional quality of higher education and promoting regional economic development and talents cultivation, fulfilling the role of higher education in the sustainable regional development and strengthening East Asia education cooperation and exchanges include the following:

* Set up standards for higher education system including standard of higher education institutions, curriculum, equipment, facilities etc.

* Revise curriculum and the delivery modes in all higher education programs to meet the labor market by promoting credit transfer and cross-border higher education.

* Promote academic exchange and mobility regional and international cooperation through bilateral and multilateral cooperation between and higher education institutions with regional and international reputation in order to share experiences and best practices and to reach international standards on a long-term and sustainable basis.

* Put in place a regional / international quality control and accreditation arrangement.

* Introduction a mechanism for a good governance and management of higher education by supporting a transparent and accountable management.

I do hope that the East Asia Higher Education Cooperation Forum could contribute to resolve the common issues and problems and strengthen our further cooperation in the field of education in general and especially in higher education for sustainable development in the region and wish a tremendous success East Asia Higher Education Cooperation Forum.

Thank you for your attention!

布恩桑·法西波利奔简历

老挝教育部高等教育司副司长。曾任万象林学院、老挝国立大学讲师。出席国际研讨会、研修班等40余次，出版专著、报告、译著等10余部。精通英语、法语、泰语和越南语。

全球教育商业化还是教育全球商业化?

马来西亚高等教育部高等教育司教育市场处处长
赛义德·阿尔维·宾·赛克·阿尔萨格夫

尊敬的主席先生，

中国教育部张秀琴女士，

嘉宾们，

女士们，先生们：

我今天的发言，要从一句中国的谚语开始——千里之行始于足下，正如上海世界贸易中心这样高楼的建设需要打好地基一样，一切工作都要从基础开始。马来西亚政府一向重视教育，多年以来，我们每年将GDP的5%以上投入教育产业。去年政府在教育产业的投入达到了GDP的8%。我们已经连续30多年投入50%的GDP用于公共事业建设，其中教育产业占了较大比例。马来西亚目前是在教育产业上的投入第二大的国家。马来西亚每年有6%的学生在海外留学，也就是说，在100万学生当中，有6万人在世界各地留学，这其中包括中国，以及其他东西方国家。

在马来西亚，教育产业是建立在政府的大力支持这一稳定基石之上的。政府今年的统计数据显示，大学毕业生的收入比未接受过高等教育的同龄人高出153%。一名本科生一年的收入可以达146000美元，其中有86000多美元反馈给社会。这差不多是政府对教育投入的3倍。从这些数据中我们知道，马来西亚向来重视教育投入，而教育作为一项产业，在经济领域也十分重要。众所周知，美国每年对教育的投入超过120亿美元，英国是 18 亿美元，澳大利亚是 12 亿美元，马来西亚的投入也很大。

那么我们教育的基础到底有多坚实呢？哈佛一位教授——哈维·路易斯曾表示出担忧：究竟当前的高等教育会把学生引向何处？他提醒我们，当前的本科生教育仅仅专注于专业知识的培养，这最终很可能会摧毁美国的国民文化。这表明教育对于一个社会的文化、经济以及政治发展具有基础性的作用。我们很多人都忽视了这一点，即高等教育如果没有一个适当的价值体系来引导学生记住并重视自己在社会中所扮演的角色以及具有的责任，将会造成个人主义的膨胀，以及对个人利益得失的过度重视。教育的国际合作与交流要关注对学生的价值观的培养。我认为，对学生价值观的培养与知识的教授并不相互矛盾。我相信没有任何一个雇主愿意聘用一个对自己人生都不负责、不成熟的大学毕业生。我们今天聚在一起也正是为了探讨一个适当的学生培养途径，让他们更趋成熟。或许我们现有的教育体系不能完全实现这一目标，但是只要能够让学生体验到真正的国际化，真正多样化的文化，这一目标的实现并不难。有调查显示，对于学生来说，选择到某高校就读，吸引他们的，一般不是跨文化的体验，或是校园生活，而是这所学校的排名，科研实力与声誉。在高等教育中加入国际元素已经不是一个新鲜的尝试。今天上午我们谈到了进行教育体制改革以适应国际化。我们总是一味地学习像哈佛、剑桥、斯坦福、耶鲁等这样的名校，却忽视了教育事业肩负着服务当地社会文化这一重要责任，这是非常遗憾的。我相信刚才提到的这些大学对他们各自所在的地区的发展之所以能够作出巨大的贡献，正是因为在他们的每一个发展阶段都纳入了国际化的教育元素。所以，我倡议，我们不要仅仅为了国际化而国际化，而应该立足于为我们的未来社会培养优秀人才而精心设计我们的国际化进程。

我们是否了解我们的历史？我们是否知道我们东亚国家的教育发展史？我们是否都仅在向前看？我们是否都忘了，世界上最古老的大学就在我们中间——在印度？剑桥大学建于 1200 年前后，与之相比其实很年轻。那么在中国呢，汉武帝建立了中国的第一所皇家大学，而在隋朝就已经有了科举制度，所有的学者和政府官员在进入政府工作前都必须经过这一考试。这是考试制度的起源。在谈及学者流动性的时候，我们是否记得中国的玄奘西行，远赴印度求真经的故事？所以，学者流动、大学制度等在我们东亚其实古已有之。所以，我们东亚的教育体系一向重视流动性，我们也一向重视对下一代的培养。我们的老师一向重视学生的培养和学术能力的提高。

马来西亚一直不忘这一根本，致力于建立培养学生价值观的教育体系。我们在开展国际合作的过程中不忘学生的发展。例如，最近马来西亚、印度尼西亚和泰国建立了一个促进学生流动性的体系。在这一体系中，我们在学分对接、教学大纲，甚至专业设置方面整合了三个国家的资源，以保证学生在这三个国家之间游学的时候没有任何学习上的障碍和损失。我相信来自泰国的代表对此会有进一步的介绍。

马来西亚政府也鼓励企业加入教育事业中。目前有一项企业投资设立了总额为 180 万美元的奖学金，可以资助 400 多名学生到中国学习。希望中国政府可以协助我们安置和照顾这些学生。

在马来西亚新的教育改革计划中，国际化发展已经成为高等教育必须展开的实践之一。目前，马来西亚赴国外留学的学生中已经有 9% 选择回国服务，从中我们强烈地感到，学生、学者的国际经历就是我们教育改革千里之行的开始。

谢谢！

（沈芸　译）

赛义德·阿尔维·宾·赛克·阿尔萨格夫英文发言 PPT

Commercialization of Global Education or Global Commercialization of Education?

Syed Alwee Bin Shekh Alsagoff
Director, Education Marketing Division, Department of Higher Education,
Ministry of Higher Education, Malaysia

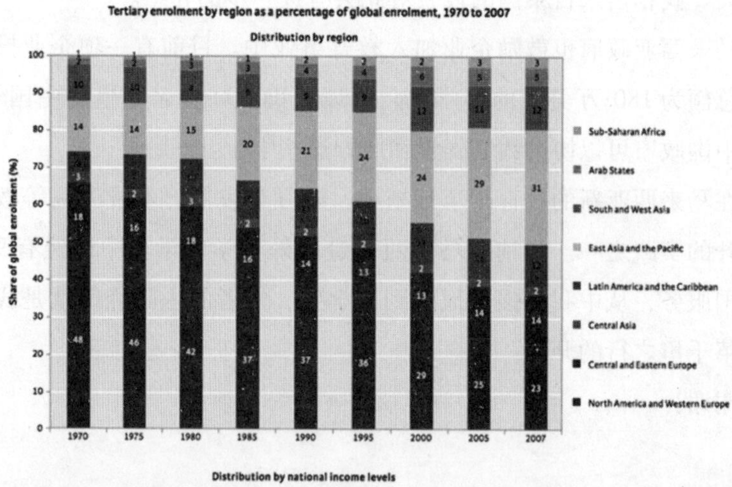

*
The Big Picture
Malaysian Government spends
USD 4.8 billion
on education infrastructure development

2%
Share of international
students choose Malaysia
(open 2003)

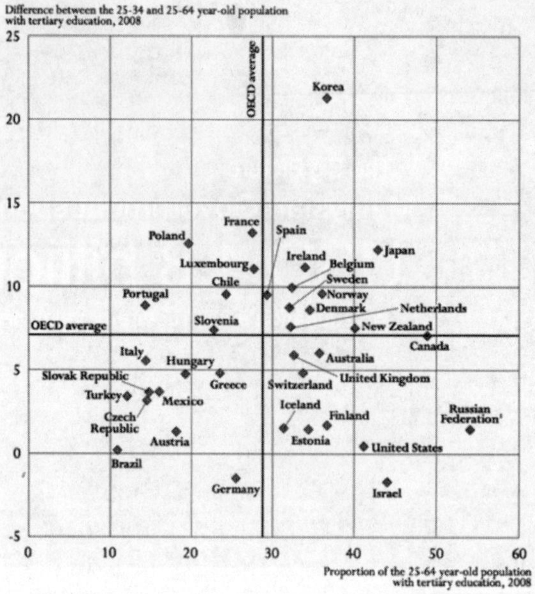

Figure 2.8. Public costs and benefits for someone obtaining higher levels of education, 2006

This figure shows both the costs and the benefits to the public purse from a male student obtaining upper secondary or post-secondary non-tertiary education and tertiary education.

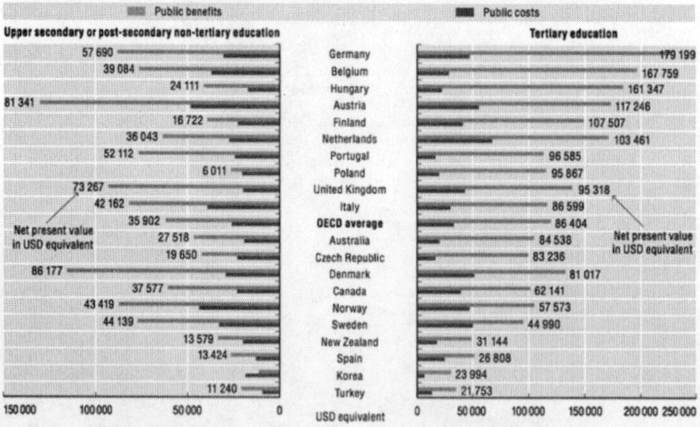

Source: OECD (2010), *Education at a Glance* 2010, Tables A8.3 and A8.4, available at *http://dx.doi.org/10.1787/888932310225*.

Figure 7
Relative importance ratings for key factors associated with learning experience

1 = Very unimportant
2 = Unimportant
3 = Important
4 = Very important
(n = 15,797)

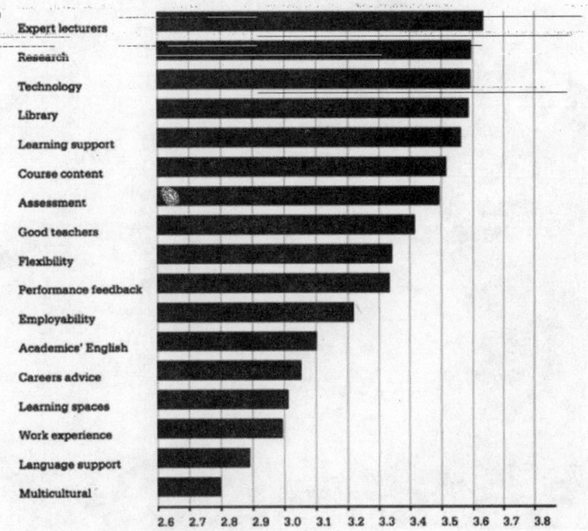

Graphic feed: visualization of national origins of THE World University Ranking top 100 (2010)
September 16, 2010 by globalhighered

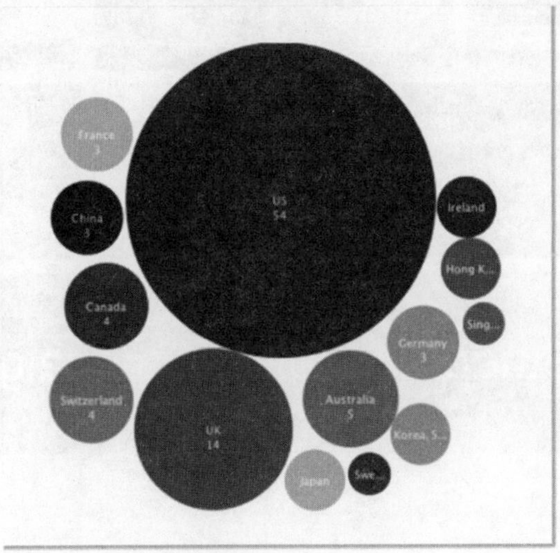

Source: *many eyes*, 16 September 2010

61%
Of students interviewed said that WORD OF MOUTH is the reason for them to choose to go to Malaysia

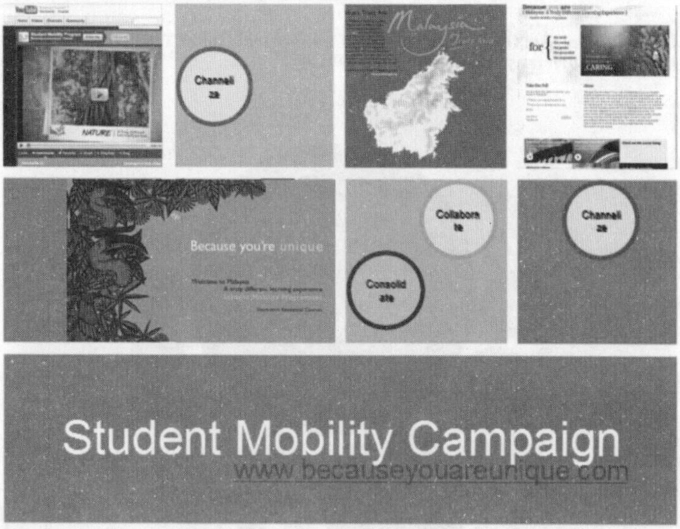
Channeli ze
Because you're unique
Collabora te
Consolid ate
Channeli ze
Student Mobility Campaign
www.becauseyouareunique.com

赛义德·阿尔维·宾·赛克·阿尔萨格夫简历

2009年7月至今，担任马来西亚高等教育部高等教育司教育市场处处长，博士。曾在马来西亚数个国家战略性特别工作组中任职，并协助出台数个国家标准。兼任英美多家学术期刊评委，发表作品50余篇，申请专利11项。

发展教育，促进国家进步

缅甸联邦驻昆明总领事　吴佐朴温

主席先生，

嘉宾们，

女士们、先生们：

我要向中国教育部以及云南省教育厅表示衷心的谢意，感谢邀请我参加在昆明召开的这次重要论坛，感谢会议主办方的盛情款待！

我也想借此机会向“东亚峰会高等教育合作论坛”组委会致谢，感谢你们在推动东亚国家间高等教育合作中所作的努力。

进入21世纪，全世界正在从信息化时代迈向知识时代，亦即向教育时代迈进。在教育时代，全民教育就是要满足人类的基本学习需求。“全民教育”已经成为当今社会每一个体的主要需求和关注的重点。所以，人力资源培训与开发在当今社会受到了极大重视。

缅甸教育部一直坚持一个信条，即通过教育建立一个现代化的发达国家。以这一口号为目标，我们提出了切合实际的战略规划以及工作进程来发展教育，从而推动国家的发展。教育质量的提高被视为实现国家稳定、社会繁荣和现代化的一个至关重要的决定性因素。

衷心期待我们的教育部以及所有相关人员能够在深入调研和与各位代表分享、交流经验的基础上脚踏实地地实现这一目标。缅甸政府于2001年开始实施“教育发展30年计划”。该计划涵盖了2001—2002财年到2030—2031财年的30年时间内的教育发展规划。该计划中的高等教育子规划有12个，其中我们设立了12个愿景和36个子项目，具体集中在以下几个领域：

（1）人力资源开发；

（2）技术转化利用；

（3）科研开发；

（4）建立终身学习型社会；

（5）提升教育质量；

（6）维护民族身份认同及国家价值观。

高等教育子规划中的每一个项目都旨在建立一个开放的教育体制。

我们在1997—2002年间为推进高等教育工作举行了一系列的研讨会，被视为缅甸教育发展的重要里程碑。这些研讨会对建立一个高效的高等教育体系起到了重要作用。通过这一体系的建立，我们可以更好地为实现我国高等教育发展目标而对人力资源提出更高的要求，并更好地迎接挑战，同时也可以更好地满足不断出现的新的学习形式的要求，以服务于现代化经济发展的需求。

为了更好地发展教育，我们在实施30年计划的同时实施“四年特别发展计划”。这一计划推动我国高等教育机构与国际同行和科研机构建立合作关系，以更好地应用国内外资源发展本国高等教育。

我们与国外的教育合作形式多样，包括签署谅解备忘录，由外方提供培训项目、研修班、合作科研项目以及参加国外奖学金项目学习等。

缅甸将一如既往地支持高等教育国际合作，并与东亚峰会框架下的国家（10+6）开展教育合作与交流。

东亚国家间紧密的高等教育合作与交流为各个国家的教育部门提供了分享、交流经验的机会以促进各国的教育发展。

我坚信“东亚峰会高等教育合作论坛”将以前所未有的力量，推动东亚（10+6）国家间的有效交流。

我衷心希望“东亚峰会高等教育合作论坛”及其他相关活动在中国教育部以及云南省人民政府的支持与引导下获得成功，并推动我们在未来建立更多合作项目。

主席先生，我希望借此机会感谢中国政府和云南省人民政府，以及来自东亚（10+6）国家的与会代表给予论坛的支持与合作。

谢谢！

（沈芸　译）

吴佐朴温英文发言稿

Develop Education and Promote National Development

U Zaw Phyo Win

Consul General of the Union of Myanmar in Kunming

Mr. Chairman,

Distinguished Delegates,

Ladies and Gentlemen,

I would like to express my warmest appreciation to the Ministry of Education of the People's Republic of China and the Department of Education of the People's Goverment of Yunnan Province for kind invitation and warm welcome extended to me and for the excellent arrangements made for the successful holding of this important forum in Kunming.

I also wish to take this opportunity to express my gratitude to the Organizing Committee of East Asia Summit Higher Education Cooperation Forum with the aim of promoting the higher education cooperation in East Asian countries.

On entering the Twenty-First century, the whole world is advancing from the information age to the knowledge age, that is, the education age.

In the education age, "education for all" is meeting the basic learning needs of human beings. "Education for all" becomes the cause and concern of each and every individual in reality.

Consequently, Human Resource Development is being given emphasis and priority in today's human society.

In the Union of Myanmar, the Ministry of Education in consonant with the motto building a modern, developed nation through education, has adopted an effective agenda and appropriate strategies to harness education for the advancement of the nation. The uplift of education quality is regarded and accepted as the most important, fundamental and decisive factor for the stability, perpetuity and modernity of the country and the people.

It is our honest desire and fervent hope that all those concerned could practically implement the aim successfully through further research and sharing of ideas and experiences among the participants of this forum.

In Myanmar, Thirty-Year Long-Term Education Development Plan was launched in 2001 and it covers the period from 2001 – 2002 financial year to 2030 – 2031 financial year. There are 12 visions and 36 programmes in Higher Education Sub-sector of the Thirty-Year Long-Term Education Development Plan for the Following areas:

(1) Human Resource Development;

(2) Utilization of Technology;

(3) Expansion of Research;

(4) Development of a Lifelong Learning Society;

(5) Promotion of the Quality of Education;

(6) Preservation of National Identity and National Values.

The component of the plan for the higher education sub-sector was formulated to develop an open education system.

The seminars related to the promotion of higher education held between 1997 and 2002 are important milestones in the annals of the education sector. Those seminars had a great impact on the crafting of higher education to satisfy the demand for better qualified human resource to meet the new challenges stemming from the increasing demand for higher education, the emergence of new modalities of learning and the need to be more responsive to the needs of a modernizing economy.

To better facilitate education promotion endeavors, the thirty-year plan has been merged with the special four-year plan. It gave impetus to higher educations to form linkages and collaborations with international higher education institutions and research organizations in order to harness both local and foreign sources for the development of higher education sub-sector.

These collaborations were in the forms of MOUs, training programmes, workshops and seminars conducted by foreign institutions, joint research programmes and invitations to participate in scholarship programmes abroad.

Myanmar will continue its participation in promoting the higher education cooperation and development programmes being undertaken in the (10+6) countries within the East Asia Summit Framework.

The enhanced higher education cooperation among the East Asian countries provides their education sectors the opportunity to share experiences and ideas and boost the education development activities.

I am confident that East Asia Summit Higher Education Cooperation Forum will contribute to facilitate the exchanges among the East Asia (10+6) Countries more effectively than before.

I sincerely hope that under the able and easy guidance of the Ministry of Education of the People's Republic of China and the People's Government of Yunnan Province, East Asia Summit Higher Education Cooperation Forum and the related activities will be successful and enable us to implement future programmes.

I wish to take this opportunity to thank the Government of the People's Republic of China and the People's Government of Yunnan Province and the delegates from the (10+6) countries for the cooperation and support that they have extended to this forum.

Thank you.

吴佐朴温简历

缅甸彬坞伦市（眉苗）缅甸国防大学理学学士。

工作经历：

1990—2005 年，缅甸国防部少尉。

2005—2007 年，缅甸外交部外语训练研究司副主任。

2007—2009 年 5 月，缅甸外交部外语训练研究司主任。

2009 年 5 月至今，缅甸联邦驻昆明总领事馆总领事。

通过国际合作
打造高品质、多样化的高等教育

新加坡教育部高等教育司副司长　林国伟

云南省教育厅厅长罗崇敏先生，

嘉宾们，

女士们、先生们：

今天能代表新加坡参加首届“东亚峰会高等教育合作论坛”，我感到很荣幸。在当前高等教育国际化进程加快，亚洲在世界高等教育领域占据重要地位的新形势下，这次旨在探讨加强东亚（10+6）① 框架下的高等教育合作的论坛的召开，无疑是非常及时的。

今天早上，我们聆听了王立英女士和凯瑟琳·坎贝尔女士的精彩演讲。她们在演讲中都提到了目前我们面临的全球机遇与挑战，并指出了进一步加强彼此之间的合作在各国政府、高等教育院校应对这些挑战时所起到的积极作用。今天我要借此机会与大家分享新加坡在打造高品质、多样化的高等教育过程中的经验，向大家介绍国际化在这一过程中所起到的重要作用。

一、打造高品质的高等教育

新加坡是一个小国家，我们的国力来源于国民的素质。要维持国家

① 东亚（10+6），指东盟十国与中国、日本、韩国、印度、澳大利亚和新西兰六国。

的繁荣以及在国际上的竞争力，我们必须保证有一流的教育机构为学生提供高质量的教育。在这方面，新加坡的三所大学——新加坡国立大学、南洋理工大学以及新加坡管理大学具有丰富的经验。他们位列本区域最好的大学之中，通过培养高素质的人才来满足经济发展、科研工作以及知识创新工作的需求，为新加坡的发展作出了突出贡献。

在发展经济的同时，我们需要通过成立更多院校来发展高等教育。这些新的院校不仅能够扩大人才培养规模，更应致力于培养具有多种技能的人才以适应日趋复杂的国际环境。这些院校包括与美国的麻省理工学院和中国的浙江大学联合建立的新加坡技术与设计大学，由南洋理工大学和英国伦敦皇家学院联合建立的全新的医学院，以及即将由新加坡国立大学与耶鲁大学联合建立的文理学院。

每一所新成立的大学都将具有自己独特的教育模式，这将使新加坡的高等教育更加多样化。新加坡技术与设计大学是一所以工学和建筑学为主的高层次研究型大学。它所提供的融汇东西方精粹，并结合企业实践经验和创新性培养的多学科课程是其标志性特征。亚洲成立的第一所文理学院偏重为政府、学界和企业界培养优秀管理人才。最后，新的医学院不仅满足国民医疗保健的需求，还将尝试利用伦敦皇家学院的经验以及南洋理工大学的技术力量，有效结合工学与医学，研发新型医疗体系和设备。

另外，我们最近才成立的新加坡理工学院将满足社会对高级技术人才的需求。这所学校将以合作办学形式为主，作为海外知名院校在新加坡的校区向理工科本科毕业生提供学位课程。学校目前的合作院校包括英国的纽卡斯尔大学和曼彻斯特大学，德国慕尼黑工业大学和美国内华达大学。理工科的毕业生可以在两年内获得学位，这既节约了费用又保证了质量。

二、国际化的重要性

这些新院校的成立从一个侧面反映了国际化对于高等教育发展的重

要性，同时也显示出亚洲在全球高等教育领域不断提升的重要性。例如，我们与麻省理工学院、浙江大学、耶鲁大学以及伦敦皇家学院的深入合作，使我们可以学习世界各国的成功教育模式和经验，使之融入亚洲高等教育领域，打开其潜在的教育市场。

目前，新加坡的高等院校与东盟成员国的高等院校有着广泛的交流与合作。例如，新加坡国立大学、中国复旦大学和韩国高丽大学建立了上海—首尔—新加坡大学联盟，向社会提供针对亚洲商业特色的商科学位课程。南洋理工大学除了与印度理工学院坎普尔校区合作开展学生交换和合作科研项目外，目前还与日本早稻田大学联合提供 MBA 双学位课程。新加坡管理大学与西澳大利亚大学签订了合作备忘录，在体育及探险教育领域开展合作。这些国际合作与交流项目不仅增加了我国教育的多样性，提高了教育质量，还拓展了在校生的国际经历和视野。

无论如何，在亚洲高等教育不断扩大的同时，我们在东亚（10 +6）框架下开展合作的领域也在不断增加。截至 2020 年，仅中国和印度两国就将共计培养出 1400 万名大学毕业生，这将是亚洲地区人才涌现的时代。亚洲各国在教育领域的合作与经验交流将为这一时代的人才培养提供有益的帮助。

三、结　语

最后，我要感谢中国教育部、云南省人民政府以及昆明人民，感谢你们的盛情款待。我希望本次论坛将取得丰硕的成果，相信论坛的举办将为东亚高等教育合作的深入提供宝贵经验。

谢谢各位！

（沈芸　译）

林国伟英文发言稿

Promote a High Quality and Diversified Higher Education sector through International Cooperation and Exchange

Peter Lam Kok Wai

Deputy Director (Higher Education), Ministry of Education, Singapore

Mr. Luo Chongmin, Director, Yunnan Provincial Department of Education,
Distinguished Delegates,
Ladies and Gentlemen,

I am honoured to represent Singapore today at the inaugural East Asia Higher Education Cooperation Forum. This forum, which seeks to enhance educational cooperation and exchanges under the (10 + 6) framework,① is timely given the rapid internationalisation of the tertiary sector and Asia's emergence as a major player in the global higher education landscape.

This morning, we have heard excellent speeches from speakers like Madam Wang Liying and Ms Kathryn Campbell who painted global challenges and opportunities and the need for more enhanced collaboration among governments and tertiary institutions on higher education to respond to these challenges.

To contribute to today's discussion, I would like to share with you Singapore's efforts to build a high-quality, diversified tertiary sector, and the important role which internationalisation plays in helping us to achieve this.

---

① The (10 + 6) framework comprises of the 10 ASEAN nations and the other 6 nations of China, India, Korea, Japan, New Zealand and Australia.

Developing a high-quality tertiary sector

Singapore is a small country. Our strength lies in the quality of our people. To maintain our competitive edge and prosper as a country we need to ensure that we have top-class educational institutions which provide our students with a high-quality education. To this end, Singapore's three universities-National University of Singapore (NUS), Nanyang Technological University (NTU) and Singapore Management University-have done well. They are among the best universities in the region and have contributed significantly to Singapore's development by producing high-quality graduate manpower to meet the needs of our economy, advancing research and creating knowledge.

As our economy develops, we will expand our university sector by establishing new institutions which will not only increase our graduate manpower, but equip our graduates with the different skills necessary to navigate an increasingly complex global environment. These include a new university, the Singapore University of Technology & Design (SUTD) that is established in collaboration with MIT and Zhejiang University, a new medical school jointly developed by NTU and Imperial College London, and a possible tie-up between NUS and Yale University to establish a liberal arts college in Singapore.

Each of these new institutions will be distinguished by a unique educational model and will add diversity to Singapore's higher education landscape. SUTD is positioned as a top-tier research-intensive university with an initial focus on Engineering and Architecture. It will offer a novel multi-disciplinary curriculum which blends the best of both east and west, with entrepreneurship and innovation as hallmarks of its brand of education. The liberal arts college, a first in Asia, will provide an education model to develop leaders of industry, academia and nations. Finally, the new medical school will not only provide for Singapore's healthcare needs but also seeks to tap on Imperial College's experience and NTU's capabilities to interface engineering and medicine to innovate better medical systems and devices for health care.

In addition, Singapore also recently set up the Singapore Institute of Technology (SIT) to cater to polytechnic upgrades. This institution is founded on the basis of collaboration. The SIT will partner reputable overseas universities to offer degrees to polytechnic graduates in the name of those universities. Partner universities include UK's Newcastle University and Manchester University, TUM, and University of Nevada Las Vegas. Polytechnic graduates can obtain these degrees in two years. This will save costs, without diluting any quality.

Importance of Internationalisation

These new institutions reflect the importance of internationalisation to the development of our tertiary sector and Asia's rising importance in the global higher education landscape. Our deep educational collaborations with MIT, Zhejiang University, Yale and Imperial College for example, allow us to draw references from successful educational models around the world which we then adapt and contextualize to Asia to tap on its emerging intellectual and commercial markets.

At present, our institutes of higher learning (IHLs) have extensive collaborations with IHLs within the (10 + 6) framework of nations. For instance, NUS together with China's Fudan University and Korea University, has established the Shanghai, Seoul and Singapore University Alliance to offer business programmes focused on Asia. NTU has collaborated with the Indian Institute of Technology (IIT) Kanpur on student exchanges and joint research, and currently offers a double MBA degree together with Japan's Waseda University. SMU has also signed a Memorandum of Understanding (MOU) with the University of Western Australia (UWA) to collaborate in sports and adventure education. These overseas collaborations not only add to the quality and variety of our educational programmes but also enhance our students' experience through the international exposure which they offer.

However, there is more scope to enhance educational collaboration within the (10 + 6) framework as the Asian higher education sector expands. With China and India expected to produce a combined 14 million graduates by 2020, there will be a surge of talent within Asia which will benefit from the exchange of ideas and diverse educational experiences offered by enhanced educational collaboration.

Conclusion

To conclude, I would like to express my appreciation to the Ministry of Education (China), Government of Yunnan Province, and people of Kunming City for your warm hospitality.

I look forward to a fruitful discussion at this forum and trust it will add valuable insights and share ideas on ways to enhance educational cooperation in East Asia.

Thank you.

林国伟简历

新加坡教育部高等教育司副司长林国伟先生戎马出身，上校军衔，步兵营副指挥官。曾任新加坡义安理工学院计划与项目主任，现任新加坡教育部高等教育司副司长。林国伟先生是新加坡公共服务委员会留学奖学金的获得者，以优异的成绩毕业于伦敦帝国理工学院，获硕士学位。曾进修过欧洲工商学院青年管理者课程。

充实高等教育和人力资源培训，积极参与东亚地区高等教育合作

菲律宾驻重庆总领事　傅查利

我对能在美丽的春城参加“东亚峰会高等教育合作论坛”深表荣幸。来自发展中国家和正在崛起的经济大国的与会代表欢聚一堂，凸显了这次聚会的多样性和特殊性。在此我要感谢中国政府邀请我出席此次会议。

我认为，中国教育部和云南大学在东亚峰会框架下发起对高等教育交流与合作这一适时、重要的主题的讨论，值得称赞。因为我们都认识到教育是东亚峰会框架下的前沿。我们都认同教育是人力资源开发、扶贫、缩小差距的要素。

随着中国这样经济空前发展的国家的崛起，21 世纪必将是亚洲的世纪。中国积极向他国学习，积极创新，同时也对其他国家予以帮助。中国无疑是当今世界发展的主要动力。

亚洲虽然是人口最多、面积最大的洲，并且还呈现出经济进一步一体化的趋势，但是我们仍然面临着巨大的挑战。今天我们仍落后于欧洲和北美，尤其是人力资源开发、拉动经济增长和社会革新方面。在全球化不断推进的情况下，亚洲已经像欧盟那样建立起了区域认同。泛亚框架的对话已开始进行，当然随后也会讨论例如建立统一货币、市场和加强文化、地缘政治和战略合作等问题。

高等教育机构为东亚（10 +6）框架下的交流与改革带来了新的力量并刺激了东亚的发展，提升了人民的素质，激发了社会的巨大潜力。

亚洲人口众多，社会多样性和教育发展不均是我们面临的主要挑战。努力构建标准化体系尤显重要，因为这样可以让大学培养更为专业的毕业生，这样将有助于区域内各国共同应对所面临的复杂挑战。人类的文明史证明了教育对于人力资源开发、人才培养的影响力，生活的质量也会随教育的发展而提高。

我要告诉大家一个好消息，菲律宾总统阿基诺三世已正式表示要优先发展本国教育。在他的就职演讲和国会演讲中，阿基诺总统强调了政府的要务是民主、政务透明、文明执政。我们相信菲律宾能够为东亚和世界贡献力量。菲律宾已成为亚洲学术、专业培训和英语教学的中心。并且，菲律宾在社会性别赋权、妇女和女童教育上一直保持着优势。但是，菲律宾目前在科学技术、基础数学、数码技术领域需要有所建树。我们希望既能获得自主技术，又能通过合作、对话和交流对我们的邻国有所帮助。

在2010年8月贵阳召开的东盟教育部长圆桌会议上，菲律宾教育部部长、高教委主席帕翠西娅·利库阿南（Dr. Patricia Licuanan）代表菲律宾对《贵阳申明》中的教育改革和区域合作作出承诺。当学生在各国间流动时，我们鼓励消除各种障碍，制定各种学位学历互认的标准化体系。我们支持中国东盟委员会关于人文交流合作的项目，诸如教育、文化、卫生、体育、旅游、传媒、艺术等。我们鼓励奖学金的设立和区域内的学生流动，特别支持中国—东盟的“双十万计划”。此外，还可以通过交换高级专家和科学家来提高教育质量。不过，我们建议应尽可能地为参与到这些交换项目的人员提供物质和精神支持，以便他们能尽快适应邀请国的生活并开展工作。

尽管我们认为基础教育应该是一种普世教育，但是高等教育也应该有所选择地提高质量。鉴于此，我们发现我们的区域缺乏一种综合考虑亚洲各国特点的对话和协商机制；一种同时兼顾亚洲教育的改革和发展，促进交流与沟通的机制。

由于亚洲国家发展程度不一，公平的原则应着眼于标准的可操作性。

菲律宾政府认为《贵阳申明》是消除亚洲教育发展不平衡、整合区域教育资源、加强教育交流重要而又振奋人心的一步。也许为了更加美好和广阔的前景，我们应该将这一倡议扩大到东亚。

有了这方面的政策，我们作为一个整体的区域竞争优势将会大大提高。我们的交流应当形成一个共有的最佳实践的资源库，并拓展我们在和平、和谐、互让的氛围中高效工作的潜能。在这一环境下，彼此依存的我们要倡导并推进低碳生活方式并为绿色亚洲贡献力量。

在瞬息万变的东亚区域内，菲律宾政府愿意与在座的各国同仁同舟共济，共同应对高等教育所面临的挑战。我们将共同扮演一个引领者的角色，带领人民过上更为富足的生活，建设更加强大的国家，最终构建一个更加繁荣、富强、和谐的东亚。

谢谢！

（何可人　译）

傅查利英文发言稿

Promote Higher Education and HR Training and Proactively Participate in Regional Higher Education Cooperation

Charles Jose

Consul General, Philippine Consulate General in Chongqing

I am deeply honored to join this distinguished group of education officials from East Asia at the East Asia Summit Higher Education Cooperation Forum in this beautiful city of Kunming. The participation at this meeting of countries from the developing world as well as emerging global economies highlights the diversity of this unique and important gathering. I thank the government of China for inviting us here today.

I should also like to commend the Chinese Ministry of Education and Yunnan University for initiating discussion on this very timely and relevant issue of cooperation and development of higher education under the East Asia Summit Framework. As we all know, education is one of the priority areas of East Asia Summit Cooperation. We all agree that education is an important factor in human resources development, poverty alleviation and narrowing the development gap.

With the unprecedented rise of countries like China in the global economy, it has become increasingly clear that the 21st century is now the Asian century. With its love of learning and invention—as well as its policy of providing assistance throughout the global South—China is undoubtedly one of the primary engines of growth in the world today.

But, as higher education representatives from the largest and most populous continent in the world and this dynamic region bracing for increasingly greater economic integration, we also confront critical challenges. Today, we continue to lag behind Europe and North America in developing human resources to spur economic growth and social transformation. In an ever-globalizing world, Asia has yet to establish its own regional identity the way the European Union has done. Initial talks on pan-Asian formations have already begun, of course, with ongoing discussions on things like the creation of a single currency and a common market, as well as the need to strengthen cultural, geo-political and strategic cooperation across the region.

Higher education institutions provide the flesh to the frameworks of exchanges, interaction and innovation that celebrate the spirit of East Asia's growth, our people's capability and our societies' enormous potentials.

Our vast population and diversity and the uneven levels of education throughout the region are one of our key challenges in this task. Standardization efforts are necessary to enable our institutions to educate trained, skilled and highly specialized graduates who can help our respective countries—and the region as a whole—cope with the complex challenges of the present century. The history of human civilization attests to the impact of education, training and research on human resource development and the quality of life is profound. Investments seeking to better equip people to rise to personal and social challenges are fundamental elements in poverty alleviation, sustainable development and social transformation.

I am pleased to inform you that the new president of the Philippines, Benigno S. Aquino III, has officially pledged to make education a top priority. In both his Inaugural and State of the Nation addresses, President Aquino also clearly emphasized democracy, transparency and good governance as priorities. We believe that there is much that the Philippines can contribute to East Asia and the rest of the world. We have become a vital center for academic and professional training in Asia, as well as for English language acquisition. Furthermore, we continue to remain fairly advanced in terms of gender empowerment, as well as in the education of women and girls. But the Philippines still needs to strengthen its programs in such areas as science and technology, mathematics, digital technology, to cite but a few examples. We hope that we will be able to acquire both the skill sets that we need, and impart those that we excel in, to and from our neighbors in East Asia, through cooperation, dialogue and exchange.

During the ASEAN-China Education Ministers Roundtable Conference in Guiyang in August, the Philippines, through Minister Dr. Patricia Licuanan, Chairman of the Philippines' Commission on Higher Education, pledged its commitment to the *Guiyang Statement* on education reform and regional cooperation. We encourage the removal of barriers in accrediting students from different countries, as well as the establishment of standardized systems for the recognition of degrees, credits and subjects. We further support the China-ASEAN Commission on Humanities Exchange and Cooperation in education, culture, health, sports, tourism, media and the arts. We also encourage scholarships and student mobility across the region, particularly in the form of the China-ASEAN 100, 000 Youth Exchange Program. In addition, the quality of education throughout the region can clearly be enhanced by the exchange of senior academics and scientists. But we recommend that those involved in such exchange programs be provided with adequate support structures so they can be properly acculturated and acclimatized to their host countries.

And while we agree that basic education should be universal, we feel that higher education should be as selective and quality conscious as possible. In this regard, we observe that our region sorely lacks a dialogue and consultative mechanism that can take into account the educational features of each Asian country, focus on the study of Asian educational reform and development, and facilitate communication and exchange.

Since Asian countries represent varying levels of development, the principle of equity should ultimately determine how standards are upgraded. The Philippines considers the *Guiyang Statement* a critical and encouraging step in the process of elimination of educational imbalances among Asian countries, the consolidation of educational resources across the region, and the strengthening of educational exchanges between and among them. Perhaps it is necessary to expand the reach of this kind of initiative to East Asia, for our common and greater good.

With these policies in place, our competitive advantage as a region should be greatly enhanced. Our exchanges should also result in a common reservoir of best practices and increase our potential to work more efficiently and effectively under conditions of peace, harmony and mutual tolerance. In this connection, those of us in the influential sector should also develop and encourage lifestyles leading to reduced carbon footprints so we might all contribute to a greener Asia.

The Philippines is committed to working with all the countries represented in this Forum in embarking upon the many profound tasks and meeting the many challenges ahead of us as higher education institutions in the fast-changing landscape of East Asia. Together we will play a guiding role in the process of empowering our peoples towards building a more fulfilling personal lives and stronger nations and, consequently, a more prosperous, more connected, more harmonious East Asia.

Thank you and Mabuhay!

傅查利简历

1960年11月出生于马尼拉。2002年，获新加坡国立大学东南亚研究硕士学位。2009年2月至今，担任菲律宾驻重庆总领事馆总领事。历任菲律宾外交部亚太司北亚处处长、菲律宾外交部亚太司副司长、菲律宾驻泰国大使馆公使/总领事、联合国亚太经济与社会委员会副常驻代表等职。

泰国有效利用现有区域交流平台，推动高等教育交流与合作

泰国教育部高等教育委员会秘书长　苏马特·亚姆农

各位东亚高等教育高级官员们，

各位东亚大学校长们，

来宾们，女士们、先生们：

我对能够参加“东亚峰会高等教育合作论坛”深感荣幸，在此我谨对中国教育部邀请我参会表示衷心感谢；在座的教育官员和学者们对于缔造东亚高等教育的未来扮演着重要角色。我还要感谢会议的组织方让我们一同分享各自关于推进高等教育合作的看法与观点。

全球化时代伴随着激烈的竞争，知识经济的重要地位日益凸显，我们都深刻地意识到了教育及其在创造性产业中起到的重要作用。我们相信教育是优质产业，高等教育是社会和经济增长与发展的巨大推动力。在新世纪之初，大部分东亚国家在社会经济方面获得了长足发展，但是我们都经历着高等教育大众化的阶段。除了入学人数的增加，东亚高等教育一个最显著的特点是跨国教育和大学师生的流动。所以，今天的论坛是一个建立合作关系的重要里程碑，在这里我们得以就构建 10 +6 高等教育合作来交流观点、分享经验。

尊敬的代表，先生，女士们：

我想和大家一同来了解目前东盟高等教育合作中业已展开、先进前沿和刚刚起步的一些合作平台。比如：

（1）高等教育体制的协调和统一。

几年前，东亚教育部长组织（SEAMEO）高等教育区域发展中心，简称“SEAMEO RIHED”，希望通过借鉴欧盟高等教育机制一体化的博洛尼亚进程，开始在东亚寻求高等教育合作的共同领域。包括共同履行教学质量保证、学分转化、资质框架设立、学历补充等。我们的共同目的是建立一个东亚高等教育体系，涵盖学历互认、统一的资格互认和学生流动平台。

（2）促进学生流动。

第二个东亚区域合作是2010年实施的马来西亚—印度尼西亚—泰国学生流动计划，简称“MIT计划”。这个计划鼓励本科生在三个国家的五个领域中进行流动，即农业、食品加工、国际贸易、酒店管理和东盟国家语言及文化。第一年计划各国在这些学科中交换5名学生，最终将学生流动扩大到东亚（10+6）国家中去。我们希望学生流动能促进东盟青年互相了解，对东盟一体化有所裨益。

（3）大学学科和教师发展计划。

第三项东盟学术合作是大学学科和教师发展。在快速迈向大范围的合作前，我们应该着眼于高等教育中的能力建设和人力资源开发的必要性。泰国与东盟大学网络（AUN）、东亚教育部长组织高等教育区域发展中心为区域内的大学学科和教师提供了许多培训项目，以此满足发展的需要

（4）推动学生参与各种活动。

第四是在东盟与泰国大学间合作，派遣学生到东盟其他国家农村社区进行锻炼。泰国学生被派到东盟其他国家的农村后将在青年营中共同工作。这样学生有了在社区服务中与他人沟通、学习领导技巧的宝贵经历。

（5）东盟科研集群的建立。

最后也是最重要的，在东盟合作中最晚建立的是科研集群。2010年11月末，泰国高等教育委员会将举办“东盟科研前沿集群会议”，将邀

请东盟的学术界人士、高等教育行政管理者参会，为期2天。会议旨在探讨科研集群的共同利益，确认哪些是我们的优势，为今后区域的发展需求服务。其他目标还有努力建立共同的东盟论文引用索引和科研期刊等。在座的各位如果对此会感兴趣，我诚挚地邀请您于2010年11月26～27日赴曼谷参会。

最后，我就区域内高等教育合作提几点建议：①“东亚高等教育合作论坛”应是一个加强各成员相互理解的平台，我们的合作应本着互惠原则进行。②我们应该认识到各成员间的差异并且尊重成员国的国情。③强国应该积极地去扶助其他成员国。④所有成员一律平等，并且机会均等。

我希望东亚（10+6）的所有成员国将来能建立一个共同的公益基金来支持缩小各成员国间的发展差距，这样我们的东亚才会是和平共处、共同繁荣的共同体。

谢谢！

（何可人　译）

苏马特·亚姆农英文发言稿

Thailand will Utilize Current Regional Cooperation Platform to Promote Higher Education Cooperation and Exchange

Sumate Yamnoon

Secretary General The Office of Higher Education Commission, Thailand

Senior Officials on Higher Education of East Asian Countries,
Presidents and Rectors of Universities in the Region,
Distinguished Delegates,
Ladies and Gentlemen,

It is my pleasure and privilege to participate in the East Asia Higher Education Cooperation Forum. On this occasion, I would like to express my sincere gratitude for the Ministry of Education of the People's Republic of China to invite me to join the gathering of the prominent education administrators and academics who had played significant roles in shaping the future of higher education in East Asian Countries. I would also like to appreciate the Organizers for this timely event to allow us to share our perspectives and to foster regional higher education cooperation.

In the competitive globalised world together with the ever-increasing importance of the knowledge-based economy, all of us are well aware the importance of education and its roles in the creative economy. We believe that education is merit goods and higher education is a great driving force for social and economic growth and development. Since the turn of the new century, most of the East Asian countries gained higher social and economic development growth, But we all experienced similar phenomenon of the massification of higher education. Except the increasing number of enrollment, one of the most obvious evidences in higher education of East Asia is the cross-border education and mobility of university staff and students. Therefore, the meeting today is a significant milestone in building our relationships and providing us with opportunities to share and exchange our views and experiences to foster closer cooperation on higher education among ASEAN + 6. I certainly hope that we will find our common understandings and mutual interest in enhancing our cooperation in higher education even further.

Distinguished delegates, ladies and gentlemen, I would like to share with you some of common platforms of Higher Education cooperation in ASEAN which are existing, pioneering, or starting. for example:

1. The Harmonization of Higher Education System.

A few years ago the SEAMEO Regional Centre for Higher Education and Development or in short SEAMEO RIHED had initiated a higher education common space in South-East Asia by adapting the Bologna Process of the European Union as a model for higher education harmonization. It is including common practices in quality assurance, credit transfer, qualifications framework, degree supplement, etc.. Our common goal is to establish a mutual recognition of degrees and common platform of qualifications and mobility of the South East Asian Higher Education System.

2. The Promotion of Students Mobility.

The second joint effort of South East Asia Region is the implementation the Malaysia-Indonesia-Thailand Mobility Programme or "MIT" Programme starting from the academic year 2010. The project promotes undergraduate students mobility among three countries in five areas namely: agriculture, food processing, international business, hospitality and hotel management, and ASEAN languages and culture. The first year aimed to exchange only five students in each discipline from each country. The goal is to expand student mobility to include ASEAN Plus Six. It is hoped that the students mobility will enhance better understandings among ASEAN youth leading toward the integration of ASEAN Community by the year 2015.

3. The Joint Faculty and Staff Development Programme.

The third ASEAN academic cooperation is in the field of faculty and staff development. Before moving fast to any platforms of cooperation, we should look back to the need of capacity building and human resource development of our higher education system. Thailand with the cooperation of Asean University Network (AUN) and SEAMEO RIHED had provided various training programmes for faculty and staff of universities in the Region. These programme were jointly developed in order to serve the needs for development.

4. The Promotion of Student Activities.

The fourth cooperation between Thai and universities in other ASEAN member countries was the exposure of students to rural and community development in another ASEAN country. Thai students were sent to rural areas of ASEAN countries and they were given opportunities to work together in a youth camp. This way, students had had good experiences to exchange their view and to learn leadership skills in community services and development.

Last, but not least, The ASEAN Research Clusters development. The latest development in ASEAN is the cooperation in establishing ASEAN research clusters. At the end of November 2010, the Thai Office of Higher Education Commission will convene a Conference on Pioneering ASEAN Research Clusters by inviting all members of ASEAN academic community and higher education management executives to participate in a two-day conference. The goal of the Conferences is to identify common interest in establishing research clusters which are our strength and serve our needs for future development in the Region. This initiative is widely accepted by members of ASEAN academic communities to work together to establish a number of research clusters hosted by members of ASEAN universities. The other objectives of the ASEAN research clusters include effort to establish a common ASEAN Citation Index and ASEAN research journal. On this occasion, I would like to invite those who are interested in the ASEAN research cluster development to join the Conference in Bangkok on 26 and 27 November 2010.

In conclusion, I would like to propose the principles for cooperation of Higher Education in the Region as follows: (1) The East Asia Higher Education Cooperation Forum should be a platform for enhancing better understanding among members and our cooperation should be for the mutual benefit of participating members. (2) We should be aware of the diversities among members and accept status of a member as it is. (3) Well-off members should earnestly offer to lend their hands to assist other members. (4) All members should be treated as equal and provide equal opportunity for all.

In the future, I wish members of the ASEAN +6 will come to a resolution to establish a philanthropic foundation to support the narrowing of development gaps among members that will lead to peaceful co-existence and common prosperity of our community at large.

Thank you.

苏马特·亚姆农简历

1951年3月出生。1984年，获美国北科罗拉多大学博士学位。2007年10月至今，担任泰国教育部高等教育委员会秘书长。历任泰国大学事务部处长、高等教育委员会副秘书长、2007年曼谷大学生运动会组委会执行主任等职。1996年至今，兼任若看公立和私立大学校务委员会委员，对改进大学管理具有浓厚的兴趣。

澳大利亚在东亚地区推动学生流动，看好中澳教育合作前景

澳大利亚教育、就业和劳资关系部副部长 凯瑟琳·坎贝尔

各位代表，列席代表，

女士们、先生们：

今天代表澳大利亚政府出席会议，我深感荣幸。东亚地区对于澳大利亚非常重要，我们重视这次就高等教育领域的合作与在座诸位交流观点的机会。

澳大利亚致力于发展国际化的高等教育并积极倡导各国通过学生、学者和教育机构的流动与交流共享互利互惠 ge 利亚致力于发展国际化的高等教育并积极倡导在高等教育机构。

今天我将就澳大利亚高等教育参与国际事务的情况进行三方面的阐述，特别需要强调的是：

（1）澳大利亚致力于区域合作以促进高等教育国际化；

（2）澳大利亚充满活力的国际高等教育行业；

（3）澳大利亚目前进行的多边合作，特别是与东亚峰会各国的合作，以实现区域内各国教育体制的协调。

一、高等教育的国际化

澳大利亚倡导一种外向型的国际化高等教育。

澳大利亚是东亚区域各国坚实而长期的教育伙伴，澳大利亚政府非常了解学生获得国际教育经历的重要性。

因此，我们一直为澳大利亚人在国外学习、从事研究或进行职业发展提供机会。当然，我们也向海外学生和专业人士在澳大利亚提供相同的机会。

通过大量的项目，有1500多名来自东亚的人员在澳大利亚学习、从事研究或进行职业发展。同时也有1500多名澳大利亚人到东亚国家学习、从事研究或进行职业发展。

这些获得赴国外学习、研究、深造机会的人将是我们国家未来的引领者，他们将会是日益全球化的世界里具有国际化视野的领导者。

作为澳大利亚政府主要奖学金项目的“澳大利亚奖学金”计划已于2009年11月公布，这一奖学金的启动将进一步加强澳大利亚与亚太地区在教育、研究和专业领域的联系。

二、教育质量和学生安全

澳大利亚推出多项举措，旨在维护澳大利亚高质量教育和培训的声誉及学生的利益。

2009年末，澳大利亚政府委托有关部门复审了与《海外学生教育服务法案》相关的法规。

这次复审的最终报告列出了19条可促进教育行业更强大、更简化和更具可持续发展的建议。

这些建议包括为改善国际学生在澳大利亚留学和生活的体验而需作出的调整。例如：

（1）为国际学生提供更多的支持服务和更全面的资讯；

（2）制定出更有力的消费者权益保护机制；

（3）澳大利亚国际教育行业实施更为严格的监管；

（4）为在澳留学、居住的人员提供更全面的支持服务。

此外，澳大利亚政府还与各州和领地政府紧密合作，出台《澳大利亚国际学生战略》，旨在提高国际学生留澳体验的质量。

三、教育的多边合作

在保障澳大利亚国际高等教育体系活力的同时，我们关注该体系与区域内其他教育体系如何进行互动。多边努力是非常有效的方式，因为我们的目的是要在各国不同的教育体系间寻求透明而简化的合作切入点。

公开、透明而协调的教育体制应该能：促进投资，学者、学生和教育机构的跨境流动；提高高等教育在东亚峰会框架下的合作质量；鼓励交换思想、技术，增进文化了解；推进区域经济一体化。重要的是，这些基于体系改革而获得的益处是具备自身可持续性的。

目前，需优先协调的领域包括质量保障、教育机构注册登记和资质认证、学历学位认可、项目内容和实施以及数据收集。

协调统一并非意味着标准化。区域内各国的教育体系必然有所不同。然而，协调统一会让这些不同的教育体系进行互动，从而增强国内教育体系的实力，让身处不同教育体系的个人能够跨体系流动，并让他们对从中获得的教育效益的基本质量和可转换性充满信心。

四、东亚峰会的教育合作

教育合作对于区域发展是一个关键领域，澳大利亚热切期望与东亚峰会各成员国就此重要领域进行合作。

东亚峰会是一个通过区域教育合作产生实际收益的出色论坛。东亚峰会成员国拥有49%的世界人口，拥有丰富的专业知识和经验，互补并具有活力的经济体。

虽然东亚峰会各成员国呈现多样性，但这恰恰也是一种优势。尽管东亚峰会成员国的发展水平不一，但是经济的活力，丰富的人力资源潜力，以及致力于将教育作为个人和集体进步的首要途径，使得这一区域独具特色。

东亚峰会的多样性是一种优势，它为教育提供了机会。区域作为一个整体，势必能从更加密切的教育合作中受益，因为欠发达成员国得益于较发达成员国的先进经验、专业知识和资源，而且，所有成员国均能得益于整个区域的迅速发展所产生的经济和社会效益。

东盟国家拥有合作和协商一致的历史悠久的区域一体化议程，它们作为东亚峰会的核心，巩固了东亚峰会的力量。此外，东亚峰会其他成员国为这个核心分组提供了规模经济，巨大的增长潜力以及更多的专业知识和资源。

在第四次东亚峰会上，澳大利亚提出与东盟秘书处共同组成高

级教育官员工作组并召开两个旨在促进东亚峰会国家间教育合作的研讨会。

这两个研讨会已分别于2010年5月和9月下旬在雅加达和普吉成功举办。两次会议的成果是一系列区域教育合作的提议，涉及教育的所有类别并包括五项关于高等教育合作的提议。

五、在科学和研究领域的合作

一些东亚峰会成员国是澳大利亚最重要的科研合作伙伴国家。最近，澳大利亚和中国庆祝了中澳两国科技合作协定签署30周年纪念。过去30年的成就清楚地表明两国皆因合作而获益。澳大利亚通过与东亚峰会其他成员国的合作也实现了类似的共赢。

随着时间的推移，澳大利亚以及其他许多国家，国际研究合作正变得愈加重要。科技进步建立在以往的研究成果之上。涉及国际合作的科学研究论文平均被引用的频率更高，这意味着这些论文对更广泛领域的其他研究人员更为有用。

六、结束语

综上所述，重中之重是我们在本次论坛中为促进东亚峰会区域内的教育合作而采取的措施，可以让学生、学者及教育机构在高质量的教育中享有更多的选择消费，或从事研究，或进行投资，从而达到互惠互利的目的。

东亚峰会各成员国更多、更好的教育对于该区域经济、社会和政治的发展是互惠双赢的。

通过区域合作可以推动协调统一、开放和透明的教育体系的建立，从而促进人员和教育机构的流动。这也将使我们可以以彼之长补己之短，同时可以通过人与人之间的联系来推动东亚峰会区域的建设。

谢谢！

（何可人　译）

凯瑟琳·坎贝尔英文发言稿

Australia Promotes Student Mobility and Envisages Great Prospects for Sino-Australia Education Cooperation

Kathryn Campbell

Deputy Secretary, Department of Education, Employment and Workplace Relations, Australia

Delegates and observers,

ladies and gentlemen,

I am honoured to be here today representing the Australian Government.

The East Asia Summit region is immensely important for Australia.

We value the opportunity to exchange ideas with you on the very important area of cooperation in higher education.

Australia is committed to an internationalized higher education sector and is a passionate advocate of the mutual benefits to be enjoyed from the mobility of, and exchange between, students, academics and institutions.

Today I will briefly outline three aspects of Australia's international engagement on higher education, in particular:

* our commitment to regional cooperation to contribute to the internationalisation of higher education.

* our robust international higher education sector.

* our current multilateral work, particularly in cooperation with the East Asia Summit, towards regional harmonization of education systems.

Internationalisation in Higher Education

Australia is committed to an outwardly engaged, internationalized higher education sector.

Australia is a substantial and long-term education partner with countries in the region and the Australian Government understands the importance of students gaining international experience.

That is why we are continuing to create opportunities for Australians to study, conduct research and undertake professional development opportunities overseas. Of course we also provide opportunities for international students and professionals to do the same in Australia.

Through a range of programs, more than 1,500 individuals from EAS countries have undertaken study, research or professional development in Australia. Over 1,500 Australians have done the same in EAS countries.

Those undertaking these opportunities will be our future leaders-leaders with an international outlook in this increasingly globalised world.

The Australia Awards initiative-the Australian Government's main scholarship program-that was announced in November 2009, will further focus on building education, research and professional linkages between Australia and the region.

Quality and Student Safety

Australia has put in place a number of initiatives to protect our reputation for quality education and training and to be responsive to student interests.

In late 2009, the Australian Government commissioned a major review of the legislation concerning Education Services for Overseas Students.

The final report arising from this review resulted in 19 recommendations to make the sector stronger, simpler and more sustainable.

Recommendations include changes to improve the experience of international students choosing to study and live in Australia such as:

* more support for international students and improved information.
* stronger consumer protection mechanism.
* improved regulation of Australia's international education sector.
* improved support for those who study and live in Australia.

The Australian Government is also working closely with the states and territories to finalize an International Student Strategy for Australia. The strategy will improve the quality of the international student experience in Australia.

Multilateral Cooperation on Education

As well as ensuring the robustness of our own international tertiary education system, Australia is interested in how that system interacts with others in the region. Multilateral efforts are a particularly efficient means for pursuing the goal of transparent and simplified interfaces between different national education systems.

Open, transparent and harmonized education systems:

* facilitate the cross-border flow of investment, academics, students and providers.
* increase the quality and quantity of education offerings.
* encourage the transfer of ideas, technologies and cultural understandings.
* increase regional economic integration.

Importantly, these benefits, being based on systemic reforms, are self-sustaining.

Priority areas for harmonization are quality assurance, provider registration and accreditation, qualifications recognition, program content and delivery and data collection.

Harmonization does not mean standardization. Education systems across the region are necessarily different. Harmonization will however allow these diverse systems to interact, thereby building the capacity of domestic systems and empowering individuals within those systems to navigate among them, confident in the basic quality and transferability of the educational benefits derived.

Education cooperation in the EAS

Education cooperation is a critical area for the region's development and Australia is keen to work with countries in the East Asia Summit on this important area.

The EAS is an excellent forum for making real gains through regional education cooperation. It boasts 49% of the world's population, complementary and dynamic economies, and a depth of expertise and experience.

The EAS region is diverse but this is also a strength. Despite the disparate levels of development to be found amongst EAS member countries, the EAS is characterized by economic dynamism, rich human capital potential and a commitment to education as a primary vehicle for individual and collective advancement.

The diversity of the EAS is a strength that presents opportunities for education. The region as a whole stands to benefit from closer education cooperation as less developed member countries benefit from the experience, expertise and resources of more developed member countries while all countries will benefit from the economic and social benefits arising from the rapid growth across the region.

The EAS is strengthened by having at its core the ASEAN countries with a strong history of cooperation, consensus and with a regional integration agenda. The addition of the +6 countries to this core grouping provides economies of scale, tremendous growth potential, and additional expertise and resources.

At the 4th East Asia Summit, Australia offered to work with the ASEAN Secretariat to form a taskforce of senior education officials and convene two workshops to progress education cooperation between EAS countries.

These workshops have been successfully held; the first in Jakarta in May, the second in Phuket in late September. The outcome of those workshops is a suite of regional education cooperation proposals, across all sectors of education, including five in higher education.

Cooperation in science and research

Some of the EAS members are amongst Australia's most important science and research partner countries.

Recently, Australia and China celebrated the 30th anniversary of our treaty on science and technology cooperation. The achievements of the last three decades show clearly the benefits of collaboration for both countries. Similar benefits have been realised through collaboration with other members of the EAS.

In Australia, and many other countries, international research collaboration is becoming more important over time. Science advances through building upon previous results. Scientific research involving international collaboration is on average more highly cited, meaning it is more useful to a broader range of other researchers.

Conclusion

In conclusion, what is most important is that the actions that we take in this forum to cooperate on education in the EAS region that will enable students, academics and providers to exercise their choices to consume, deliver and invest in high quality education to our mutual benefit.

More and better education in the EAS is a win-win for economic, social and political development in the region.

Regional cooperation to promote harmonized open and transparent education systems which promote the movement of ideas, people and providers will allow us to share our strengths and address our weaknesses, while building the EAS region through people-to-people links.

Thank you.

加强双边学生交流，促进国际化进程

——日本大学国际化所面临的挑战

日本文部科学省高教局副局长　加藤重治

首先我想告诉各位，日本高校具有明确的国际化发展诉求。日本也已经出台了一些创新政策，以便与东亚地区的其他大学进行交流。

一、日本高校为什么要国际化?

为什么日本政府鼓励高校进行国际化，而且高校本身也愿意为之奋斗呢?第一个原因是对于高等教育而言，多样化是至关重要的要素。因为学生和教职员工的文化差异实际上能够对学术活动提供质量保证。来自不同文化背景的师生可以激发新的观点，创造新的价值。但是，目前日本高校的外国留学生和外籍教师所占比例很小。因此对于日本的高校和日本教育部门而言，增加在日本大学就读的国际学生以及外籍教师的数量是首要任务。

第二个原因在于日本的制造业和服务业都迫切地需要国际化人才。在日本，国际化人才的含义是什么呢?我们在去年的工业一学术界联合会中确定了这样一个定义：国际化人才只了解文化的差异性是不够的，他们必须能够积极地从文化的差异性当中发现新事物并创造新价值。

二、日本高校怎样国际化?

在日本大学国际化的过程中，我们具体是如何运作的呢?

首先，我们从增加国际教师和学生的数量入手。从两年前自民党执政开始，设法增加外国留学生人数已经成为一项国策，现在日本全国的外国留学生人数是13万，我们力争能在2020年达到30万。这个量化目标已于2010年6月被民主党政府写入了《新经济成长策略》中。为增加在日本的外国学生人数，我们各个政府部门通力合作，在以下五个方面不懈奋斗：

（1）在海外施行激励措施并提供“学在日本”的一站式服务；

（2）改善入学流程及移民政策；

（3）促进大学全球化；

（4）对外国学生提供强有力的支持；

（5）宣传日本用工环境，改进签证申请程序。

其次，文部科学省也已经根据这些大学的国际化项目来确定了一批核心大学进行国际化的运作，并且给予其财政支持。这些项目包括开设一些只用英文授课的必修课程，聘用一些外国教师来教授英语或者进行国际化运作和留学生招生工作。这个计划被称为“全球三十强”，因为我们原本打算指定30所大学加入这个计划。但在2009财年我们只确定了13所，而且截至目前，这个数字也没有增加。我们现在的目标就是要对这13所大学进行为期五年（从2009年到2013年）的支持，而不是在数量上有所增加。这源于最近日本政府推出的一些新的倡议，稍后我会再给大家介绍。

再次，激励日本的学生到国外求学。很遗憾的是，在现实中，大多数的日本学生不愿意去国外求学或是作研究。本身，日本学生愿意到国外求学的人数要比中国和韩国的少，而且在国外留学的日本学生人数也在日益减少，尤其是在美国留学的日本学生人数可以用锐减来形容（2000年近5万人，2006年只有不到3万）。哈佛大学的校长德鲁·福斯特女士今年春天来日本的时候不无担心地提到，今年哈佛大学的大一新生只有一人来自日本，而来自中国和韩国的有好几十人。这种担忧使得日本不仅是学术界，政府及工业领域也给予了广泛的关注。在《新经济成长策略》中提出了一个非常具体的量化目标，即到2020年，日本应有30万年轻人在国外留学。

为迈出整个计划的第一步，日本文部科学省在明年的财政预算计划中提出了新的短期、三个月以下和两周交流项目。我们期望参加这些短期访问项目的学生能够了解到在亚洲、美国和欧洲，他们的同龄人正怀着明确的目标努力学习，能够体验不同的文化，在时机成熟时去国外学习甚至获取学位。同时，我们也准备吸收7000名外国留学生来日本学习，反过来也能提高日本学生出国留学的积极性。

三、重点发展东亚地区的交流合作

目前，日本已经越来越侧重于开展东亚地区大学间的交流合作项目。统计表明在日本的外国留学生中，90%的学生来自亚洲，这也就是我们认为亚洲非常重要的一个很自然的原因。在这部分学生中，来自中国和韩国的学生占总人数的将近80%，也有少部分学生来自越南、马来西亚、泰国和印度尼西亚。

我们之所以重视东亚地区的另外一个原因，是东亚地区在经济领域的国际化进程日趋迅猛。现在，越来越多的日本公司雇佣亚洲其他国家的员工在各分支机构甚至公司总部负责行政、管理及运营工作。此外，区域合作在处理全球性问题上尤为重要。大学间的交流活动不但可以帮助我们培养人才，而且可以通过区域合作为这些问题提供解决方案。

四、推动国际化的新政策

2009年以来，日本提出了很多新的政策。在2009年10月举行的中日韩三方会谈、东盟与中日韩（ASEAN+3）领导人会议以及同月在泰国华欣举办的第四届东亚峰会上，日本前首相鸠山由纪夫先生建议加强东亚地区高水平大学间的交流合作。在此，我对所有参加此次论坛的代表表示感谢，感谢你们及你们的国家领导人对他提出的这一建议的支持。日本、中国和韩国有数千所高校，鉴于其中的数十所高校之间已经开展了一些学生交流项目，我们成立了一个委员会，旨在制订具体措施来进一步推动中日韩三国学生间的交流与合作。这个委员会主要由政府官员、大学校长及企业家代表组成。2010年4月在东京召开了第一届会议，会上代表们建议实施“亚洲大学生集体行动交流计划”（CAMPUS Asia），并成立了两个工作组来为项目具体化提出建议。所有代表还一致同意在2011年开展一些试点项目。在此我非常感谢中国将在今年秋天作为东道主来举办委员会第二届全体大会。还有一项举措是在东亚地区大学学生交流互访方面举行一个专题研讨会。此项提议也是由鸠山由纪夫先生于2009年10月在东亚峰会上提出的。专题研讨会将于明年，即2011年3月17、18日或24、25日由日本、中国、韩国共同主办。我们都已意识到东盟大学联盟（AUN）及其他机构在学分互认及联合培养项目中都做了大量开创性的工作，而且在这一区域中关于学分互认及联合培养项目的需求也会继续增加。另外，这一区域中的各个国家在质量保证方面的发展情况不尽相同。认识到上述几点后，我们再来讨论如何促进东盟地区学校之间的互访，同时又保证质量就变得非常有意义了。而这就是这个专题研讨会的主题。在座的各位，欢迎你们能够参加这个研讨会并发挥积极的作用。

五、结　语

最后，总结一下我的发言：当今社会正面临着很多问题。在这种环境下，既要发展经济，又要保护环境，消除贫困，控制传染病，确保水的供给等，我们怎样才能解决这些问题，以便拯救我们赖以生存的地球呢？我相信答案就是全世界的年轻人来进行合作与竞争，而这种合作与竞争的基础就是彼此之间的互相理解与尊重。

大学的社会责任是什么？或者说全球化的责任是什么？当然，人们希望大学能让学生学习世界上最先进的知识，获得最优秀的技能。但仅仅这样是不够的。真正重要的是要培养学生成为一名世界公民的态度与期望，以合理的方式进行合作和竞争。为实现这一目标，我们必须加深大学的国际化，加强大学的对外开放。我希望我们每个国家的每所大学都能招收尽可能多的外国学生，能够有越来越多的教职员工、学生交换项目为他们打造一个提升自身能力的平台。我们必须意识到这样做并不仅仅是为了大学的经济利益，更是为了培养人才以期解决各种全球性的问题。对于来自学术界和政府部门的我们更需要进一步加深合作。我们始终不能忘记，保证项目质量对开展成效显著的大学交流合作项目来说是不可或缺的基础，至少，我们不能让学生成为没有质量保证的大学交流合作项目的受害者。

谢谢各位！

（刘飞　译）

Enhancing Tow-way International Students Mobility to Promote the Process Challenges of Internationalization: challenges for the Internationalization of Japanese Universities

Shigeharu Kato

Deputy Director-General, Higher Education Bureau, Ministry of Education, Culture, Sports, Science and Technology (MEXT), Japan

Internationalization of Japanese Universities: Why

Why does Japanese government encourage universities to internationalize, and are universities themselves struggling to do so?

For one thing, Needless to say, diversity is an essential ingredient of higher education, because cultural diversity of students, as well as of faculty, is a source of quality of academic activities. It is the interaction of players with different cultural background which brings about new idea and value.

However, fraction of international students and faculty is very low in Japanese universities, as you can see in the slide, "Why Internationalization of Japanese Universities". It is the first order business for Japanese universities and my ministry to increase international students and faculty.

Second, strong demand for global talents is rapidly eminent in Japanese industries, not only in manufacturing industry but also in service industry.

In this connection, the author wants to introduce what kind of people is meant by "global talent" in Japan. The slide "what 'Global Talents' Meant in Japan" shows the definition reached in the Global Human Resource Development Committee of the Industry-Academia Partnership for Human

Resource Development this April.

An important thing in this definition is that, to be a global talent, it is not enough to understand cultural difference, but he/she has to be an active person as to make capital of cultural diversity of members of the group to which he/she belongs and to produce new thing and new value.

Internationalization of Japanese Universities: How

The first avenue the Japanese government and universities are pursuing is to increase the number of international students and faculty.

Since two years ago, when the LDP was in power, it has been a government policy to increase international students to 300 thousand in 2020, the current number of which is about 130 thousand. This numerical target has been succeeded in Japan's "New Growth Strategy" decided June this year under Democratic Party Administration.

In order to increase international students in Japan, relevant government Ministries are working together, so that international students enjoy easy access to and comfortable stay in Japan. The efforts are concentrated in the five principal components: (1) offering incentives and one-stop service for Study-in-Japan; (2) improving admission process and immigration regulation; (3) globalizing universities; (4) robust support to international students, including their housing, welcoming local community; (5) promoting employment in Japan, improving visa status procedure.

As the second pillar, MEXT designates core universities of internationalization, and gives them financial support. The designation is based on competition of specific programs, such as opening the courses where you can get degree only with English, employing foreign faculty for teaching in English or administration of international nature, implementing international recruiting, etc.

The program is called "Global 30", since it was intended for thirty universities to be designated. However, 13 universities were designated in FY2009, according to budget availability, and no additional designation has been made in this fiscal year.

It is the intention of MEXT to support 13 designees steadily for five years, rather than try additional designation, because of new policy initiatives mentioned later.

The third one is to facilitate study abroad for Japanese students.

In these days of internationalization of higher education all over the world, majority of Japanese youth will not go abroad to study, to conduct research, whatever.

The slide "How to globalize Japanese universities (2/2)" shows some evidence. Japanese students want to study abroad less than Chinese and Korean colleague. The number of Japanese students abroad is decreasing; in case of those in the US, sharp decline like this.

This concern is of course widely shared in Japan, among academia, as well as government and industry. When Harvard University President Drew Faust visited Japan, Prime Minister Hatoyama and university leaders raised this concern. According to Harvard statistics, the number of Japanese students (across all faculties) at Harvard over the past decade dropped from 151 in 1999 to 101 in 2009.

In the "New Growth Strategy", numerical target was set: in 2020, 300 thousand Japanese youth are studying abroad.

As the first step, MEXT are proposing new short-term (less than three months) two-way exchange program in next FY budget. It is expected that students taking part in this short visit program recognize how hard their colleagues in Asia, the US, Europe or any place in the world are studying with clear objectives, experience different culture, and seek another, full-fledged occasion of studying abroad, for example seeking degree abroad or taking part in longer, substantive exchange programs. Also incoming 7,000 international students will be good stimulus to Japanese colleagues.

Japan's Emphasis on East Asian Region in its University Exchange

The slide "International Students Coming to Japan" shows that more than 90% of international students in Japan are from Asia. That's the first, natural reason to put importance on Asia. The slide "Japanese Students Abroad" shows that about one third is Asia, with the North America is the number-one destination.

The slide "Emphasis on East Asian Region" shows break-down of Asian students in Japan. Those from China, Korea and Taiwan consist of about 80%. Vietnam, Malaysia, Thailand, and Indonesia follow.

Another factor for Japan to put emphasis on East Asian region is rapid globalization of economic activities in the region. More Japanese companies employ Asian people in executive and managerial, as well as operative, positions in their affiliates in Asia, and even in their headquarter in Japan.

Furthermore, regional cooperation is essential to dealing with global issues. University exchange is important in training human resources to work on that effort, as well as providing solutions to the issues through collaboration with colleagues in the region.

Japan's New Policy Initiative

In this context, new policy initiatives have been put forward since last year. Former Prime Minister Hatoyama made proposal to enhance university exchange with quality assurance in East Asian region.

He made it in Japan-China-Korea summit meeting in Beijing last October, and in ASEAN + 3 and EAS summit meetings in Cha-am Hua Hin, Thailand same month. His proposal was warmly supported by leaders in these summit meetings.

Since there are already student exchanges in several tens of thousands among Japan, China, Korea, the three countries set up a committee to discuss specific measures to promote university exchange and cooperation among the three countries with quality assurance. The committee comprises of government officials, university presidents and professors, and industry executives.

The first meeting was held in April this year in Tokyo. It was agreed to launch CAMPUS Asia, and set up two working groups to come up with specifics. Through the discussion in the working groups, it is a consensus among the three to start some pilot programs during 2011.

Another specific activity is an international symposium on university exchange in East Asian region, the proposal of which is described in the slide "International Symposium on Exchange among Universities with QA in East Asian Region (proposal)".

The symposium will be jointly organized by Japan, China and Korea. The date will be either 17 ~ 18 or 24 ~ 25 March 2011.

In East Asian region there already are pioneering activities by ASEAN University Network (AUN) and Regional Center for Higher Education and Development, Southeast Asian Ministers of Education Organizations and other organizations, in the area of quality assurance (QA), credit transfer, and joint programs. On the other hand, university system, QA system and state of its development are diverse in this region.

Having these in mind, it would be meaningful to discuss how to promote university exchange in East Asia with proper QA. That's the intention of the symposium.

Conclusion

Today, the globe faces many issues: to attain economic growth with environmental protection, to get rid of poverty, epidemic, and to assure supply of water, energy and food, etc.

What will save the Earth by solving these issues? The author believes that it will be collaboration and competition among youth of the world, and this has to be based on mutual understanding and respect among them with multi-cultural background.

Then, in this context, what is the Universities' "global" social responsibility? Of course, universities are expected to equip students with state-of-the-art knowledge and skills. But that's not enough. The important thing is to equip them with attitude and aspiration necessary for global citizens, necessary for them to be global citizens, necessary for them to collaborate and compete in a sound manner with colleagues in the region and all over the world.

Now what we have to do is clear: to open up universities. Let us realize more mobility of students and faculty and make every university be a platform of capacity building in the global era. The author stresses that this has to be realized for the sake of the supreme cause of bringing up human capital fighting to solve global issues, not with university's economic sake as the primary cause.

Further international collaboration among those in academia and government is required. In that instance, it should be remembered that quality assurance is indispensable foundation for fruitful university exchange. The last thing we want is to make students victims of inadequate QA in university exchange.

加藤重治简历

1957年6月生于东京。2009年7月至今，担任日本文部科学省高教局副局长。获美国哈佛大学公共政策硕士学位。历任日本科学技术振兴机构处长、日本经济产业省处长、日本理化研究所处长、日本文部省处长、日本经济产业省副局长等职。

加强高等教育合作，促进东亚地区繁荣

韩国驻华使馆参赞　申竣浩

谢谢主持人，今天我的发言分为两个部分：第一部分将介绍韩国与东亚峰会各成员国之间的高等教育合作方向及发展情况；第二部分将详细描述韩国在推广高等教育领域国际交流与合作方面所作出的努力。

一、韩国与东亚峰会各成员国之间的高等教育合作方向及发展情况

从目前全球形势来看，亚洲国家有必要进行人才储备，因为亚洲很有可能在将来领导全世界的发展，先锋即是各种人才。因此，对于东亚国家来说，如何整合资源，联合培养人才并充分发挥他们的作用变得越来越重要。毋庸置疑，各所大学肩负着这一历史使命并完全有能力完成。以东亚各国人才之间的相互了解为基础，大学与大学之间的合作与交流应当得到进一步加强。在此背景下，东亚峰会的各个成员国讨论如何在高等教育领域建立起一套行之有效，且可持续发展的体系是非常重要的。

各成员国的专家可以进一步考虑在高等教育合作领域各个大学之间建立起一个多边合作平台的建议。比如建立一个“东亚大学校长论坛”，在这个论坛上，参会代表可以讨论一些行之有效的合作交流方式，例如多所学校间进行学生互换项目，共同出版学术刊物，组织国际夏令营，或者网络教学，等等。同时，在这个论坛上还可以举办一次国际会议来讨论全球性或者亚洲地区的某些问题，比如我们所有国家都面临的气候变化问题等。通过加强东亚国家间的交流与合作，同时也有利于促进全世界的繁荣与发展。

二、韩国在推广高等教育领域国际交流与合作方面所做的努力

（一）不断完善国际化教育服务，积极引进留学生赴韩学习

近期，韩国政府已经公布了优先发展完善国际化教育服务的计划，为外国留学生提供更好的教育服务，旨在为实现韩国大学和国外学生双赢打下坚实的基础。韩国将会建立起一整套的一站式（从入境到出境）支持和管理系统来保证在2012年前吸引来自各个国家的超过112000名留学生来韩国学习。

（1）在招生和选拔留学生阶段，韩国将会提供给这些留学生“韩国政府奖学金”和各级“政府奖学金”。2010年，近700名奖学金生中的27%，共196人来自东盟国家。另外，为保证外国留学生的学术水平，韩国将建立起包括韩语熟练程度在内的具体准入标准。

（2）在他们入学之后，我们给这些留学生提供更好的居住条件，并且帮助他们尽快适应新的学习环境。韩国大学会尽量将宿舍优先分配给留学生，在地方政府和大学的共同努力下解决住宿问题。在留学生管理方面有经验的学校在帮助留学生办理签证手续时非常简单，可以直接在网上申请签证和提交录取通知书。2010年4月由韩国国际教育协会成立了一个专门的留学生服务中心，延长了办公时间并能提供多种语言服务。在此机构的帮助下，留学生可以与韩国学生建立一种亦师亦友的关系。

（3）韩国大学会采用各种方法积极帮助和鼓励留学生学习，比如开设用外语授课的课程或讲座，或者直接定制个性化课程，等等。

（4）韩国会采取多种措施帮助留学生毕业回国后找到合适的工作，比如提供假期培训项目为在校生提供实习机会，或者在四年的学习中进行一些职业技术培训，以便他们能够学有所用。

（二）高等教育领域国际合作的几个案例

（1）韩国与东盟各成员国之间建立的“网络大学”。在2009年举办的韩国—东盟峰会上，双方都同意建立一所“韩国—东盟网络大学”。经东盟国家同意，韩国将在2015年前分三步实施这个项目。韩国与东盟

国家通过网络平台来实现学分互认和学生交流。2010年12月，韩国还在四个东盟国家中为高级别官员开展国际研修班，讨论制定出一个整体的框架和计划。

（2）韩国还针对来自东亚峰会成员国的学生设立了一个非常特别的学习项目。为介绍韩国的经济、文化、社会、商业环境并共享韩国在经济发展方面的经验，建立与东亚峰会成员国之间的经济合作。2010年5月，韩国为40名东亚峰会成员国的学生开设了这一学习项目。

（3）我要向大家介绍一下中、日、韩三国之间的“亚洲大学生集体行动交流计划”，即刚才我们的同行加藤重治先生介绍的“校园亚洲”计划。这个2009年在北京签署的中、日、韩三国高等教育合作的协议旨在增强中、日、韩三国大学间的合作以及学生流动，包括改进大学教育质量，以及完善相关细节，例如各国大学间如何相互承认学生的课程学分。它可以进一步促进和提高亚洲学生的国际竞争力与人才的培养。它主要包括学生交流活动、联合教学和学分互认等等。还有一个关于高等教育合作的高级委员会会议也在2010年举行。中、日、韩三国在高等教育合作领域进行的多种多样的合作必将提升彼此的学术竞争力，为适应未来社会的发展奠定良好的基础。

（4）我想特别向大家介绍两个活动。一个是韩国于2006年启动了一个科技帮扶志愿者项目（又名“科技与和平支援队”），主要是提供给其他国家一些科技支持。我们的伙伴国可以提出具体的需求，选择某个科学领域，由我们指派一些相关领域的专家去进行科技指导和帮助。截止到2009年，这个项目共向位于亚洲、非洲和南太平洋的职业学校、学术机构和研究所派出了126名专家、学者。他们的志愿服务期为一年或多年，费用全部由韩国教育科技部承担。2010年我们将派出61位专家、学者到15个国家进行科技帮扶，其中有6个是东盟成员国。

另外一个是第五届“世界人力资源论坛”将于2010年10月26~28日在韩国首尔举办，此次论坛的主题为“以开放的姿态迎接明天”。三天的研讨会将为与会代表提供一个非常好的平台来进行沟通和交流，探讨有关人力资源发展的问题。在这个研讨会上还可以体验东西方不同的文化，建立起一个广泛的合作网络，以探究如何更好地培养具有全球化视野的人才，实现全世界共同繁荣。

谢谢大家！

（刘飞　译）

申竣浩发言稿

Increase Higher Education Cooperation and Promote Regional Development in East Asia

Shin Jun Ho
Education Counselor, Korean Embassy in Beijing

Thanks to Mr. Chairperson. I'd like to introduce Korea's policy directions and international cooperation on higher education. My presentation today is composed of two sections. One is about the direction of cooperation and development of higher education within the EAS. And the second is about Korea's efforts for international cooperation and higher education. Now I'll start with the first section: the direction of cooperation and development of higher education within the EAS.

In the advent of the year of Asia, it seems to be necessary for Asia to prepare a reservoir of talented people of Asia, since Asia is likely to lead the world, spearheaded by talented people. Therefore, first of all, it is increasingly important for the East Asian countries to come up ways of co-prosperity through jointly nurturing and making full use of talented people. In this vein, it seems to be quite certain that universities in East Asia are responsible and well qualified for this mission.

As mutual understanding among talented people from East Asia nations are essential, exchanges and cooperation among universities in the East Asia should be further strengthened. Against this backdrop, it is significant for the East Asia Summit members to discuss how to build an effective and sustainable cooperation framework in the higher education area.

The experts from the East Asia Summit members could further consider the idea of launching a multilateral platform of discussion on higher education cooperation among East Asian universities, like the so-called East Asia universities president forum. At the forum, participants could discuss effective ways of cooperation in higher education, such as the introduction of multilateral university students exchange programs among East Asian nations, issuance of academic journals, the launch of international summer schools, the operation of e-learning curricula, and so on.

In parallel with the forum, an international conference could be held to discuss global and all Asian issues, like climate change, with which the East Asian nations is faced in common. Through galvanizing exchanges and collaboration among of East Asian universities, the East Asian summit member countries could contribute to the development and prosperity of the world as well.

Ladies and gentlemen! From now on, I will introduce Korea's efforts for international cooperation on higher education. The first one is about the promotion of globally oriented education services to expand foreign students in Korea. Korea has recently announced priority plans to promote globally oriented education services, which are expected to lay groundwork for a kind of win-win situation for both Korean universities and foreign students. Korea will establish a whole gamut of support and management system, from entry to exit, for attracting 112, 000 qualified foreign students from various countries by 2012. At the first stage of abstraction and selection of foreign students, Korea will expand Korea's scholarship program or its governmental scholarship program. In 2010, 196 (27%) students out of about 700 beneficiaries were from ASEAN members. Also, in order to induce academic quality assurance of admitted foreign students, Korea will set up concrete admission criteria, including certain level of Korean language proficiency. At the second stage of domestic stay of foreign students, Korea will provide them with better stable life conditions and help them to adjust to the new overseas studying surroundings as quickly as possible. Korean universities will try to assign university dormitories to them in the first place, while expending dorms through the joint efforts between local government and universities. Korean universities, which have excelled at assisting and managing international students, will be granted much simplified visa assurance procedure, such as on-line visa application, submission of only college acceptance letters and so on.

A counseling center for the international students, which was launched by the National Institute of International Education of Korea in April 2010, will expand its current operation hours on certain languages. Foreign students will be encouraged to form mentor-mentee relationships with Korean students. At the third stage of studying at universities, Korean universities will be encouraged to assistant foreign students in facilitating their studies in Korea by several measures, including expanding classes, lectures in foreign languages, establishing Korean language courses and providing information on customized classes.

The fourth stage, when graduates return to their countries, Korea will support foreign students' effort to seek jobs, through providing vocational training programs for foreign students in colleges and customized job placement programs for foreign students in four-year universities by linking universities with businesses and so on.

Second, I will briefly talk about some cases of international cooperation related to higher education. First is about the establishment of a "Cyber University" of ASEAN members. At the Korea-ASEAN Summit in 2009, both parties have agreed to establish a "Korea-ASEAN Cyber University". Based on the consultation and agreement with ASEAN, Korea will implement this project in three steps until 2015, with the goal of exchanging credits among Korean and

ASEAN universities, through the Cyber University as an accredited university. At present, Korea is pursuing curricular surveys in four countries of the ASEAN members in an international workshop, which will take place in December this year, in order for senior officials from Korea and ASEAN members to make consultations about designing a framework and establishing a master plan.

Second is about organization of a special study program for the university students of the EAS. To introduce Korean economy, culture, society, business environment, to share Korea's experience on economic development and to facilitate economic cooperation between the EAS countries, Korea has held a special study program for about 40 university students from the EAS in May 2010.

Third is about introduction of Korea-China-Japan university students' well-developed program, or Campus Asia Program, which has already been introduced by our colleague, Mr. Kato. Korea-China-Japan university students' well-developed program or Campus Asia Program is the follow-up initiative to the agreement at the trilateral summit in Beijing in 2009 on the strengthening of international cooperation in higher education among the three countries. The Campus Asia Program, which stands for a collective action for motility program of university students in Asia, will contribute to the competitiveness of Asian universities and human capital development, through the initial adoption of student exchange programs, including college credits recognition and control of joint degrees among the three countries. To realize this program, at the coming meeting of the export committee for higher education exchange in China this year, the three countries are trying to iron out a pilot project which is expected to be operated in 2011, based on a consecutive and comprehensive guideline for college credit recognition and quality assurance. This program will be a stepping-stone for full-fledged implementation in East Asia in the near future.

Finally, for your information, I'd like to introduce two activities. Firstly, Korea launched a scientific and technological support program or Techno Peace Corp in 2006. This program is a volunteer program, which is designed to provide vigorous and effective support in science and technology to Korea's partner nations, by sending Korean technological personnel and advisors or Korean consultants to nations, based on specific demands for assistance and guidance in the relevant scientific and technological fields. Under the program until 2009, 126 Korean consultants had been dispatched to qualified vocational schools, academic institutions and research organizations in Asia, Africa and South Pacific for one or more years with full funding from the Ministry of Education, Science and Technology of Korea. This year, Korea dispatched 61 Korean consultants to 15 countries, out of which six are ASEAN members.

Secondly, the "5th Global Human Resources Forum 2010" will be held in South Korea from October 26th to 28th, 2010. Under the central theme of Open and Ready for Tomorrow, this three-day forum will provide a pivotal platform for the international community to exchange best practices and to develop policy agenda on human resources development. Participants will also be able to gain deeper understanding of different cultures of the East and the West and to build a wide-reaching network for the development and utilization of global talents who will serve as a foundation on which equal global prosperity can be pursued.

Thank you for attention.

申竣浩简历

1993 年 4 月—1995 年 8 月，科学技术部气象厅企划科与气象研修院事务官。

1995 年 8 月—1999 年 5 月，科学技术部企划管理室行政管理与企划预算负责事务官。

1999 年 5 月—2002 年 9 月，科学技术部科技协力局东北亚技术合作科与美洲技术合作科事务官。

2002 年 9 月—2004 年 7 月，科学技术部科技政策室技术开发支援科与政策总括科书记官。

2004 年 7 月—2005 年 9 月，科学技术部科技创新本部准备企划团与科技信息科书记官。

2005 年 9 月—2006 年 11 月，科学技术部企划法务组组长。

2006 年 11 月—2007 年 7 月，总统直属国家均衡发展委员会区域创新局科长与科学技术部科长。

2007 年 8 月至今，韩国驻华大使馆教育科学参赞。

第三部分　大学校长发言

Section III: Speeches by University Administrators

提升东亚高等教育合作水平，
搭建留学生就业服务网络平台

北京师范大学校长　钟秉林

女士们，先生们：

东亚地区作为全球最具发展活力和潜力的地区之一，“10＋6”框架成员在世界格局中具有重要地位和作用。经过5年的发展，东亚峰会及其相关合作论坛已成为东亚区域合作机制的创造性模式之一。

放眼未来，东亚一体化是历史前进的必然趋势，是东亚和平与稳定、经济良性发展的战略性抉择。在2009年第四届东亚峰会上中国政府总理温家宝先生倡议加强东亚高等教育合作，这是东亚区域合作的重要内容。东亚各国地域相邻、文化相似、诉求相近，通过高等教育合作可以更好地加强和平共处、共同发展的联系纽带，可以有力地促进东亚国家的可持续发展。

迄今为止，北京师范大学已和“10＋6”框架成员的大学签署了128份协议，积极开展学生互换、教师交流、共同研究、联合举办研讨会等形式多样的合作项目。我校在新加坡开展“汉语言文学”及“学前教育”专业的大专、本科、硕士的联合办学项目，已有10多年的历史，培养的1300余名毕业生在当地得到了广泛认可。自2005年起，我校每年与澳大利亚昆士兰科技大学联合举办教育类博士论坛，每年有30余名博士生参与该活动。我校连续几年派遣对外汉语教学专业硕士研究生，到日本、韩国、泰国、新西兰等国家进行教育实习，均获得高度评价。2008年，我校教育学部与日本早稻田大学、韩国高丽大学的相关学院实

施全面合作计划，互派师生交流，进行合作研究。今年9月，我校主办了东亚教师教育国际研讨会，来自中国、日本、韩国以及香港特别行政区的30余所大学的校长参加了会议。

国际金融危机的发生和应对使我们更加深刻地认识到，在东亚一体化深入发展的今天，人才资源特别是留学生这一高端人才资源是可持续开发的资源，对推动经济持续发展、实现平衡增长，具有基础性的重要意义。东亚各国大学必须加强交流合作，协力解决留学生资源开发和管理中的深层次、结构性问题。促进留学生充分就业，是我们应该高度关注并切实解决的问题之一。

目前，东亚各国、各地区之间的留学生规模显著增长，留学生教育质量不断提高，成为东亚高等教育合作的直接成果和重要载体。以北京师范大学为例，2010年注册就读的来自“10+6”框架成员国（新加坡、越南、菲律宾、马来西亚、泰国、老挝、缅甸、印度尼西亚、文莱、日本、韩国、印度、澳大利亚、新西兰）的留学生共1540名，占我校外国留学生总数的82.8%。必须引起重视的是留学生毕业后的就业问题。由于长期在海外生活，不少留学生在及时获得就业信息上遇到困难，信息量小、成本较高；有些聘用单位与留学生求职者及其就读学校之间在信息沟通方面程序繁复、工作量大、时效性弱。因此，关注留学生学成后的回国创业或跨境就业，尊重他们开放性、多样化的选择权，成为东亚各国留学生教育发展的战略需求和必然趋势。我们有理由相信，“东亚峰会高等教育合作论坛”是东亚教育交流与合作的主渠道，应该在推进教育领域的务实合作方面作出贡献。留学生教育合作已经具备了良好的基础，网络技术已经提供了便捷的条件，我们应该为留学生的创业、就业提供支持。为此，我提议政府、社会、用人单位、大学、个人共同参与，搭建留学生就业服务网络平台，不断提升东亚高等教育合作水平。

第一，紧扣时代特点，发挥平台价值。当前，后国际金融危机时期全球深度调整对东亚留学生就业的多方面影响已经凸显出来，留学生就业服务网络平台应能在分析全球化进程对东亚经济结构调整带来的巨大挑战的基础上，准确判定就业、创业领域；应能在分析全球经济再平衡调整中东亚国家产业转型升级的基础上，预测就业、创业方向；应能在把握国际社会要求东亚国家分担更多义务的主动权的基础上，引导留学生承担就业、创业责任。

第二，瞄准实际需求，合理设计网页。留学生就业服务网络平台应围绕求职者、用人单位的实际需要，设计招聘信息、实习信息 、创业机会、创业大赛、就业动态、就业政策、就业法规、求职策略、职业测评、典型案例等栏目，提供满足留学生、用人单位等不同对象个性化需求的内容和信息。

第三，健全维护制度，释放服务效能。建立实时上网制度，汇集更多涉及留学生就业、创业的供需信息，突破时空限制，扩大信息量，克服传统搜索形式的局限性，降低信息获取成本，提高对接效率。建立留学生就业网络议题应对制度，促使相关各方对各自工作领域内热点议题进行积极回应和正确引导，及时解疑释惑、回应诉求。

第四，缜密规划进程，确保实际效果。充分尊重各国国情和特点，构建政府倡导、社会参与、主体多元、形式多样的留学生就业服务网络共建共享机制。可先由各国完成基础性建设工作，边建设边使用，再进行交互接入和并网；先运用多种语言，再共同商定通用语言；先各自管理和维护，再适时由东亚峰会轮值主席国或专设秘书处协调统筹，适时调整优化，不断增强实效。

女士们、先生们：东亚高等教育合作正面临着前所未有的机遇。让我们携起手来，搭建好技术合作平台，不断提升高等教育合作水平，为造福东亚各国留学生和促进东亚高等教育发展作出贡献。

祝本次论坛取得圆满成功！

谢谢大家！

钟秉林简历

北京师范大学校长，教授，博士生导师，留英博士。全面主持学校行政工作；兼管继续教育、教师培训、网络教育工作，兼管继续教育与教师培训学院。

北京师范大学和东南大学教授、博士生导师，清华大学兼职教授，英国卡迪夫大学名誉研究员。

担任第五届国务院学位委员会委员，国务院学位委员会机械学科评议组成员，中国教育国际交流协会副会长，中国高等教育学会常务理事，中国振动工程学会理事，中国机械工程学会理事，《振动工程学报》、《机械工程学报》、*Neural Computing and Applications*（英国）杂志编委等职。享受政府特殊津贴。

转变教育模式　培养合格学生

文莱大学校长　哈吉·祖尔卡耐恩·哈纳菲

21世纪的高等教育总是面临着各种机遇与挑战。我们生活在一个经济与社会都高速发展的时代，面对着气候变化、环境恶化、食物污染甚至金融业和银行业的危机等各种问题，该如何去应对这一系列的挑战呢？对绝大多数国家来说，教育将发挥着非常关键的作用，帮助我们解决问题，应对各种挑战。

应对现在面临的各种问题需要各个国家更紧密联系起来，互相学习。两年一次的论坛就给我们提供了这样的机会，让大家聚到一起，就如何解决现今社会中我们面临的挑战进行讨论，交换各自的观点与看法。大家在这里分享各自的知识，互相学习新的知识与技术，并且有机会跨越空间和时间的间隔，及时获取和交换各国最新的信息。

为应对当今形势，经过全面和科学的审视，2009年，文莱大学对教育体系作了一次全面改革，取消了40多个本科专业，增设了4个崭新的非常有潜力的本科专业。这样做的目的是为了帮助学生为今后可能担负的工作作好准备。文莱大学教育秘书长曾经说过："2010年最吸引人的10大职业或许不会出现在2014年的名单里。"在学生今后的人生中，他们的职业生涯将面临很多不确定的改变，该怎样帮助学生去面对这样的未来？"下一代成长"项目是一个广博学习项目。在此项目中，学生55%的学习时间用于进行理学、医学、商学或者其他社会学科专业知识的学习，另外45%为广博学习，教师将带领学生到服务性企业进行实际能力的培养，例如动手能力和协作能力，并教会他们如何学习。学生可以通过这样的学习获得更多实用的知识。广博学习项目提倡三个主要方面，即领导才能、创业精神和环境意识。学生首先学习如何成为一位创新者，体验成为创新者的整个过程，然后成为一个领导者。没有领导意识，创新者就无法联系实际来进行改革，无法带来持续性的发展。创新精神为工作提供动力，学生首先学习如何使用现有的资源去寻找机会，迅速开展工作，最后进行谈判并建立合作网络。“下一代成长”项目特别注重跨学科教育。由于现在很多新知识都是跨门类的，促使文莱大学最终决定取消所有的系。这个举措招致学校很多教授的不满，因此，文莱大学开发了一些多学科教育项目来替代原来的教育体系，让我们的教师得以选择在多个项目中任职。另外，“下一代成长”项目是一种体验式学习，带学生走出课堂，到其他环境中去学习。在新项目中，攻读四年制学士学位的学生，在大三的时候会经历被我们称为“探索年”的一年，学生可以走进所有项目中进行学习，参加文莱大学与其他合作院校共同开展的学生交流项目，到企业去实习，参与策划一些社会活动，并开展一些创新项目。

研究生“UVD”项目的开展是文莱大学的另一个关键性的发展。这个项目的其中一个目标就是使文莱大学在读研究生人数占到学生总人数的30%。文莱大学在能源研究、作物种植技术、抗衰老问题的研究和新型材料的研究等领域开展了一些新的研究生项目。为了吸引人才，文莱大学还为本国和外国留学生设立了300个很有吸引力又充满竞争的博士/硕士研究生奖学金。在此，我代表文莱大学诚挚地向在座各个大学的代表、学生和工作人员发出邀请，欢迎大家申请我们的研究生奖学金项目。东亚国家的一些领导人在很多正式的场合都指出，为了大家的利益，各国应采取集体行动来应对气候变化、能源危机、环境污染等挑战，以获得更大的成效。文莱大学一直将能源和生物多样性研究作为最重要的项目来开展，另外一个重要的研究是食品安全问题。

众所周知，文莱是一个天然气生产国，经济在很大程度上依赖于此。为此，文莱大学将能源研究扩展到再生能源和替代能源等方面的研究。

东亚的很多国家也面临能源方面的问题，并且这些问题和国家经济问题、环境问题都是分不开的。大家应该认识到，这些问题光靠一个国家的力量是无法解决的，我们应该积极寻找多方合作方案，用大家的知识和技术共同解决问题。

在生物多样性方面，文莱是有优势的，我们有60%的国土被热带雨林覆盖，拥有6000个特有物种。对生物多样性和热带雨林的研究也一直是文莱大学的重点研究课题，这也给我们带来很多研究压力，我们同样意识到在这方面所面临的各种问题也不是我们自己可以解决的。

因此，为了更好地应对我们面临的各种挑战，我们的学生应学会从跨学科、全球化的角度去看问题。“东亚峰会高等教育合作论坛”让大家加深了解合作与交流的意义，推动各个大学间开展更多交流与合作。文莱大学邀请今天在这里的各个大学和我们开展各种本科及研究生交流、科研及教师互换等各个方面的项目。

最后，再次感谢这次“东亚峰会高等教育合作论坛”让我们有机会对我们所关心的政治和经济等方面的问题进行对话与交流，这对培养东亚各国下一代的领导人、决策者和企业家都发挥着非常积极的作用。

（方芳　译）

哈吉·祖尔卡耐恩·哈纳菲英文发言 PPT

Change Educational Modle and Train Qualified University Students

Haji Zulkarnain Hanafi

Vive Chancellor, University Brunei Darussalam

GEOGRAPHIC	
Land Size	5765 km²
Coastline	161km
Rainforests	Over 70% of total land area
Climate	Tropical, humid, rainy

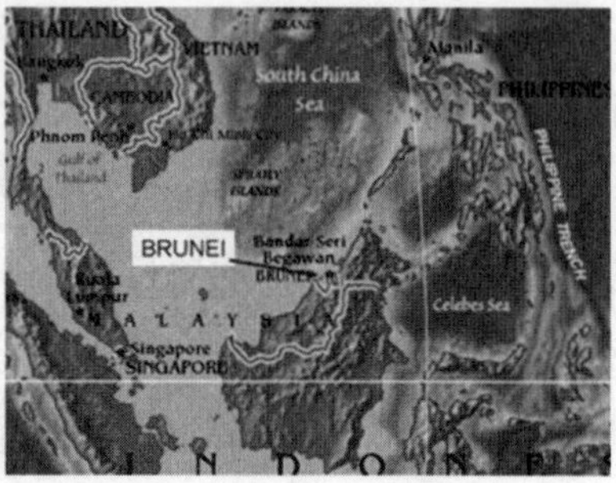

Universiti Brunei Darussalam, Our National University

DEMOGRAPHIC	
Population (2009)	406,000
Language	Malay/English
Labour Force (2008)	188,800
Unemployment rate (2008)	3.7%

ECONOMIC	
Currency	Brunei Dollar (pegged to Singapore Dollar)
GDP (2008)	BND$20.3 billion
Per Capita GDP (2008)	BND$51,300

Universiti Brunei Darussalam, Our National University

Universiti Brunei Darussalam. Our National University

Universiti Brunei Darussalam: Our National University

哈吉·祖尔卡耐恩·哈纳菲简历

文莱大学校长，耳鼻喉头颈外科专家，受教于英国。

1999—2007 年，文莱 RIPAS 医院外科手术顾问医生和耳鼻喉科主任；2003—2005 年，东南亚耳鼻喉和颈部外科手术联盟主席；2007 年 5 月，被授予英国皇家全科医生学院荣誉会员资格，这是在全科诊疗外皇家全科医生学院授予个人的最高荣誉。该奖项专门颁发给那些为皇家学院作出杰出贡献的人，他们有的提高了全科诊疗技术，有的对英国甚至是世界的全科医生都产生了影响。2008 年 8 月，任文莱大学校长，曾任 RIPAS 医院的药物部主任，临床诊断标准委员会主席，专业能力维持和标准计划主席和文莱药品委员会成员。文莱大学药物研究院的创始院长。

高等教育的重要性及对如何提高高等教育的质量和效率的几点建议

柬埔寨皇家金边大学副校长　索斯·曼

尊敬的校长、教授，主席，

尊敬的主持人，

女士们、先生们：

我很荣幸出席由中国教育部和云南省政府共同主办的“东亚峰会高等教育合作论坛”，我谨代表柬埔寨皇家金边大学对主办方致以深深的谢意。

这确实为来自东亚各国的高等教育工作者相互交流经验和共同探索教育方面的发展，共商高等教育合作提供了一个平台。通过这次论坛，我们会看到过去的成就、不足以及机遇和挑战，继续发扬优良品质，最大限度地提高效率和促进社会发展，这确实是一次历史性的会议。这标志着东亚地区各国正在加大培养有能力、有才华的人才，从而加快社会经济发展的进程。

我们一如既往地深刻认识到，高等教育和培训工作需要投入大量财政和精力，同时需要充分的耐心。而结果却是无形的，甚至有时候需要一代人才能看到具体的结果。这意味着我们目前对高等教育和培训工作所作出的努力，不仅关系到这一代人，对于我们后代的可持续发展也是潜在的社会资本。因此，东亚地区各国政府一直把高等教育和培训工作作为在当前全球一体化的形势下，以可持续发展为前提，提高生产力和工作效率的首要工作和决定因素。

人力资源开发的成功，主要基于各部门的能力，特别是培养创造性人才的高等教育院校。同时，高等教育院校作为进修场所，确定了学生能力、技术、自信、职业和综合社交网络等的发展方向，为个人生活、家庭乃至整个社会奠定基础。关于这点，各高等教育机构应进一步重视培养学生理论和实践相结合的能力。

同时，人力资源开发的成功，离不开市场经济形势下各部门积极主动的参与，这被喻为“经济增长的火车头”。随着时间的推移，高等教育国际化的趋势与自由化政策正在积极影响着东亚地区的社会发展，特别是柬埔寨。这一影响在私立教育机构的增加、改善服务质量和竞争力的强化等方面表现显著，这将有利于人民和整个社会。不仅如此，尽管我们的经济年均增长受到全球经济的影响而导致财政萎缩，但是工业、贸易和就业率的活力仍然保持在一个可控的水平，使我们能够高效处理失业问题，缓和其他对经济和社会可能产生不利影响的矛盾。高等教育的发展在其中功不可没。

除此之外，基于世界发达国家的经验，各方面的繁荣和进步主要取决于知识资本。知识资本是解决当前一切问题的关键，同时它通过文学成就、科研论文、著作和其他研究资料为社会、个人提供高等教育的学习资料，共享有用的知识。21 世纪是知识和信息技术的时代，因此，知识资本对社会起到更加重要的作用。

关于进一步提高高等教育的质量和效率，我有以下一些建议：第一，坚持贯彻确保高等教育机会平等的各项政策。第二，坚持深化机构改革，完善教材和课程资料、文献，定期开展训练项目，开展科研活动，改善和提高高等教育的质量和效率，力图达到最好。第三，坚持以公共部门和私人企业合作模式（PPP）与国内外机构、发展伙伴以及各种重建和发展高等教育的赞助者建立更加密切的联系。第四，继续推动高等教育中的科研竞争。

事实上，这些工作将从理念和精神上有助于整个论坛乃至与会的校长、教授、主任、讲师、学术研究人员以及来自高等教育领域的各位女士们、先生们，帮助大家确立目标、任务和计划，以进一步促成东亚社会进步。

最后，我想再次向来自东亚地区参加本次论坛的各位呼吁，让我们一起积极分享信息资源、知识和经验！

预祝论坛取得圆满成功！

谢谢！

（付蕾　译）

索斯·曼英文发言稿

The Importance of Higher Education and Some Advice on How to Promote the Quality and Effectiveness of Higher Education

Suos Man

Vice Rector, Royal University of Phnom Penh Ministry of Education, Youth, and Sport Kingdom of Cambodia

Rectors, Professors, Director Generals,

Distinguished Speakers,

Ladies and Gentlemen,

It's my honor and pleasure to participate in the East Asia Summit Higher Education Cooperation Forum, held in Kunming, Yunnan Province, PRC, which is jointly hosted by the Ministry of Education of China and the People's Government of Yunnan Province. On behalf of the Management of Royal University of Phnom Penh (RUPP) of Kingdom of Cambodia, I would like to express my deepest thanks and profound gratitude to the PRC's ministry of education for inviting me and Cambodian delegates to attend this important forum.

This event indeed allows all of us, in particular, rectors, professors, director generals, lecturers, academic researchers, ladies and gentlemen from East Asia to exchange dialogues and experiences to explore development options for education sector, especially higher education. Through this forum, we can truly evaluate our past achievements, drawbacks, opportunities, and challenges in order to ensure quality improvement, efficiency and social development at maximum level. I think this is a truly proud and memorable gathering, showing that our region is on the accelerated path of building competent and talented human resources to accelerate the pace of socio-economic development.

As always, we are fully aware that higher education and training are investments that require huge amount of budget and time, along with degree of patience, but will provide intangible result which sometimes take even a generation for the result to be materialized, meaning that higher education and training, for which we are making effort today, will not only bring result for society of this generation, but also are potential social capital for sustainable development and continuity of our people generations. That's why the governments in this region have always considered higher education and training as priority sector and key determinant for increased productivity and work efficiency with objective to ensure success for sustainable development process in the context that the world is being characterized by strong current of globalization at the present.

Moreover, the success of human resource development is primarily based on the capacity of the institutions in all levels, especially the higher education, which is the place for creative intellectual training. Along with that, higher education institutions are the places for workshops to orientate students towards development of capacity, skills, confidence, professions and comprehensive net works to be a foundation for each individual's living, families and society as a whole in the future. In this regard, all higher education institutions should pay further attention to train our students in both theories and practices.

At the same time, in the context of free market economy, the success of human resource development cannot be separated from the active participation from the private sector, which is considered as the "locomotive of economic growth". For the time being, the trend of globalization and liberalization policy on higher education has been positively affecting the regional societies, especially Cambodia. This effect could be clearly shown through the increase of private education institutions and the strengthening of the competitiveness for the improvement of quality of services, which is the good advantage for the people and the society as a whole. At the same time, although our annual economic growth has been affected by global economic and financial downturn, the activities of industry, trade and employment generation for the people can still be maintained in a level that is manageable, which makes us able to cope with the issue of unemployment with high efficiency as well as mitigating from other problems that may cause adverse impacts to the economy and our society. These successes are truly the advantage gained from the priceless contribution by the growth in higher education sector.

Along with that, based on the experience of developed countries in the world, prosperity and progress of all sectors primarily depends on knowledge capitals. It plays a key role in solving every confronting problem, and the knowledge capitals also provide higher education and share other useful knowledge to every individual in the society through literature achievements, research papers, books, and other research documents. This 21th century is the era of knowledge and information technology, thus knowledge capital has a more crucial role to play in society.

To further strengthen the quality and efficiency in the higher education sector, I would like to provide a number of recommendations to be carried out in this sector as follows: First, continue to implement policies that ensure equitable enrolment in higher education. Second, continue to implement policies that improve and raise the quality and efficiency of higher education through deepening reforms of institutions, curriculum and materials, documents and research activities by regularly carrying out training programs, aiming for perfection. Third, continue to implement policies of public-private partnership (PPP) as well as having closer relationship with the national and international organization, development partners and various donors in mobilizing resources to rebuild and develop higher education sector. Fourth, continue to promote the competition on research in higher education.

In fact, these tasks will ideally and spiritually contribute to the whole conference as well as rectors, professors, director generals, lecturers, academic researchers, ladies and gentlemen in higher education sector to put into objectives, obligation and action plans to double the fruitful result and progress for our East Asian societies.

Before ending, I would like to appeal once again to the rectors, professors, director generals, lecturers, academic researchers, ladies and gentlemen from East Asia and the whole conference to actively share information, knowledge and various experiences.

At this end, may I wish you all a more fruitful discussion!

Thank you!

索斯·曼简历

柬埔寨皇家金边大学副校长。

教育背景：

1988—1993 年，柬埔寨皇家金边大学外语学院对外英语教学专业教育学学士。

1995 年，澳大利亚堪培拉大学对外英语教学研究生班学习。

工作经历：

1985—1988 年，柬埔寨教育部外语学校现代语言教育处主任。

1993—1994 年，柬埔寨皇家金边大学外语学院英语讲师。

1994—1995 年，柬埔寨皇家金边大学外语学院英语语言研究所主任。

1996—2002 年，柬埔寨皇家金边大学外语学院英语系主任。

2002—2009 年，柬埔寨皇家金边大学外语学院副院长。

2009 年至今，柬埔寨皇家金边皇家大学副校长。

对在东亚峰会框架下开展国际合作与交流项目的几点建议

印度尼西亚哈山诺丁大学副校长　德瓦伊·阿里斯·提娜·普鲁布胡

根据哈山诺丁大学2006—2010年战略规划，在过去的四年，国际学术合作都被定为最优先开展的项目之一。开展各种活动和项目，制定出相关日程表都是为了在以下四个方面得到提高：①使教学质量尽量贴近国际标准；②用国际化的眼光开展各种学术研究，增加在各种国际学术刊物上的论文发表数；③使学生能够在更多国际学术竞赛中获奖；④在各种国际论坛中宣传哈山诺丁大学出版的刊物，提高哈山诺丁大学的知名度。

一、取得的成就

可以从以下几个方面来衡量哈山诺丁大学在2010年是否取得了进步：

（1）哈山诺丁大学与更多的教育机构开展了合作项目。合作的目的在于便于双方机构开展工作，支持教学和科研质量的提高。哈山诺丁大学需要向一些来自东亚国家的合作伙伴学习，例如与一些来自日本、韩国和中国的大学进行学习和交流能够帮助教师、研究人员和学生提高他们的学术竞争力。

（2）通过加强与国际高等教育机构的合作，我们更深刻地认识到自己的使命：把哈山诺丁大学建成一所社区大学，即贴近社区的目标任务的大学。这个使命的战略意义在于使哈山诺丁大学在提高国家竞争力方面发挥更大的作用。

（3）来哈山诺丁大学学习或授课的外国留学生及客座教师的数量显著增加。这些学生和客座教师来自美国、德国、中国、日本、韩国、意大利、法国、英国和埃及。来到哈山诺丁大学的外国留学生、客座教师和研究人员可以增进他们对自己在原籍国和印度尼西亚的不同身份的认同感。

（4）在国际学生竞赛中赢得胜利。例如在艺术领域，哈山诺丁大学的学生在奥地利格拉兹、韩国首尔和中国厦门举行的比赛中都赢得过民俗类比赛的优胜奖。

二、经验与建议

通过认真审视哈山诺丁大学与外国高等教育机构开展合作项目的经验，我们总结出一些在东亚峰会框架下开展国际合作与交流项目的建议：

（1）经济全球化为印度尼西亚乃至整个东亚地区提供了更多的就业机会。这也使印度尼西亚的大学毕业生（东亚其他国家也有相同情况）面临与其他国家毕业生在本国或者国外一起竞争工作机会的问题。在这种情况下，东亚各国的高等教育机构应在相同框架下制定一个课程、学习质量及其他学术方面符合国际化劳动力市场需求的标准。

（2）加强高等教育机构在同一个研究路线图下的合作科研。这是引用2010年7月在越南河内召开的会议上东亚国家外长们所强调的内容。研究路线图应有助于推动东亚国家在经济上的迅速崛起，缩小发展差距，加强东亚各国的相互联系。除此之外，东亚各国还将面临一些问题，包括一些常见的问题，例如，食品安全、气候剧变、能源危机和安全、身份识别问题导致的冲突、灾害管理及其他一些重要的问题。

（3）学生、教师和研究人员积极参加各种交换项目能够极大地帮助他们提高自身的国际竞争力。这种交换项目的进一步作用应该是努力在东亚地区达成共识，从而增进区域安全，尽力通过和平手段解决一切争端。

（4）政府和利益相关方应作出更大的贡献。

（方芳　译）

德瓦伊·阿里斯·提娜·普鲁布胡英文发言稿

A Few Thoughts to Share for Developing the Cooperation and Exchange Program under East Asia Summit Framework

Dwia Aries Tina Pulubuhu
Vice Rector for Planning, Development and Cooperation Affairs
Hasanuddin University, Indonesia

International Academic Cooperation has been defined as one of the priority programs in Hasanuddin University for the last four years based on the Strategic Planning for the year of 2006 to 2010. The activities are focused to carry out several agendas, these are to improve: (1) the learning quality to appropriate in international standards; (2) the research activities within international perspectives and increasing its publication in international academic journal; (3) student performances in winning international academic competitions; (4) international promotion and publication of Hasanuddin University in international forum.

The achievement of these agendas in 2010 can be measured by several indicators as follows:

1. Increasing numbers of Higher Education institutes to those that have been cooperating with Hasanuddin University. The cooperation aims to support the implementation of learning quality and research activity undertaken in respective institution. Some partners from universities in East Asia countries such as Japan, South Korea and China have been considered as bench mark

institutions for Hasanuddin University whereas lecturers, researchers, and students are possible to improve their academic competencies in those universities.

2. By improving the collaboration with international Higher Education, it has significantly contributed to realizing one of Hasanuddin University missions, which is to become a communiversity, which means a university in the vicinity of community goals and agendas. The strategic issue in this mission is to improve the role of Hasanuddin University in enhancing the nation's competitiveness in the international level.

3. Increasing numbers of students from abroad and guest lecturers who come to study and lecture at Hasanuddin University. They come from several countries like USA, Germany, China, Japan, South Korea, Italy, France, Scotland and Egypt. Accepting students, guest lecturers and researchers from abroad is also beneficial for bridging an identity gap between Indonesia and their origin countries.

4. Winning some student international competitions. For instances in the field of Art, Hasanuddin University students won the Folklore Category in the competition held in Graz (Austria), Seoul (South-Korea), and Xiamen (China).

By looking at the experience of carrying out cooperation programs between Hasanuddin University and Higher Education abroad, there are a few thoughts to share for developing the Higher Education cooperation and exchange program under East Asia Summit Framework:

1. The economic globalization has emerged job and employment opportunities across the country and entire region. This has made the university graduates from Indonesia (similar to other countries in EA) to compete tightly with the university graduates from other countries, either for job in their own or outside the country. This situation reminds us of the need to establish

curriculum, learning quality, and other academic standards for higher education under the same framework in East Asia countries which meets with the international character of labor market.

2. Reinforce the collaboration scientific research undertaken by the Higher Education institutions under a road map research. Refers to the need that is highlighted by East Asia Foreign Ministers in the meeting in Hanoi in July 2010, then research road map should contribute to strengthening the rapidly emerging economies in East Asia countries, bridging development gaps, and promoting connectivity in EAS countries. Besides that, there are the issues including matters of common problems that faced by East Asia countries, such as food security, dramatic climate change, energy crises and security, identity-based conflict, disaster management, and some other important issues.

3. The student, lecturer and researcher mobility attending the exchange program is very significant to increase their international competencies. However, the exchange programs furthermore have to address on significant endeavor to build a shared identity in EA region that in turn will bring increased security to a region and resolve all disputes by peaceful means.

4. Contribution from the government and stakeholders are highly needed.

德瓦伊·阿里斯·提娜·普鲁布胡简历

印度尼西亚哈山诺丁大学社会学和政治学学院讲师，博士，副校长，分管规划、发展和对外合作工作。

工作经历：

1992—1995 年，哈山诺丁大学人口研究中心研究员。

1995 年起，哈山诺丁大学性别研究中心研究员。

1998 年起，哈山诺丁大学社会学和政治学学院讲师。

1999—2000 年，南苏拉威西岛小型灌区管理项目性别专家。

2001 年起，哈山诺丁大学人权中心争端解决所协调员。

2001—2002 年，基于社区的都市基础设施管理项目社区专员。

2003 年至今，世界银行第二期消除城市贫困项目苏拉威西岛区域负责人。

2006 年至今，哈山诺丁大学副校长，分管规划、发展和对外合作工作。

构建大学网络　加强教育合作

印度尼西亚大学副校长　穆罕默德·阿尼斯

早上好！

我们很荣幸能够来到美丽的中国昆明参加本次“东亚峰会高等教育合作论坛”。我是印度尼西亚大学主管教务的副校长穆罕默德·阿尼斯博士，随行的还有我们印度尼西亚大学护理学院的院长德伟·伊拉瓦提博士。

我将与大家分享我校的国际学术合作。印度尼西亚大学是印度尼西亚历史最为悠久的大学，2010 年 QS 版世界大学排名第 236 位。我们在印度尼西亚的大学排名中名列榜首。目前，印大拥有在校学生 49000 名，他们均是印度尼西亚莘莘学子中的佼佼者，全都经过精挑细选。他们分布在下列学院：医学院、牙医学院、护理学院、公共卫生学院、心理学院、社会与政治科学院、法学院、经济学院、工程学院、计算机科学学院、数学与自然科学学院以及研究生部。

目前我校共有 1143 名学生就读国际学位课程，其中 37 名为外国留学生，分别来自马来西亚、缅甸、日本、中国、韩国、东帝汶、巴基斯坦、土库曼斯坦、阿塞拜疆、伊拉克、伊朗、也门、巴勒斯坦和法国。

我们也开展学生交流活动。2009—2010 年度，我们派出 43 名学生前往日本、韩国、马来西亚、澳大利亚和俄罗斯参加交流项目。我们也接待了 30 名国外交换生，他们来自泰国、日本、韩国、朝鲜、中国香港、中国大陆、尼泊尔、德国、荷兰、波兰、俄罗斯和美国。

就我们的国际合作而言，我们是 9 个国际教育协会的成员，即 AUN

（东盟大学网络）、APRU（环太平洋大学联盟）、ASAIHL（东南亚高校协会）、AUAP（亚太大学联盟）、ASEA－UNINET（东盟—欧洲大学网络）、FUIW（伊斯兰世界大学联合会）、GUNI（全球大学创新网络）、SEAMEO（东南亚国家教育部长组织）、APL（亚太领袖）。我们也是一些国际论坛的成员高校，如东京财团、亚洲大学校长论坛（AUP）和“立命馆亚洲太平洋大学”。

目前，有54所外国高校与印大签署了学生与学术交流协议。这些院校来自马来西亚、泰国、澳大利亚、日本、中国、法国、挪威、意大利、英国、伊朗、沙特阿拉伯、德国、东帝汶。印大有25个本科和研究生层次的国际联合学位课程，专业包括经济学学士、法学学士、理学硕士和工商管理硕士学位。

我们非常赞成在高等教育合作东亚（10＋6）框架下扩大我们的国际合作。我们希望开展任何形式的教师交流、学生交换、联合办学、合作科研项目。

谢谢大家，我们期待着与各位共同开辟新的教育合作。

注：目前印大与澳大利亚、日本、法国、加拿大、葡萄牙、韩国，沙特阿拉伯及瑞典的大学开展了72研究与学术合作项目。

（赵高顺　译）

穆罕默德·阿尼斯英文发言稿

Build University Network and Strengthen Education Cooperation

Muhammad Anis

Vice Rector for Academic Affairs, University of Indonesia

Good Morning!

It is a pleasure for us to be here to attend the East Asia Summit Higher Education Cooperation Forum in a wonderful place of Kunming, China. I am Dr. Muhammad Anis, Vice Rector for Academic Affairs, University of Indonesia, accompanied by Dr. Dewi Irawati, Dean of Faculty of Nursing, University of Indonesia.

I would like to share with you about our Academic International Cooperation. We are the oldest University in Indonesia and placed 236 in the 2010 QS World University Ranking. We are the highest rank among Indonesian Universities. Currently UI has 49,000 students. They are among bright scholars in Indonesia and have passed the very selective process. They are studying in Faculties of: Medicine, Dentistry, Nursing, Public Health, Psychology, Social & Political Science, Law, Economics, Engineering, Computer Science, Mathematics & Natural Sciences, and Graduate Program.

Currently we have 716 students enrolled in our international degree programs. Among those students, 57 are foreign students. They are from Malaysia, Myanmar, Japan, China, South Korea, Timor Leste, Pakistan, Turkmenistan, Azerbaijan, Iraq, Iran, Yaman, Palestine, and France.

We also have student exchange activities. In 2009 - 2010 we have 31 students going aborad for exchange programs in Japan, South Korea, Malaysia, Australia and Russia. We also host 27 foreign students from: Thailand, Japan, South Korea, North Korea, Hongkong, China, Nepal, Germany, Netherlands, Poland, Russia, and USA.

For our international cooperation, we are member in 9 international education associations: AUN (ASEAN University Network), APRU (Asia Pacific Rim University), ASAIHL (The Association of Southeast Asian Institutions of Higher Learning), AUAP (Asia University America Program), ASEA-UNINET (The Austrian South-East Asian University Partnership Network), FUIW (The Federation of the Universities of the Islamic World), GUNI (Global University Network for Innovation), SEAMEO (The Southeast Asian Ministers of Education Organization), and APL (Asia Pacific Leaders). We are also member in International Forum: SATU President Forum, The Tokyo Foundation, and Asian University Presidents (AUP), and Ritsumeikan Asia Pacific University.

Currently, there are 54 international universities engaged in agreement with UI① on Student and Academic Exchange. Those institutions are from: Malaysia, Thailand, Australia, Japan, China, France, Norway, Italy, England, Iran, Saudi Arabia, Germany, Timor Leste. UI has 24 International Joint Degree Programs, Undergraduate and Graduate level, ranging from Bachelor in Economics, Bachelor of Law up to Master of Science, and Master of Business Administration.

We are very supportive to increase our international cooperation under the Higher Education Cooperation 10 + 6 Framework. We would like to foster and we welcome any faculty exchange, student exchange, joint degree program, and also joint research program. Thank you for your attention, and we welcome to entertain new cooperation in education from all of you.

---

① UI currently have 72 research and academic cooperation with Universities from Australia, Japan, France, Canada, Portugal, South Korea, Saudi Arabia, and Sweden.

穆罕默德·阿尼斯简历

英国谢菲尔德大学博士。2007 年至今，担任印度尼西亚大学副校长，分管教学和学生工作，印度尼西亚大学学术委员会委员。曾任印度尼西亚大学工程学院教学副院长、印度尼西亚大学工程学院分管合作的副院长、印度尼西亚大学工程学院冶金与材料系主任、印度尼西亚大学教育主管等职。

国际教育合作的作用
——苏冯那翁大学的视角

苏冯那翁大学校长　坎姆菲·斯萨旺

尊敬的主持人，

各位来宾，女士们、先生们：

我很荣幸能够参加本次论坛。首先，请允许我向出席本次论坛的所有嘉宾转达苏冯那翁大学的问候。苏冯那翁大学位于老挝的世界遗产城市琅勃拉邦。

老挝通过培训、进修，学术经历、教学、科研、教育管理交流，课程及学历互认等形式，继续促进同国外及国际教育发展组织的交流与合作。

过去二十年中，老挝教育部非常重视实施友邦之间的双边合作，如越南、中国、日本、澳大利亚、泰国、印度、德国、韩国、法国等等。老挝教育部也同区域性及国际性的捐资机构保持着紧密的多边关系，如亚行、世行、联合国教科文组织、联合国儿童基金会、东南亚教育部长组织及各种非政府组织。

老挝五所大学及其他高等技术与职业学院积极开创并扩大与国外高校的学术交流与合作。

合作范围涵盖了主要的学术活动，如通过大学的管理人员与学者（教授、讲师或研究人员）的考察访问交流知识与经验；通过组织单边或多边的会议展现学生在学术、艺术/文化、体育比赛中的风貌来开展学生交流；就特定的双方共同感兴趣的主题组织合作研究或研习；交换学术信息或教学资料；交换学术期刊；共同主办国际研讨会、论坛、研修班或会议以及其他一些由相关大学商定的学术交流，例如大学间互认各自国家授予的学位、学分及学分转移。

因为琅勃拉邦是老挝的一个世界遗产城市，我们特别希望就旅游商务管理、国际商业化及世界遗产的保存和保护等领域与亚洲邻国的高等学校交流知识与技能。

直到2015年，我校都将继续接受亚行的资助。我们很高兴，承担部分费用派遣我们的教师到我们的友好/合作院校攻读硕士学位。我们将开展生物多样性、高山农业、食品加工的合作研究；开发工民建、室内装潢的课程与教学材料，并更新工商管理教材。为了加深学生对东亚各国的了解，我们有意建立越语、汉语、韩语、日语语言学校或中心，只要这些东方文化受到学生或特定目标人群的欢迎。

我坚持认为，教育合作在加深友谊与和平、国际的理解及各民族的团结方面发挥了重要作用。多亏友邦通过教育提供的信息，老挝人民逐渐享受到了宪法与国家法律赋予的权利与自由，改善了生活质量，2020年将实现从欠发达到发达的飞跃。这使得社会经济的发展以非常理性的方式通过工业化与现代化顺利推进。目前，老挝正在大步迈向区域的乃至世界的经济一体化。

借此机会，我谨向所有参加论坛的代表致以衷心的祝愿，祝各位家庭幸福、事业发达、心想事成！

愿我们大学间的友谊与合作万古长青！

（赵高顺　译）

坎姆菲·斯萨旺英文发言稿

The Role of International Education Cooperation: A Perspective of Souphanouvong University

Khamphay Sisavanh
President, Souphanouvong University, Lao PDR

Your Excellency Ms. Chairperson,

Distinguished guests,

Ladies and Gentlemen,

It is my great honour to attend this international forum. First of all, I would like to convey friendship and solidarity from Souphanouvong University in World Heritage City of Luang Prabang, Lao PDR, to all participants of this Forum.

Lao PDR continues to promote the relationship and cooperation with foreign countries and international organizations for education development through training, upgrading qualification of personnel, exchange of academic experiences, teaching, research, education administration and management, recognition of curricula, diploma, and so on.

Last 20 years MOE has paid attention to realizing the bilateral cooperation with friendly countries, like: S. R. of Vietnam, P. R. of China, Japan, Australia, Thailand, India, Germany, R. of Korea, France, etc. MOE also maintains tight multilateral educational cooperation with regional and international donors: ADB, WB, UNESCO, UNICEF, SEAMEO, and various NGOs. Five universities and other tertiary technical and vocational schools of Laos are dynamic in establishment and extending academic relationship and cooperation with foreign institutions.

The cooperation scope covered main academic activities such as exchange of knowledge and experiences through study visits of university's executives and scholars (professors, lecturers, or researchers); exchange of students by organizing bilateral or multilateral meetings to present student's performances in academic, art\cultural, sportive contests; organization of joint research or study on specific topics of mutual interest; exchange academic information, and instructional materials; exchange of periodical academic publications; co-host-ting international symposia, forums, seminars and conferences; and other academic exchange that various Universities agree to such as "mutual recognition of academic degrees conferred in the respective countries and on credit recognition and transfer among universities".

Since, Luang Prabang is one of world heritage cites in Laos, we are interested in specific exchange of knowledge and skills on the tourism business management, international commercialization, and conservation and protection of world heritage along with higher education institutions of our Asian neighbor countries.

From nowadays to year 2015, our University is granted scholarships from ADB. We are pleased to send our lecturers to upgrade their qualification of master degree to our neighbor \ twin universities by sharing cost. We intend to do joint research on biodiversity, upland agriculture, food processing; to develop curricula and instructional materials of civil engineering, interior decoration and to update business management materials.

In order to boost international understanding among various nations in the region, we are interested in establishing Vietnamese, Chinese, Korean, Japanese Language schools \ centers where the eastern culture could be proliferated among our students and other target groups.

From this great-honor podium, it is fair to confirm that education cooperation plays a role of strengthening friendship, peace, international understanding and solidarity among the nations. Thanks to information through education from friendly countries, Lao people gradually enjoy their rights and freedom given by the Constitution and State laws better, improve quality of life for shifting from underdeveloped to developed status in 2020. This made the socio-economic development through industrialization and modernisation process move forward smoothly and in a most rational way. In present time, Laos is convincingly stepping forward to economic integration into Region, and World as well.

By taking this solemn opportunity, I would like to express our best wishes to all of the Forum delegation happiness, prosperity and great success.

Long life to the friendship and cooperation among our universities!

坎姆菲·斯萨旺简历

老挝苏冯那翁大学校长，副教授，博士。

教育背景：

1984 年，获教育学硕士学位。

1987 年，获语言学博士学位。

工作简历：

1979 年，任法语、俄语教师。

1980—1987 年，老挝教育局教育研究所研究员。

1987—2000 年，老挝教育局教育学研究所副主任。

1992—2001 年，老挝教育局海外改革与科技协会管理委员会成员。

1996—2003 年，联合国教科文组织老挝委员会成员。

2000—2003 年，老挝教育局教育学研究所主任。

2003 年 9 月至今，老挝苏冯那翁大学校长。

东亚峰会框架下的高等教育合作与发展

新加坡国立大学副教务长　陈添顺

我们的发展是在东亚峰会的框架下进行的，我们必须要了解，现在高等教育的趋势是什么样的？我们面临一个问题，我们要为我们的学生开发出什么样的高等教育，以便他们在全球化的竞争中更有竞争力？

现在我们看到在教育方面出现了一些转变，这样的转变，是两种力量推动的结果，就是全球化和知识社区的出现。知识社区的出现，比如说现在出现的许多新的知识，有助于全球化的进程。全球化展现出一个全新的市场，这个市场很庞大，我们要在其中进行一些创新，我们要进行技术的创新。世界出现了许多变化，对我们教育者提出了挑战。这样的变化，迫使教育在不断演变。我们的学生要学习相应的知识，以便能够适应变化。

随着经济的变化，我们的知识也要不断地变化。只有我们的知识不断变化，我们才能够顺应经济的发展，不断迈上新台阶。这就是说，我们大家可能在经济发展中处于不同的阶段，但是大学所扮演的角色是一致的。我们要提出一个核心的问题，我们的学生，他们的优势在什么地方？在未来的10年当中，我们的学生要作好充分的准备，以便能够迎接终身的职业生涯。这一点，刚才的发言人已经强调过了。所以我们一定要强调创新的重要性。将来很多工作可能是新型的，目前并不存在的。而现在我们所看见的一些工作，在今后也会消失。所以，我们要研究一下，这个世界需要什么样的技能技巧，这个社会以后会出现一些什么样的变化。

在东亚区域经济发展的阶段，各个国家可能是不一样的。但是学生培养出来的能力，应该是永远都有用的。我们要进行什么样的高等教育的合作呢？如何满足这种预期呢？如何发展高等教育行业呢？由于我们现在碰到的变化如此迅速，它们对我们的文化、经济的影响是不一样的。我们要确保我们的高等教育能够让我们的毕业生充分地应对各种各样的改变和变化。而且在这个方面我们要互相学习和借鉴。我们要进行广泛的合作与交流。我们要发掘一些方法，在工作层面进行一些交流活动。

我们在具体地设计和制定一个学校的培养目标的时候，我们要给大家一些充分的交流的机会。现在我们的合作交流的方向是非常正确的。我们要进一步加强学习借鉴的合作。我们要根据需求举行定期的会议，尤其是邀请一些负责培养目标和课程的人来参加，让他们能够参与这样的活动。这样的话，效果会更好。

谢谢大家！

（赵高顺　译）

陈添顺英文发言稿

Cooperation and Development of Higher Education under the East Asia Summit Framework

Tan Thiam Soon

Vice Provost (Education), National University of Singapore, Singapore

As we think about cooperation and development of higher education under the East Asia Summit, it is important to understand some of the key trends driving changes in higher education today. The key question we should pose is what kind of education we need to develop for our students to face a globalised world confidently and competently, and how we can enhance this through cooperation and development within this particular community.

Just like everything else around us, we are witnessing major shifts in the educational landscape. This titanic shift has been driven by two different and often overlapping forces-globalization and the rise of knowledge societies. The rise of knowledge societies, in particular, the many varied new technologies that have been developed have contributed greatly to the pace of globalization, and globalization itself with its huge market opportunities has been the prime catalyst for the many innovations that have come in recent years. With globalization and technological innovation come interconnectedly rapid flows of everything, from the information we use and exchange, to the transactions we make and the food we eat! But this also spells a particular challenge for educators, this fast pace of change also means a constantly evolving market and our graduates need to be equipped with the right skill set and knowledge to know how to steer in that changing wind.

As the economy evolves, the demand on knowledge and innovation keep going up the ladder, and in this, the higher education institutions have a big role to play to help its graduates, and thus by extension, the economy move up the ladder and ensure that the graduates produced can stay relevant as the economy changes its focus. Each of us may be in a different stage, but this role of the university is still the same.

In this current stage where the competition is about innovation, then the key question that should be asked is what should our graduates be prepared for?

One obvious point that is increasingly evident in the last decade is that all our students need to be prepared for a "lifetime of careers" and not a "career-for-life". Underpinning this trend is that with innovations, many in-demand jobs of the future may not even exist today, and hot jobs today will vanish tomorrow. This is driven both by the moving out of lower level industry to less expensive locations as well as the rapid pace in which skills have become obsolete. While the stages of development of the economies in the East Asian region may not be even, this trend applies to all, though the skill set displaced may not be the same.

With this context in mind, what kind of cooperation can we envisage that can help the higher education in the region be able to cope with this expectation, and in this process help to develop the higher education in the region?

As the changes are coming fast and all of us are reacting in different ways because of our economic and cultural differences, to ensure that the education delivered can help our graduates to be ready for these changes, it is important that we strengthen our dialogue and learn from each other, filtering out some of the best practices that we can then adopt in our own curriculum. In a smaller grouping such as this, there are shared values and this makes some of the cross learning easier. A summit of the nature we are having now is one such helpful forum.

More importantly, we need to think of ways to strengthen the exchange at the working level, where the people who are actually doing the design and delivery of the curriculum can have this exchange. The healthy exchange of academic and administrative staffs amongst partner universities in this region in the last 5 years is a testament that this is the right direction. But as the global competition heats up, we need to further strengthen this mutual learning. A regular conference of key people involved in the development of curriculum to share and exchange ideas and experiences is something worthwhile to pursue.

陈添顺简历

新加坡国立大学土木工程系教授，副教务长，分管教育。协助校长制定学校教育方针政策，确保高标准学术研究和教学质量；兼管注册办公室、招生办、教学发展中心和教育科技中心。曾获得美国试验材料学会 C. A. Hogentogler 奖、日本岩土工程学会颁发的最佳研究论文奖等。

南洋理工大学的现状与未来

新加坡南洋理工大学副教务长　许谦益

尊敬的主持人，

各位来宾：

大家好！

南洋理工大学（南大）成立于1991年。南大的建校起缘及其发展历程可以追溯到1955年，前身是东南亚第一所中文大学——南洋大学，是由东南亚民间各阶层人民筹款建立起来的。1991年南洋理工学院进行重组，将国立教育学院纳入旗下，更名为南洋理工大学。

我们有一个园林式的校园，被称为“云南园”，校园内中西式建筑物交相辉映。我们还有一个名为“纬壹校区”的校园，毗邻新加坡的核心研发区域。我们现有在校生共33100名，其中有1/3是博士和硕士研究生，2/3是本科生。南大的外国留学生人数在不断增长，而且我们的教职员工来自67个国家。我们现有14.3万名校友，其中有15000多人来到中国，南大有19个校友会分布在中国的各大城市。

南洋理工大学有工、理、商、文四大学院。相对来说，南大是一个年轻的大学，我们所有的教职员工都在为之努力，争取在未来几年带领南大取得更高的成就。目前，我们成立了拉惹勒南国际研究院，在亚洲排名第三（国际著名公共政策研究机构“ Go-To Think Tanks”2009年度排名）。另一个可喜的成就是，我们还与英国伦敦学院合作成立了新的医学院，为新加坡大型传染病医院陈笃生医院提供了关键的医疗技术研究基础。从这个方面来说，南洋理工大学在病理研究、科学技术和生物医学的发展上发挥着重要作用。另外，我们还有一所孔子学院，是一个自主办学的学院，主要是培养新加坡的汉语教师，为他们提供中文学历学位教育。

我们把南大看做是一个学术生态系统，其责任是培养学生，让他们准备好应对21世纪的各种挑战。21世纪不仅给我们带来了巨大的经济挑战，也给我们带来了技术领域的挑战。这就需要我们开创新的教育模式，培养优秀的工程师、医生、科学家、艺术家、设计师等等。所以，我们看到科技在转变年轻毕业生的思维方式中具有关键作用。

在科研方面，我们正努力开展多学科研究。五年来，我们继承和发扬了南大深厚的科研传统，进行了高难度的研究工作，取得了骄人的成绩。在新加坡国立研究基金会和教育部的资助下，我们成立了两个高级研究中心，一个是新加坡地球观测研究所，致力于了解地震、火山和大气变化的运动规律。另外一个中心是今年成立的新加坡环境生命科学工程研究中心。该中心拥有一批污水净化技术方面的专家，以及美国著名的基因工程先锋学者，他们一起从事开拓性的研究，主要是环境微生物学的研究。

继往开来，南洋理工大学确立了2010—2015规划，即在未来的五年中，我们确定了五个巅峰作为奋斗目标，包括“可持续发展的地球”、“未来的医疗护理”、“新创意媒体”、“新丝绸之路”和“创新型的亚洲”。首先“可持续发展”是我们南大发展的首要方向，这是我们的最终目标；关于“保健医疗体制科技”，正如我前面提到的，我们与伦敦学院合作成立了新医学院，致力于卫生系统和临床医学领域的研究工作；“新丝绸之路”意指在21世纪东西方思想交流的新模式；在建设“创业创新生态模式”方面，我们目前成立了南洋公共管理研究研究生院、南洋中国研究中心，此外我们还将与印度建立学术联系。

最后，我想谈谈南大的国际合作与交流现状。我们与海外许多知名高校建立了博士学位联合培养项目，最近我们与欧洲、中东和美洲的部分顶尖高校签署了合作备忘录，跟亚洲国家高校间的合作规模正在不断扩大。我们将继续努力，不断前进。

谢谢大家！

（毕媛媛 译）

许谦益英文发言稿

Nanyang Technological University: Present Achievements and Future Goals

Michael Khor Khiam

Associate Provost, Nanyang Technological University

Dear Madam Chair,

fellow colleagues,

Nanyang Technological University (NTU) was established in 1991, which has a distinguished lineage with roots that go back to 1955, when Nanyang University (Nantah), the first Chinese-language University in Southeast Asia, was set up with donations from people of all walks of life. In 1991, NTI became Nanyang Technological University with the absorption of the National Institute of Education.

We have a garden campus which is called "Yunnan Garden Campus", in this campus we have a mix of old and new architecture. We also have a campus done in the one-north area which is next to the R&D heart of Singapore.

We currently have 33,100 students with about 1/3 studying PhDs and masters, and remaining 2/3 of undergraduates. We have a growing international student population, as well as a diverse international faculty from over 67 countries. We have currently 143,000 alumni; more than 15,000 of our alumni are in China, spread across 19 NTU Alumni Associations in major cities in China.

We have four major colleges of Engineering, Business, Science, and Humanities. NTU is a relatively young university as I said, and these colleagues are all well poised to take NTU to greater heights in the coming years. We also have an "S. Rajaratnam School of International Studies" which is ranked 3rd among Asian think tanks (Global "Go-To Think Tanks" 2009 Rankings). A very exciting development in NTU is the establishment of a New Medical School, in partnership with Imperial College, London. This will have a critical base in Tan Tock Seng Hospital which is a hospital for infections of diseases. We see NTU as a well position to contribute to the new development in medical studies with a very strong technology base, and so Biomedical Engineering is crucial in the development of these curriculums. We also have a Confucius College which trains our teachers in Singapore with degrees and diplomas.

We see NTU as an academic eco-system as one that prepares students for the challenges of the 21st Century. 21st Century comes with severe economic challenges as well as technological demands that require us to develop new paradigms in teaching the engineers tomorrow, not just the engineers, but the scientists, doctors, artists, and designers. We see that technology having a very crucial element in the development of the mind-set of the young graduate students.

In research, we strive a multi-disciplinary research, we have only began the intensive research about 5 years ago, and we are striving to inherit the discipline and restring the steps of the development of NTU. We are very proud that we have two of the Research Centers of Excellence (RCE) founded by National Research Foundation and the Ministry of Education: the first is "Earth Observatory of Singapore (EOS)", dedicated to understanding basic processes that produce natural hazards such as earthquakes, tsunamis, volcanic eruptions and climate change. Another RCE was established this year, "Singapore Centre on Environmental Life Sciences Engineering (SCELSE)", here we have established experts in the bio-films along with U. S. genetic pioneer professors to work on the global breaking research on Environmental

Micro-biology.

Moving forward, NTU has the 2015 vision, in which, we see five peaks of excellence as something we strive for, in the areas identified we would like to develop excellence in: Sustainable Earth, Future Healthcare, New Media, New Silk Road, Innovation Asia. "Sustainable Earth" is our Mount Everest of NTU; And "Future Healthcare", I already mentioned Imperial-Nanyang Medical School, we also developed research in health system as well as experimental medicine; the "New Silk Road" is really looking into the 21st Century paradigm of exchange of ideas between East and West. On "Innovation Asia", here we have Nanyang Centre for Public Administration, Nanyang China Institute, and we will open up new academic links with India.

Lastly, on International Collaborations, we have established many joint PhD programs with prestigious overseas universities. We have recently signed MOUs with some fabulous universities in Europe, Middle East and America. We have a growing partnership with Asian countries and we strive to extend this even further.

Thank you very much!

许谦益简历

澳大利亚莫纳什大学博士，新加坡南洋理工大学副教务长，教授。

1989年，执教于新加坡南洋理工大学（NTU）之前，是墨尔本联邦科学与工业研究组织（CSIRO）的实验科学家。主要研究领域：为人工角膜移植、骨科、牙齿移植提供纳米生物陶瓷和纳米结构复合；为航空航天设备以及固体氧化物燃料电池提供纳米材料的火花电浆烧结（SPS），纳米能源，金属陶瓷，薄膜，热喷涂层，热障涂层（TBS）。

2001年，受邀担任日本国家防卫学院访问学者，最近又被中国浙江大学聘为客座教授。2004—2008年，担任南洋理工大学研究主任和新加坡—麻省理工联盟（SMA）的副院长。2008年，作为项目主管参与由总理办公室（PMO）推动的国家研究基金会（NRF）。兼职担任日本科学技术局（STA）研究员，日本产业技术综合研究所（AIST）研究员，材料国际组织主席（IMEA），材料、矿物、采矿研学会（IOM3）电子研发部主席。

在东亚“10+6”框架下促进区域性教育合作与发展

——以清迈大学为例

泰国清迈大学副校长　彭音·拉卡利亚桑

东亚峰会各成员国教育部的各位领导及代表，

各位高校校长及副校长，

各位尊贵的来宾，

女士们、先生们：

迄今为止，清迈大学已与世界各地的多所院校开展了150余项学术合作项目。这些项目涉及科研、教学、课程设计、联合学位、短期课程，当然还有国际学术会议。

在“10+6”框架下，清迈大学积极致力于开展区域内的合作项目，造福高校学生，带动师资交流。为此我校采取了一系列措施，包括引入“质量保证”管理和学分互换机制，采纳促进学位互认的资格体制，以及开展涉及交流、联合科研和奖学金等的各类项目。“10+6”框架下的各国政府、国际组织和高校对我们的这些项目给予了大力支持。

泰国国际开发合作署全力资助清迈大学与老挝国立大学联合开展“发展研究国际硕士学位培养项目”（2009—2015年）。同时，在2010—2012年间，我们还将与老挝苏冯那翁大学开展三个合作项目，分别是食品加工学士学位项目、苏大图书馆建设项目和人力资源开发项目。

为确保上述项目的顺利开展，我们采取了一系列措施，包括课程设计，校际学术研讨会，提供硕士、博士学位奖学金，配备相关师资力量，培训项目负责人，购置书籍，创建数据资源库。

此外，清迈大学还直接向柬埔寨皇家艺术学院和琅勃拉邦的苏冯那翁大学提供建筑硕士学位奖学金，并自2004年起累计向老挝国立大学、苏冯那翁大学和琅勃拉邦信息和文化发展中心捐赠100余台计算机。我们还继续给予苏大工商管理学院教学指导，并共同开展涉及工商管理领域的合作项目。我们也与印尼布劳爪哇大学签署协议，共同培养生物技术双学位硕士。

目前，清迈大学已接纳了100多名“10+6”成员国的高校师生攻读硕士和博士学位。我校还积极鼓励本校学生和海外学生进行互换交流。2009年，通过学生互换交流项目，有10余个国家近250名学生到我校交流学习。交流项目有益于各高校，也有助于拓展学生的国际视野，并加强他们对学术和社会的了解。我们的交流项目还使就读我校的学生获得一些与世界领先的院校可比的资格证书。近年来，我校赴海外学习的学生数量也持续增长。仅2009年就有50多名学生离开泰国，前往海外的10余所大学交流学习。我们还有其他一些项目帮助我校师生赴国外学习，包括泰国与周边国家师生交流项目（也称“大湄公河次区域项目”）和亚太大学交流项目。后者承认学分转换机制，并包含软件工程科学学士学位项目、机械工程学士学位项目、生物制药工程硕士学位项目、环境科学硕士学位项目、应用地球物理硕士学位项目和石油地质硕士学位项目等。

自1994年起，清迈大学与日本三重大学和中国江苏大学共同举办“三国三校国际学术研讨会”。该研讨会由三校每年轮流承办，也成为青年科学家和学生获取国际化专业知识的重要平台。鉴于研讨会广受好评，其他高校也希望加入其中。清迈大学将于2010年11月10~13日承办第17届“三国三校学术研讨会”，其主题是“亚洲在区域和可持续发展方面的作用”。目前已有日本、中国、印尼、越南、孟加拉和泰国等国家和地区的13所高校师生报名参会。

清迈大学还与日本三重大学和香川大学于2007年起共同举办教育研

究交流联合研讨会。今年的年会积极鼓励三校师生广泛开展学术和科研交流，并加强科研合作。研讨会同样由三校每年轮流主办。

清迈大学区域可持续发展中心每年都向越南、柬埔寨和中国等国家和地区的学生提供可持续发展国际硕士学位奖学金。该中心同时还资助大湄公河次区域内的专家学者与清迈大学共同开展科研合作。

此外，清迈大学还积极发挥其国际影响力，力求成为国际知名高校和大湄公河次区域的学术高地。为此，我校与次区域内的多所高校签署了谅解备忘录，分别在云南师范大学、河内农业大学和皇家艺术学院设立了三个教育研究合作中心。我校还将在琅勃拉邦苏冯那翁大学设立一个中心。该中心的任务就是发布清迈大学的有关信息，鼓励所在地高校师生通过合作研究项目到我校继续深造。

清迈大学将一如既往地重视发展与次区域内各高校的友谊和合作关系，以增进各国人民的相互了解。与此同时，我们已在云南师范大学和成都大学建立了泰国语言文化中心，并计划在温州医学院也设立一个中心。我校持续派遣教师前往这几个中心教授泰语并开展学术活动。这个项目得到了泰国高等教育委员会办公室的大力支持。清迈大学还建立了具有影响力的孔子学院。我校通过设立孔子学院来教授中文课程，传播中国文化，为一些在泰国北部从事汉语教学的中学和大学教师提供培训。

2008 年 9 月 18 日，清迈大学主办了第一届大湄公河次区域高校的国际会议，以加强该地区高校间的学术发展和国际合作。来自五个大湄公河次区域国家的 7 所高校参加了会议。召开这次会议的目的在于讨论如何推动与会高校间的学术合作，以及合作的途径和手段，从而建立区域性的高校国际合作网络，这个网络可缩写为“GMS - UNIC”（GMS University Network for International Cooperation），即大湄公河次区域高校国际合作网络。

清迈大学和澳大利亚新南威尔士大学在材料科学、农业环境水源管理、森林环境火灾控制、登革热疾病防控、生物医学材料、电子化学等方面开展了合作科研项目。在不久的将来，我们希望建立学位联合培养项目。

我们清迈大学的所有教职工将持之以恒地建设一个研究型的清迈大学。围绕这个目标，清迈大学在各个学术领域都设立了高水平研究成果的激励机制。自2005年以来，校园里逐渐形成了良好的学术氛围，通过长期组织学术研讨会来鼓励学者们加大科研产出，积极发表学术论文。为此，我们设立了“清迈大学金象奖”，专门表彰科研成果突出的教职工。

毋庸置疑，我们清迈大学作为一所本土大学，会继续开发我们的教育和学习项目，以建立一个跨学科的、符合国际标准的教育模式，培养一批高质量的、具有优良学术背景的毕业生。换言之，我们的挑战来自如何建立一个享誉国内外的重点高等教育学府。

综上所述，我们清迈大学希望在东亚“10+6”框架下与各国政府、国际机构和高校建立多边合作体系，从而使我们与合作院校能够长期有效地开展国际交流与合作。

（毕媛媛　译）

彭音·拉卡利亚桑英文发言稿

Regional Cooperation and Development of Higher Education within the East Asia "10 + 6" Summit Framework

Pong-In Rakariyatham

Vice President, Chiang Mai University, Thailand

Directors General and representatives from the Ministry of Education from 10 + 6 East Asia countries,

Presidents and Rectors from 10 + 6 Universities in East Asia,

Vice Presidents and Vice Rectors from 10 + 6 Universities in East Asia,

Honorary guests,

ladies and gentlemen,

Until today, Chiang Mai University has undertaken more than 150 academic projects in collaboration with numerous institutions around the world. The range of collaboration encompasses research, teaching, curricula development, joint degree programs, short training courses and seminars, and, certainly, international conferences and symposia.

Within the context of the10 + 6Framework, Chiang Mai University manages many collaborative projects to support higher education of students and increase staff mobility in the region. These measures have included so far the development of quality assurance and credit transfer systems, qualifications frameworks leading to mutual degree recognition, as well as exchange, joint research and scholarship programs. These projects have been supported by 10 + 6 governments, international organizations or the University itself.

The Thailand International Development Cooperation Agency (TICA) approved funds for Chiang Mai University to undertake projects covering the Development of the International Master's Program in Development Studies at the National University of Laos in Vientiane from 2009 – 2015. Also, during the period 2010 – 2012 three projects were undertaken at Souphanouvong University which are 1) Development of Food Processing Curriculum for Bachelor's degree level 2) Development of a Souphanouvong University library, and 3) Human Resources Development.

In order to warrant sustainability of all the projects just mentioned, various activities were initiated, such as curriculum development, organizing joint workshops within the frame of university partnership arrangements, provision of scholarships at the level of Master's and Doctoral degree, making expertise available for these programs, arranging training programs for those in charge, purchasing books and the creation of a database system including the establishment of relevant ICT for the Library.

In addition, Chiang Mai University has been providing directly scholarships to staff from the Royal University of Fine Arts in Phnom Penh and Suphanouvong University in Luang Prabang to study Master's degree at Chiang Mai University in the field of Architecture, along with the provision of some 100 computers to the National University of Laos, Souphanouvong University, and the Department of Information and Culture in Luang Prabang, since 2004. We continue to support its Faculty of Business Administration to undertake academic services programs to provide advice for curriculum development including collaboration to develop business-related research projects with Souphanouvong University. With Indonesia we have an arrangement for a double degree program at Master's level in Biotechnology with Brawijaya University.

As I speak, more than 100 staff and students from 10 + 6 East Asia

Countries are studying Master's and Doctoral degree at Chiang Mai University. We actively encourage interaction between our own students and those from overseas. In 2009, the student exchange programs enabled almost 250 students to travel from more than 10 countries to study at Chiang Mai University. Participants in these programs have proven to make valuable contributions to the University community, affording a global outlook in both academic and social contexts. These programs also warrant that those studying at Chiang Mai University obtain qualifications comparable with some of the world's leading institutions. The number of Chiang Mai University students involved in exchange programs abroad is continuously increasing. In 2009 alone, more than 50 Chiang Mai University students left Thailand to study at 10 overseas universities. Other initiatives that support students and staff exchange overseas include:

Faculty and Student Exchange Programs between Thailand and neighboring countries (e. g. the so-called Greater Mekong Subregion Program)

University Mobility in Asia and Pacific (also called UMAP) which includes credit transfer systems. The programs involved are: Bachelor of Science in Software Engineering, Bachelor of Engineering in Mechanical Engineering, Master of Science in Biomedical Engineering, Master of Science in Environmental Science, Master of Science in Applied Geophysics, and Master of Science in Petroleum Geoscience.

Chiang Mai University, Mie University from Japan, and Jiangsu University of Science and Technology have been organizing the so-called Tri-University International Joint Seminar and Symposium since 1994. Each university takes turns to be the host of this annual event. The event offers young scientists and students a unique opportunity to update their knowledge on experience with the global issues of the theme. Due to its popularity, other universities intend to participate as well. In 2010, during November 10th-13th,

Chiang Mai University will host the 17th Tri-University International Joint Seminar and Symposium under the title "The Role of Asia in Communities and Sustainable Development". Students and staff from 13 universities from Japan, China, Indonesia, Vietnam, Bangladesh and Thailand are now registering to attend.

Chiang Mai University, Mie University and Kagawa University from Japan have been organizing the so-called Educational Research Exchange Joint Symposium (EDUREJS) which started in 2007. This yearly event encourages staff and students of the three aforementioned universities to exchange both academic and research knowledge, as well as to intensify research collaboration. Each university takes turns to be the host.

The Regional Center for Sustainable Development (RCSD) of Chiang Mai University grants yearly scholarships for students from Vietnam, Cambodia and China to participate in an international Master's degree program on Sustainable Development. The Center also enables staff in the Greater Mekong Subregion to conduct research, including joint research, with staff of Chiang Mai University.

In addition, Chiang Mai University is playing a significant role internationally, pursuant to its goals to become a "University of Excellence" and become a Higher Learning Hub for the Greater Mekong Sub-region. This has meanwhile resulted in the signing of memoranda of understanding with various universities in the Greater Mekong Sub region, and examples are: Three Chiang Mai University Education and Research Coordination Centers at Yunnan Normal University, its Royal University of Fine Arts, and Hanoi Agriculture University. The next such centre will be set up at Souphanouvong University, Luang Prabang. The aim of these centers is to disseminate information on Chiang Mai University and to encourage students and staff from those countries to continue their study at Chiang Mai University with the possibility of conducting joint research.

Chiang Mai University will continue to give significant priority to friendship and collaboration arrangements with countries of the Greater Mekong Subregion in order to promote cultural understanding among all people in the GMS. More in particular, two Chiang Mai University Thai Language and Cultural Centers were established at Yunnan Normal University and Chengdu University, while the next center will be at the Wenzhou Medical College. Continuously professors from Chiang Mai University visit these centers to teach Thai and arrange activities. This project is supported by the Office of Commission on Higher Education of Thailand. Lastly, Chiang Mai University is one of the most effective universities with a Confucius Institute offering language courses and distributing information on Chinese culture. As of today a number of secondary teachers and university professors who teach Chinese in Northern Thailand have been receiving training.

As recently as September 18th 2008, Chiang Mai University organized the 1st International Conference on Academic Strengthening and International Collaboration among Universities in the GMS, attended by 7 universities from 5 GMS countries. The objectives of the conference were to discuss and exchange ideas about the promotion of academic cooperation between the respective university administrations in order to determine ways and means to build up cooperation, as well as to establish a GMS University Network for International Cooperation, also shortened to GMS-UNIC.

Chiang Mai University and the University of New South Wales in Australia have conducted joint research in the field of Material Science, along with other research in such fields as Water Management in agricultural environments, Environmental management of forest burning, Dengue fever, Biomedical materials, and Electro ceramics. In the near future, we do hope to have joint degree programs as well.

We at Chiang Mai University continue to pay attention to establishing a sustained research institute. To this effect the university has already set up a working mechanism to stimulate quality research production in all fields of study. A research atmosphere has been established by organizing academic events in order to encourage researchers to produce and publish more academic works on a continuing basis, ever since 2005. As you may be aware, a "CMU Golden Elephant Award" is given to honor those persons who produced excellent research results.

It is clear that our university, as a local university, will continue to develop its teaching and learning programs in order to be able to offer access to an international standard of multidisciplinary education, and to produce graduates with academic excellence and quality at world standards. In other words, our challenge is to become a "University of Excellence".

In ending, we at Chiang Mai University look forward to entering into mutual collaboration arrangements with 10 + 6 governments and international organizations, which would enable us and our partner universities to manage our activities effectively and sustainably.

彭音·拉卡利亚桑简历

泰国清迈大学社会科学学院地理系教授，副校长，分管教学。

教育背景：

1974 年，泰国清迈大学土木专业工学学士。

1976 年，泰国清迈大学地理学、理学学士。

1978 年，荷兰恩斯赫德国际地理信息科学与地球观测学院摄影测量学硕士。

1984 年，法国保罗沙巴岛大学遥感专业博士。

工作经历：

1976 年起，任清迈大学地理系教师、社会科学院院长、地理信息与空间技术开发中心（北部地区）主任、教务副校长，兼任泰国国家研究委员会成员。

加强区域性高等教育合作，应对全球教育事业新挑战

泰国宣素南塔皇家大学校长　楚昂科特·布恩图为特

尊敬的朱拉隆功大学副校长卡拉亚·廷萨巴先生，

各位大学校长，

尊敬的各位来宾，

女士们，先生们：

大家好！我非常荣幸能参加“东亚峰会高等教育合作论坛”，与大家共同探讨合作交流事宜。与各位一样，我们泰国同样意识到必须加强区域性高等教育合作，以应对全球教育事业新挑战，特别是要在东亚峰会高等教育合作行动计划中所提出的四个领域展开合作。

在过去二十年里，中国—东盟之间的合作让我们都受益匪浅。诸如“中国桥夏令营”等活动在年轻人中建立起了长久的友谊，构建起了影响深远的交际网路。

东亚和中国合作的另外一个重要平台就是“东亚峰会高等教育合作论坛”。我们关注的焦点是如何增强地区竞争力？利用现有的全部教育资源来推动经济和社会发展，其中灵活性和流通性是主要因素。

我们知道，教育是东亚地区发展的基石。因此，东亚社会—文化群体致力于发展人力资源。协调本地区高校间的评估标准，采纳普遍的学分转换系统，并实行学位及资格互认，定将能促进本地区师生流动。目前，东盟、东南亚教育部长组织和东盟大学联盟正在进行的项目，能帮助我们增加教育机会，促进技术、知识和思想的自由交流，打造一个高

级智囊团，为本地区的人民提供更多的择业机会。

女士们，先生们，我代表着泰国 40 所“Rajabhat”大学和 9 所“Rajamonkala”大学。“Rajabhat”大学系列的最初办学定位是“师范学院”，而“Rajamonkala”大学系列的办学定位是“理工学院”。

我们的主要职责是为泰国的城乡社会发展服务。我们致力于为所有泰国学生提供教育途径。绝大多数学生都来自穷困和中等家庭，有超过 60% 的泰国本科学生是由我们培养的。

同样，在东亚各国的本科生中，有超过 70% 的学生都来自贫穷家庭或中产家庭。这是东亚各国政府的首要问题之一，也是“东亚峰会高等教育合作论坛”提上日程的一个重要任务。

东亚国家在教育领域必须支持和领导的另一个领域是制定一个在教育系统普遍通用的“东盟教师培训标准”。那些选择了以教书育人为职业的东盟人民定能从中受益，从而在不久的将来提高社会劳动力的整体素质。

如果“东亚峰会高等教育合作论坛”同意将“东盟教师培训标准”作为论坛的一项成果，那么宣素南塔皇家大学提议在 2011 年 12 月，暨庆祝宣素南塔皇家大学建校 75 周年之际，在曼谷主办一次研讨会。

女士们，先生们，当我们都将大部分注意力投放在高等教育水平上时，我们不应该忽略作为基础教育的共同责任。我们将致力于教育的可持续发展，继续努力提高不同层次的教育质量。因此，我们希望在东亚（10 +6）框架下一起合作探索并改进终身学习途径，确保本地区及其人民的可持续发展。

女士们，先生们，“东亚峰会高等教育合作论坛”给我们提供了非常多的宝贵机会，借此提升教育质量，增加教育机会，造福东亚各国学生。能参加这次论坛，我们深感荣幸和感激！

谢谢！

（毕媛媛　译）

楚昂科特·布恩图为特英文发言稿

Develop Regional Education Cooperation To Meet Global Challenges In Education

Chuangchote Bhuntuvech

President, Suan Sunandha Rajabhat University, Thailand

Vice President of Chulalongkorn University , Dr. M. R. Kalaya Tingsabadh,
Presidents Rectors of Universities in the Region,
Distinguished Delegates,
Ladies and gentlemen,

Greetings to all participants of The East Asia Summit Higher Education Cooperation Forum. I am honored to be here to participate in this forum and to discuss strategies for implementing areas of cooperation and collaboration. Like you, we, too recognize the need for regional education cooperation to meet global challenges in education, particularly in the four areas named by the East Asia Summit Higher Education Cooperation Taskforce.

Over the past two decades, China-ASEAN cooperation has brought benefits to us all. Activities such as the "Chinese Bridge-Summer Camp" allow our young people to build long friendships and establish networks which will continue far into the future.

Another important forum for ASEAN and China to work together on is the East Asia Summit Higher Education Cooperation. Attention has focused on how to enhance regional competitiveness, gathering all the available educational resources to promote economic and social development. Mobility and flexibility are key factors.

We know that education is fundamental for the development of Eastern Asia. Thus, the Blueprint for East Asia Socio-Cultural Community is focused on Human Resource Development.

The harmonization of standards of assessment among higher education institutions in the region and the adoption of a common credit transfer system for the mutual recognition of degrees and qualifications will enhance mobility of faculty members and students in the region. Projects are currently underway by ASEAN, SEAMEO and the ASEAN University Network. These efforts will help us to increase educational opportunities, promote the free flow of expertise, knowledge, ideas, build a skilled and talented workforce, and provide alternative career paths for the peoples of the region.

Ladies and gentlemen, I represent of 40 Rajabhat Universities plus 9 Rajamonkala Universities in Thailand. Rajabhat universities were originally designed as "Teacher's Colleges", while Rajamonkala Universities were designed as technical colleges.

Our main mission is to serve and develop urban and rural communities throughout Thailand. We are crucial in offering access to education for all students of Thailand. Most of students are from poor and middle class families, and more than 60% Thai undergraduate students are our responsibility.

I also believe that more than 70% of the undergraduate students in East Asia countries are from the poor and middle class families.

This is one of the main issues for the East Asia government and the East Asia Summit Higher Education Cooperation to consider as an important agenda.

Another area that the East Asia must support and provide leadership in the field of Education is in the development of an "ASEAN Teacher Education Standard?" in order to? formulate a standard for all teaching areas. It would of great benefit to the ASEAN people who have chosen teaching as a career in order to support the labor mobilization in the near future.

If the East Asia Summit Higher Education Cooperation agrees with ASEAN Teacher Education Standard? as outcome of this forum, Suan Sunandha Rajabhat University would like to propose to be the hosting venue for the workshop in December 2011 in Bangkok, which will be the 75th Anniversary Celebration of Suan Sunandha Rajabhat University.

Ladies and Gentleman, While a great deal of attention is focused at the higher education level, we must not forget our shared commitments with regard to basic education. We and The Education for Sustainable Development will contribute and continue to strive for overall quality improvements in education at all levels. For this reason, we would like the East Asia (10 + 6) cooperation to explore and develop lifelong learning opportunities to ensure sustainable development in the region and among its peoples.

Ladies and Gentleman, The East Asia Higher Education Cooperation Forum has presented many wonderful opportunities for advancing the quality and of education for students throughout East Asia. We look forward to building and strengthening the relationship with East Asia Education Cooperation. We are proud and grateful to be part of this exciting time.

Thank you!

楚昂科特·布恩图为特简历

泰国宣素南塔皇家大学校长，博士。

教育背景：

1974 年，泰国斯里纳卡琳威洛特大学教育学学士。

1979 年，菲律宾科技大学管理学硕士。

1986 年，美国纽约大学技术与工业管理专业 博士。

工作经历：

1988—1991 年，泰国宣素南塔师范学院 计算机科学系 主任。

1992—1995 年，泰国宣素南塔皇家学院 理工学院院长。

1996—2003 年，泰国宣素南塔皇家学院 教务副校长。

2004 年至今，泰国宣素南塔皇家大学 校长。

高等教育合作：实现共同发展的议程

印度旁遮普大学校长　琅勃·钱德尔·索博蒂

一、引　言

发展中国家的高等教育领域正经历着巨大变迁。这些国家的政府着力通过加强对初等教育的资源配置，改变高文盲率普遍的现状。世界发展报告（1998—1999）在一篇题为《知识促进发展》的文章里精辟地指出："知识好比光线。没有重量、不可触摸，它能轻松地周游世界，启蒙各地的民众。但上亿的人民仍然生活在黑暗中（文盲）——这其实是可以改变的。"初等教育作为中等和高等教育体系的源头供给者，国家扫除文盲的做法是必要的。但是，由于资源匮乏，绝大多数的发展中国家一直以来都忽视了高等教育。大多数公立大学极度依赖政府日益减少的拨款，这种螺旋效应冲淡了教育自主权，也带来了过多的干预。一个国家的知识首都只能发展成为高等学府所在地。因为只有人力资本才能使一个国家成为一个知识动力库，在当今动荡的经济环境下，只有劳动者的知识和技能才是一个国家保持可持续竞争优势的源泉所在。

东亚地区自远古以来一直都是教育的中心，它欢迎思想与观点的自由交流。在全球化的当代，高等教育合作早已不是一种选择，而是势在必行。在兼容并包、互通有无、自由往来的环境里，思想方能开花结果。教育是区域合作的重要内容。政府和学校都做了大量工作以达到共赢。为了培养适应一体化的经济要求的人才，如何使教育内容和教授方式全球化成为合作的一个重要推动力。这个目标可以通过师生交换实现。

作为公民的一项基本权利和公共利益，联合国《世界人权宣言》第二十六条庄严申明："人人都有受教育的权利。"教育应当免费，至少在初级和基础阶段应该是无偿的。小学教育应属于义务教育。职业和技术教育应当普及，高等教育应当在择优的基础上对人人平等开放。同样，"千年发展目标"和"巴黎宣言"都在关注高等教育和科学合作以达到人才全面、均衡的发展。

二、高等教育的嬗变

全球范围内教育正经历着格局性的转变。全球经济的一体化催生了信息爆炸，在教育领域则反映为越来越多的课程通过因特网和远程方式教授。同时，学术机构的企业化趋势也日益加剧。这种变化日益要求高校及时了解地方、国家和全球三个层面上社会对高校当前和将来的需求。经济生存压力下，高校也面临合并的危机。这种转变对受过良好教育、技艺精湛的工作者也提出了更高的要求，扩张了的中等教育系统使更多的学生选择接受高等教育；教育不断加强与国际的联系，使其有流动性，并外包教育。教育过程的终端用户，企业需要的是具有技术头脑的知识型劳动者，这样吸收他们进入企业时就不用投入太多的培训。此外，还有一种明显的变化就是人们更加普遍地关注和期待跨学科学习环境培育出的人才素质。

这些变化伴随着政府渠道的资助的急剧减少。现在对高等教育的看法有一种观点认为，高等教育不是公益性质的产品而是个人福利，不是一种投资而是一种代价。大量学生无力支付学费的现实迫使学校提供更多的奖学金和助学金。

这些巨变要求高校制定战略规划。要求高校不断审视和分析其自身和它所服务的外部环境。因此，在技术型知识经济中，高校必须不仅教授学生专业知识而且还要加强他们的行业必备技能和知识，这样他们将来才能在岗位上提高效率。不同的利益相关者对学习的需求不仅仅是"顺应时代"的学习，而且还是量身定做的"一切为了你"的学习方式。

竞争促使高校探索出路，完善服务模式，以保证自己在市场上的竞争地位。同时，也是竞争使高校得到更好的生源和教师以及资金，保证学校的研究任务和支持院系的发展。大多数发展中国家的高等教育目前正进入一种市场主导、收入驱动的重组阶段。为了能为学生提供最好的学习服务，为家长和未来的雇主提供最优质的服务，高等教育必须回应社会课题和自己客户的需求，成为一个包罗万象的实体。

三、印度高等教育的转变

自1947年独立以来，印度的高等教育有了巨大的发展。

印度高等教育指数增长表

	1947 年 8 月	2010 年 7 月
大学(所)	20	504
学院(所)	500	26064
教师(个)	15000	5900000
接受高等教育学生(个)	100000	13600000
接受高等教育人口	1%	12.5%

*资料来源：印度政府（2010）人力资源发展部数据。

运用SWOT分析模型（从压力、弱点、机遇和威胁四个方面分析）对印度高等教育的分析表明，印度社会对高等教育入学率的需求在不断增长，对新兴的、先进的不同学科的多样性的专长、能力和技术的需求也在扩大。随着巨大的教师队伍智囊团，合理配置的基础设施和物质资源，先进的技术设备、信息、通信和技术、远程课程及校友基地等等条件的出现，高等学府也面临巨大机遇。但是，这些高校的一些弱点包括欠缺长期的政策和战略，缺乏协调、角色冲突阻碍了他们的发展。由于没有教学评估和审议机制，导致了一些陈旧的不适应市场需求的课程长期存在。教育技术方面陈旧的系统、迟缓的改善和发展导致教学不能与时俱进，满足产业的需求。

挑战 一：受教育的机会与教育扩张。

挑战二：公平与包容。

挑战三：质量与优秀。

挑战四：学术和管理改革。

挑战五：国际化与私人力量参与办学。

作为完成中等教育的学生有机会接受高等教育的指针，印度的毛入学率为12.5%，较之美国和加拿大的60%低得可怜，在欧洲一些国家这个比例超过40%，甚至在一些发展中国家也超过20%。国际经验表明，如果一个国家的高等教育毛入学率低于20%，那么这个国家绝不能跻身经济发达国家行列。因此，印度的教育政策制定者的首要任务是将毛入学率提高到20%这个门槛，这样才能实现经济的可持续发展。在印度，教育被列为并行的事项，所以它需要中央和地方政府的共同努力。

关于教育机会的公平性，存在着巨大的城乡差异，邦内的多样性，性别及宗教内部、种姓内部的差异。印度政府一直着力通过诸如预留名额、免学费和提供奖学金等诸多的公平政策鼓励教育落后的群体如女孩和低种姓族群得到更多的受教育机会。

印度有很多大学办学成绩卓著并且在世界上取得一席之地，诸如印度理工学院、印度管理研究所、全印度医学研究所、昌迪加尔医学研究院、贾瓦哈拉尔·尼赫鲁大学、德里大学、孟买大学和旁遮普大学。然而，就质量而言，在印度有1/3 的大学，超过60%的学院以及所有私立学院都达不到国际标准。政府一直在努力改善投入不足的公立教育机构的办学条件。为了吸引并留住最好的教职人员，学校设立了综合型的研究基金。此外，大学和研究实验室之间必须充分配合以便将教学、研究及指导学生融为一体。学校应该建立一种持续的质量评估、反馈及完善体系，这种文化体系在学校层面创造强有力的质量保证程序，主要仰赖教师的专业技能，同时也融合了学生、产业界和相关人员的意见。

为了使招生、考试、教师和管理等相关方面的制度更加协调，很多高校已经开始了改革。这些改革包括统一的课程设置，通过引入学分课程和持续的考试与评估体系，鼓励学生流动和学分交换。引入辅导式的和讨论课形式的授课方式，促使学生更多地参与学习过程，从而提高分析能力、创造能力和应用能力。一些知名学校的改革措施包括经常性和定期的修订与完善教学大纲，使大纲具有弹性和活力，增加跨学科的课程以跟进职场的需求。还有一些学校通过重组以确保透明度、自主权和问责制的实行。

为了应对印度高等教育行业面向国际教育集团开放的必然趋势，将印度发展为教育中心，印度的高校采取了联盟的办法吸引国外学生，并与各国高校联合进行合作研究。将来，印度的大学有可能获准与国外知名学校联合颁发双学位，允许国外大学在印度建立分校，而不是特许办学权和课程租用。印度政府也可能会成立一些委员会把印度的教育资源推向海外市场。

四、加强高等教育合作

一体化的全球经济要求培养能够应对各种不同环境的人才。很多因素使得我们的世界变得更平坦（差异缩小），这对高等教育也有影响。因此，劳动者需要训练有素，对社会和文化方面的问题有更好的理解和更高的敏感性。所以，学校需要更广泛的合作开发相应的课程。以下是一些促进合作的建议：

（1）合作要与全球人力资源的要求相一致和匹配。可以通过联合评估地区能力，开发教材等实现。

（2）通过专业的管理和学校建设，加强核心能力，提高系统和结构的透明度与开放度，防止人才流失。鉴于此，可以开发东亚国家间的合作项目。

（3）采用组合的办法实现成员国间的教师和研究人员的人力资源流动。通过更快捷的交换模式，例如内联，可使领先的领域在东亚区域的不同国家间得到推广。

（4）可以通过培育区域间可共享的系统科学知识网络实现合作和建立伙伴关系。这种合作方法可以成为学校自身能力发展的一个渠道，合作基于双方的强项，并且从文化和科学角度都有益于双方。这种合作也可成为经济发展的先驱。

（5）建立知识和技术前沿领域的孵化中心和知识中心。这不仅能为成员国带来经济的繁荣而且还能加强技术和商业合作。

（6）开发联合学位项目，教师和学生能够在一所学校参与课程的一部分。此外，定期的工作团队、暑期项目和联合申请研究基金、建立研究型交流合作伙伴关系都能发展成为建立合作的方式。

相对缓慢的合作关系的建立可以归因于文化和意识形态的冲突。高校感到他们的首要任务是教学生和传播知识。由于奖励和晋升机制都看重学术水准的成果，高校形成了一种较多关注基础性研究的思维定式。这种模式导致信息不畅、闭门造车的局面。为了实现普遍的发展，高校的领导和决策者需要引导、培育合作。

（马理　译）

琅勃·钱德尔·索博蒂英文发言稿

Synergistic Collaboration in Higher Education: Agenda for All Pervasive Growth

Ranbir Chander Sobti

Vice Chancellor, Panjab University, Chandigarh (India)

A. Introduction

Higher education scenario in developing countries is in a flux. The focus of these countries is on removing high levels of illiteracy prevailing by allocating resources towards universal primary education. World Development Report (1998 – 1999) entitled "Knowledge for Development" has very succinctly remarked "Knowledge is like light. Weightless and intangible, it can easily travel the world, enlightening the lives of people everywhere. Yet billions of people still live in the darkness (of illiteracy) -unnecessarily". This is essential as the primary education acts as the feeder to the secondary and higher education systems. However, there has also been a neglect of higher education in most of the developing countries due to scarcity of resources. Most public universities are highly dependent on governments for their financial resources, which is getting scarce. The spiraling effect is also dilution of academic autonomy and undue interference. Intellectual capital of a nation can only be developed in institutions of higher learning. It is the quality of human capital which can lead to emergence of nation as a knowledge powerhouse. In today's turbulent economic environment, skills and knowledge of the workforce can be the only source of sustainable competitive advantage for the nations.

East Asia has been the hub of education since times immemorial. It has been receptive to and welcomed free transfer of ideas and opinions. In this era of globalization, need for cooperation in higher education is no longer a matter of choice, but a compulsion. Ideas bear fructification in an environment of openness, exchange and free flow. Education is an important constituent of regional cooperation. Numerous efforts have been made, both at the government and institutional levels to develop integrated approach for mutual gains. An important thrust towards collaboration is the need to globalize educational content and delivery systems so as to provide training to the students for the emerging integration of economies. This is also possible through exchange of students and faculty.

As a basic right and public good, education is firmly established by Article 26 of the United Nation's *Universal Declaration of Human Rights*: "Everyone has the right to education. Education shall be free, at least in the elementary and fundamental stages. Elementary education shall be compulsory. Technical and professional education shall be made generally available and higher education shall be equally accessible to all on the basis of merit." On similar lines, *Millennium Development Goals* (MDGs) and the *Paris Declaration* have focused on higher education and scientific cooperation for balanced, all round development.

B. Seismic Changes in Higher Education

Education is witnessing paradigm shifts globally. With the global integration of economies, there has also been an information explosion as reflected through increasing popularity of courses offered through internet and telecommunication. There is also now increasing corporatization of the academic institutions. Institutions of higher education are increasingly being required to be sensitive to the current and future needs of society, at the local, national and global levels. There are also pressures for institutional mergers and acquisition so as to be economically viable. There is a paramount requirement for highly skilled and educated workers, expansion of secondary education systems making more students opting for higher education; increasing links to the international system, with mobility and outsourcing of higher education. End users of the educational process, i. e. the corporations demand for knowledge workers that are technologically savvy so that minimal efforts are required to absorb them in the organizations. There is also a perceptual shift in the learning environment & expectations with interdisciplinary learning outcomes becoming more widespread and essential

Such changes are coupled with significant decrease in funding from government sources. There is now a shift in perception with education not really being treated as a public good but a private benefit, and that it is not really an investment but a cost. Inability of many students to pay high fees has led to demand for more scholarships and grants on campuses.

These upheavals require that the institutions of higher learning develop strategic planning orientation. This necessitates continuous analysis of the points of interaction between the institution and the external environment in which it functions. Thus, in the technology-enabled knowledge economy, institutions have to not only impart subject knowledge but also to enhance requisite skills and knowledge so as to enhance their effectiveness and efficiency in the work place. Demand of the various stakeholders is not only for "just in time" learning but also customized "just for you" learning.

Competitive forces force higher education to search for ways to improve their service delivery in order to remain competitive in the market place. Such competition is also for better students and faculty as well as for grants in order to further their research mission and support their faculty. Most developing countries are moving toward a revenue-driven, market-responsive restructuring of higher education. Higher Education must respond to demands society projects and their own customers in order to transform itself into an all-inclusive entity that provides superior services and learning to students, parents, and in turn, future employers

C. Higher Education in India: Harbinger of Transformation

Higher education has witnessed tremendous growth and development since India gained independence in 1947.

Exponential Growth of Institutional Capacity in Higher Education in India

	August, 1947	July, 2010
Universities	20	504
Colleges	500	26,064
Faculty	15,000	5.90 lacs
Students in Higher Education	1 lac	136 lacs
Access to Higher Education	1%	12.5%

* Ministry of Human Resource Development, Government of India (2010).

A SWOT Analysis for Indian Higher Education reveals that there is an increasing social demand for enrollment in higher education as well as trend towards new and advanced set of diversified specializations, competencies and skills in different sectors. Institutions of higher learning present immense opportunities as there is the presence of a huge think tank of faculty members, reasonably well established infra-structure and material resources, advanced technical & technological facilities besides direct overseas connections through ICT, Distance Learning Programmes, alumni base etc. However, some of the weaknesses of these institutes impeding the growth process include absence of a long term policies and strategies, lack of coordination and conflicting roles and responsibilities for higher education sector's institutions and organizations. The near absence of operational mechanisms for reviewing and evaluating academic programs has led to continuance of many obsolete programmes having poor marketability. Aging of systems, slowness of enhancements and developments in educational technologies has resulted in teaching not keeping pace with the industry's expectations.

There are tremendous challenges facing Higher education.

* Challenge 1: Access and Expansion;
* Challenge 2: Equity and Inclusion ;
* Challenge 3: Quality and Excellence ;
* Challenge 4: Academic and Administrative Reforms ;
* Challenge 5: Internationalisation & Private Participation.

The gross enrollment ratio, which is an indicator of access to higher education to students who have completed the secondary education is only 12.5% which compares very poorly with 60% in USA and Canada, over 40% in several European countries and even more than 20% in many developed and developing countries. International experience shown that no country has been able to become an economically advanced country, if its enrolment ratio in H. E. < 20%. Thus, foremost priority for educational planners in India is to enhance access to a minimum threshold level of about 20 % for sustained economic development. In India, education is in the concurrent list. Thus, it requires joint efforts of both the central as well as the state governments.

With regards to equity in educational opportunities, there are huge rural and urban disparities, inter-state variations, gender as well as inter-religious and inter-caste disparities. Indian government is making special efforts to encourage educationally backward sections like girls, caste groups through affirmative actions like reservations, freeships and scholarships.

Many seats of higher learning have excelled and made their mark internationally like IITs, IIMs, AIIMS, PGI and universities like Jawahar Lal Nehru, Universities of Delhi, Bombay and Punjab etc. However, only 1/3rd universities and over 60% colleges and all of the self-financing institutions are cannot be considered up to the international ranks in terms of quality. Efforts have been made at strengthening of public educational institutions, which have suffered from underinvestment. In order to attract and retain best brains as faculty members, comprehensive research fellowship programs have been developed. In addition, collaboration between universities and research laboratories must be harnessed in order to integrate teaching and research and offering application oriented teaching to students. Institutions need to build a culture of ongoing quality review, feedback, and improvement by creating robust quality assurance processes at the institutional level which rely heavily on faculty expertise and incorporate the views of students, industry and different stakeholders.

Many institutions have embarked upon institutional reforms so as to harmonise admission, examination, faculty and governance related practices. Some of these include following uniform academic calendar, encouraging student mobility and credit transfer through introduction of credit based courses and continuous examination and evaluation system; introduction of tutorial and seminar-based lecture to promote more involved learning with focus on analytical ability, creativity and application oriented learning. Salient feature at reputed institutions include regular and periodic revision and up gradation of syllabi, making them flexible and dynamic, promoting inter-disciplinary courses to be in tune with the job-market dynamics. Many institutions are also restructuring to ensure transparency, autonomy and accountability.

Responding to the inevitable opening of Indian higher education for international service providers as well as promoting India as an educational hub, institutions are adopting consortium approach to attracting foreign students and networking with global institutions for collaborative research. It is likely that Indian universities may be allowed to offer dual degree in collaboration with reputed foreign institutions as well as permitting foreign universities to set up their full-fledged campuses rather than resorting to franchising and courseware renting. Government may also set up council to market Indian educational facilities abroad.

D. Strategies for Cooperation in Higher Education

Integration of global economies has also necessitated training workforce to handle multitude of divergent situations. Many of the forces that have made the world a flatter place also have an influence on higher education. Thus, workers need to be trained for better appreciation and sensitization on social and cultural aspects. Thus, institutions need to collaborate on development of programmes, through establishing larger alliances and partnerships. Some of the recommendations to enhance collaboration include:

1. Harmonization and alignment with the international requirements for global workforce. This could be achieved through joint appraisal of the distinctive competencies of the region, developing instructional material etc.

2. Discouraging Brain drain by developing and managing institutions professionally, harnessing core competencies, bringing transparency and openness in the systems and structures. Thus collaborative programmes among East Asian nations could be developed.

3. Brain circulation by ensuring mobility of the faculty and researchers among the member nations through a cluster approach. With faster modes of

communication and transportation, such inter-linkages can lead to development of niche areas of excellence spread across different nations in the region.

4. Cooperation and partnerships can be developed by fostering knowledge networks which allow systematic scientific knowledge sharing at the regional levels. Such an approach can be a source of institutional capacity development and cooperative mindset that is based on the partners' strengths and is beneficial for both sides from a cultural and scientific standpoint. Such cooperation in education can be precursor to economic development.

5. Establishing Incubation and Knowledge centres which may act as centres of excellence in distinct domains of knowledge and skills. This can not only bring economic prosperity to member nations but also increase technological and business collaborations.

6. Developing twin programmes wherein faculty and students can undertake\ impart part of the course in one institution. Besides, regular working groups, summer programs, joint applications for research funding, establishing a partnership for research exchange could lead to development of a mind set of collaboration.

The relatively slower rate of relationship building can be attributed to the conflict of cultures and orientation. Institutions of higher learning feel their primary responsibility is towards students and in dissemination of knowledge. They have a mindset which focuses more on basic, fundamental research as the reward and promotion systems are based on publications having high academic content. This has led to emergence of a situation where non-sharing of information and working in closed castles is paramount. Captains of premier institutions of higher learning and the policy makers need to take a lead in fostering collaboration for all pervasive growth.

东亚峰会框架下的高等教育合作与发展

——以东京大学为例

东京大学副校长　小岛宪道

我非常荣幸能有机会向各位介绍我校在东亚峰会框架下开展的一些活动。

东京大学始建于1877年，是日本历史最悠久的大学。东大现有10所学院、15所研究院以及32家研究所和研究中心；4000名教师，4000名管理及教辅人员；14000名本科学生及同等规模的研究生。财政方面，每年有近25亿美元的预算。

东京大学有2872名留学生，占全校学生人数的10%。学校与东盟峰会框架下的国家建立了密切的合作关系，71%的留学生均来自东盟国家。

东京大学与东盟峰会框架下的国家签署了120项双边合作协议，占学校协议总数的1/3。其中一项于2010年10月实施的协议，是关于与新加坡国立大学合作开设公共政策专业双学位项目的。

三方的合作框架中，东京大学与中、韩两国有着积极的合作，尤其值得一提的是，我们与北京大学和首尔大学在多个学科领域定期举办三方专题论坛。自2005年以来，我校的材料工程系与清华大学及首尔大学合作举办了多次纳米材料学术研讨会。在通识教育方面，东京大学自1999年以来与北京大学、首尔大学和越南河内国家大学共同组建了一个名为“BESETOHA”的“东亚四大学论坛”（取四所大学英文名的前两个字母组成）四方论坛机制。上周我们刚在河内成功举办了第12次年会。通过这些交流取得的成果，已经以四种语言出版了关于通识教育的通用教材和书籍。

2005年东京大学发起了一个名为“伊来”（EALAI）的海外教育计划。它代表“东亚文科教育创新组织”，旨在通过与东京大学在东亚的合作高校进行讲座交流从而分享知识。为此，我们邀请东亚大学的教师到校给我们本科一、二年级的学生授课，我们主要依靠与南京大学的合作推动EALAI的各项活动。

我们与东亚国家多边合作的另外一个例子是始于2001的ASNET项目。ASNET是一个针对亚洲的教育与研究的网络，旨在使研究人员在关于日本及亚洲的教育和研究方面开展合作、信息共享及开发新项目。这个网络用来支持研究人员的研发，培育教育与研究方面的新兴合作。东京大学正在尝试建立一个亚洲和日本的数据库，通过多个系所间开设的“日本—亚洲研究”课程深化学生对亚洲的理解。

此外，作为东亚研究型大学协会（AEARU，由东亚几所主要的研究型大学组成）及环太平洋大学协会（APRU，由亚太几所主要的研究型大学组成）的成员，东京大学还致力于推进东亚以及亚洲及太平洋的区域交流。

另外，我们正在研发网络之网络，目标在于通过将全世界现有的各种大学和研究部门的网络连接起来，加强这些大学和研究部门之间的合作，从而使其能够对解决国际问题发挥更大的作用。

以上是东京大学在东亚峰会框架内的一些主要活动，我希望将来我们能对促进东亚高校的合作发挥更大的作用。

非常感谢各位！

（马理　译）

小岛宪道英文发言稿

Cooperation and Development of Higher Education within the East Asia Summit Framework: The University of Tokyo's Case

Norimichi Kojima

Managing Director and Vice President, The University of Tokyo, Japan

It is my great honor to be given an opportunity to address you on our activities concerning the East Asia Summit Framework.

The University of Tokyo, established in 1877, is the oldest university in Japan. We have 10 faculties, 15 graduate schools and 32 research institutes and centers.

Our personnel consists of about 4,000 faculty members and about 4,000 administrative and supporting staff. We have about 14,000 undergraduate students and about the same number of graduate students. Our annual budget is approximately 2.5 billion US dollars.

The University of Tokyo has 2,872 international students, which make up about 10% of our whole student population. It has close relationships with East Asia Summit countries, from which 71% of its international students originate.

The University of Tokyo also has 120 bilateral exchange agreements with EAS countries. These account for about one third of our total number of agreements. One agreement, which just started in October 2010, concerns the double degree program in the field of public policies with the National University of Singapore.

As for our three-party framework, we have active cooperation with China and South Korea, particularly with Peking University and Seoul National University, with which we have three-party symposia periodically in various academic disciplines. The Department of Materials Engineering has had student workshops on Nanomaterials with Tsinghua University and Seoul National University since 2005.

We have had four-party symposia called BESETOHA since 1999 with Peking University, Seoul National University and Vietnam National University, Hanoi, on liberal arts education. We have just held the 12th symposium successfully in Hanoi last week. Based on the outcome of these activities, we have been producing some common teaching materials as well as books on liberal arts education in four languages.

We established an international education program, named EALAI in 2005. EALAI, which stands for East Asia Liberal Arts Initiative, aims at sharing knowledge with East Asia, through lecture exchanges with affiliated East Asian universities. To this end, we invite faculty from East Asian universities to our university to give lectures to first and second-year undergraduates, and we cooperate particularly with Nanjing University in promoting EALAI activities.

Another example of our multi-lateral projects concerning EAS countries is ASNET, which started in 2001. ASNET is the network for education and research on Asia, and its aim is to enable researchers to collaborate, share information and explore new possibilities in education and research related to Japan and Asia. This Network acts to support the studies of individual researchers and cultivate new collaborations and exchanges in research and education. We are trying to make a database on Asia and Japan, and deepen students' understanding of Asia through the cross-department "Japan-Asian Studies" educational program.

In addition, we promote regional exchanges within East Asia as well as

Asia and the Pacific as a member of AEARU, which comprises of major research universities in East Asia, and of APRU, which comprises of major research universities in the Asia-Pacific region.

These are the main activities of the University of Tokyo within EAS framework and I hope we can make further contribution in strengthening collaborations and networks among universities in EAS countries in the years to come.

Thank you very much for your attention.

小岛宪道简历

东京大学常务董事，常务副校长，博士，教授。

研究领域：

物性化学、配位化学。

工作经历：

1977—1978 年，日本放送协会（NHK）放送科学基础研究所博士后研究员。

1981—1984 年，日本神户常盘短期大学学院讲师。

1984—1992 年，日本京都大学理学院助理研究员。

1992—1994 年，日本京都大学理学院副教授。

1994—1996 年，日本东京大学文理学院教授。

1996—2005 年，日本东京大学文理研究院教授。

2005—2007 年，日本东京大学文理学院教授兼文理研究院副院长。

2007—2009 年，日本东京大学文理学院教授兼文理研究院院长。

2009 年至今，日本东京大学常务董事、常务副校长。

21 世纪韩国的大学愿景

韩国祥明大学校长　李铉清

我认为21世纪的高等教育正经历着巨大转变，正进入一个学习型组织的世纪，一个流动性学习的世纪，以及一个教育发展为产业的世纪。

传统的大学模式已经快速地转变为3S模式，所谓3S，指的是没有校园、没有书籍的图书馆以及没有教师的课堂的大学。从这个意义而言，国际合作应该成为这个地区高等教育的关键战略。我们所说的无边界的、跨国界的、跨边界的教育，应该成为每一所大学在这个区域的国际战略。不断加剧的国际竞争和不断加强的合作，即所谓的2C（竞争与合作）战略，要求我们的政府使全球范围内的高等教育体系取得更大的一致性。从大学体系的角度而言，基于校园的教育概念应当转变为全球性的学习型组织概念。同时，大学必须考虑为学生提供利于创新的不同环境，即所谓的流动性学习的世纪。根据联合国教科文组织的数据，流动性学习越来越广泛。当今世界有1万所大学，其中每十名学生中即有1人在国外留学，即全世界总计有270万学生在国外留学。因此，拓展东亚大学间的合作应该优先成为这种趋势中的主要形式。就各所大学的历史、地理位置、规模、教育使命以及新时期的适时的战略这些因素而言，区域性的、政府间的合作交流战略十分必要。

根据我过去近20年来国内国际的工作经历，我希望与各位分享以下几方面：

第一，为了成功地实施或者启动东亚高等教育合作论坛，我们必须认真地分析双边和多边的合作与交流中可能存在的障碍，比如我们这个区域大学间存在的语言方面的障碍、奖学金问题、签证问题、住宿问题、质量保障问题、不同的质量体系等等问题。例如，我们认为英语是世界通用的语言，然而在你的大学里有多少课程是用英语授课？这就是一个现实的关键问题。

第二，我们可以同时进行多项工作。首先，建章立制，众所周知这是成功的保障。其次，大学和政府都需要更加重视提高大学人员和决策者的积极性。当我们考虑什么是国际合作项目的优先内容时，以大学基础设施为例，我们必须考虑多方面的因素，管理一个国际项目，需要考虑包括资金、资源、人事、政策以及培训技能等因素。在我担任主席的各种机构，我都告诉我的同事，少说话多做事。

第三，其他联盟机制的做法值得我们借鉴，比如，欧盟在欧洲教育方面有很好的经验，他们提出了“一个欧洲，一个欧盟”教育政策。例如，伊拉斯姆斯·蒙杜斯计划、苏格拉底计划、达·芬奇计划。这些都是很好的范例。在亚洲，我们有 UMAP（亚太大学流动组织）、UCTS（UMAP 研发的大学学分转换系统）。联合国教科文组织地区大会批准了 20 多个国家的文凭和辅助文凭互认项目，以推动这些地区的大学间的合作。一些问题在经合组织、东盟及亚太经合组织反复讨论，这次会议我们也在重复这些话题。昨天我的同事提到韩国、中国和日本发起了“亚洲大学生集体行动交流计划”（Campus Asia Project），这也是一个区域合作的范例。

第四，我们需要建立信息交换机制，因此，我们在这个地区建立了 90 个信息交流中心。另外，在这个区域的大学间实现必要的信息共享。

第五，我想提两点建议。“东亚峰会高等教育合作论坛”拟在东亚地区的大学间建立双边和多边的合作，为了达到这个目标，我们需要做两件事。首先，缩小贫富差距，缩小教育发达国家和欠发达国家之间的差距。这是主要问题，换言之，教育质量保障问题和全球教育福利政策必须得到高度重视。其次，缩小教育输出国和供给国之间的教育逆差。我个人认为，在亚洲，我们必须追求教育福利，也就是说，必须实施人才资源共享的政策，而不是遭受人才流失（流入与流出）的损失。达沃斯论坛预测21世纪是亚洲的世纪，如果各位同意这个预测，亚洲的教育家包括我本人在内，都应当积极、热切、毫无保留地投身这个地区的高等教育合作，这样我们方能建立一个亚洲地区的教育理想国。

谢谢大家！

注：伊拉斯姆斯·蒙杜斯计划（ERASMUS MUNDUS program），这个计划是欧盟委员会于2003年提出来的高等教育交流项目计划。

苏格拉底计划（Socrates program），是欧盟设计的综合教育计划，其内容包揽从幼儿教育到成人教育的全部教育内容。（http：//www. chinamission. be/chn/sbgx/jy/jhxm/）

达·芬奇计划（LEONARRDO DA VINCI program），是欧盟旨在促进欧盟成员国之间的职业技术教育项目。此计划的中心目标是促进职业融合；改进职业技术教育培训质量和提供更多的培训机会；通过提供培训促进革新。

"亚洲大学生集体行动交流计划"（Campus Asia Project），由中日韩三国政府共同实施，该计划旨在增强东亚三国大学间的合作以及学生流动，其他目标包括改进大学教育质量，以及完善相关细节，如各国大学间如何相互承认学生的课程学分。

（马理　译）

李铉清英文发言 PPT

The 21st Century University Visions and Policy Issues in South Korea

Hyunchong Lee

President, Sangmyung University, South Korea

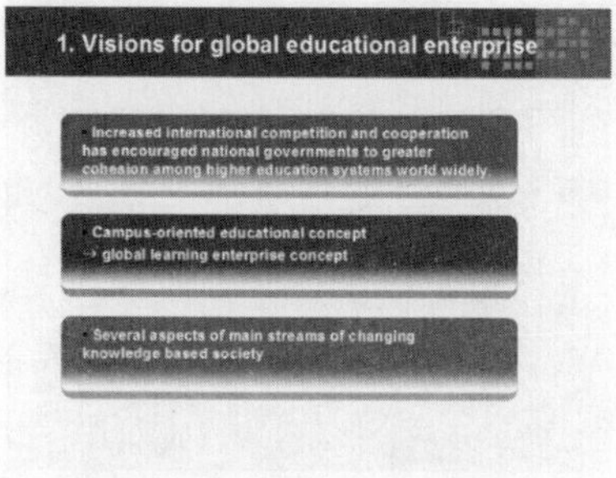

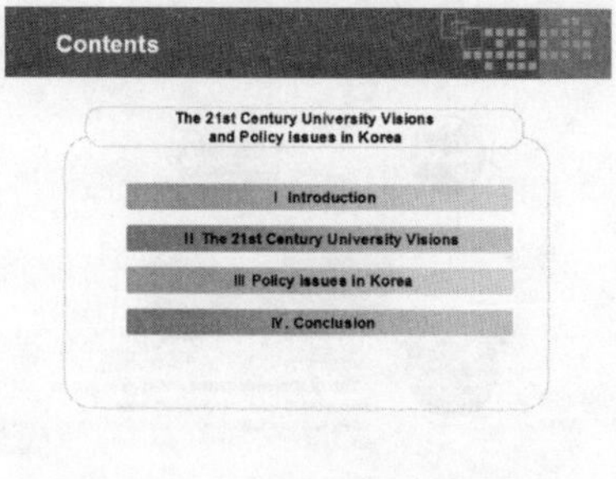

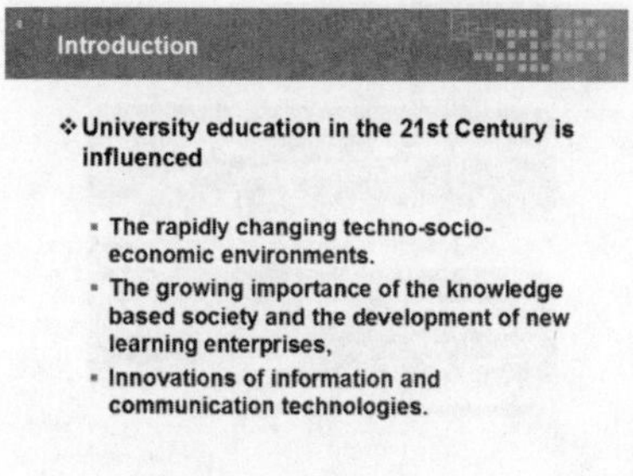

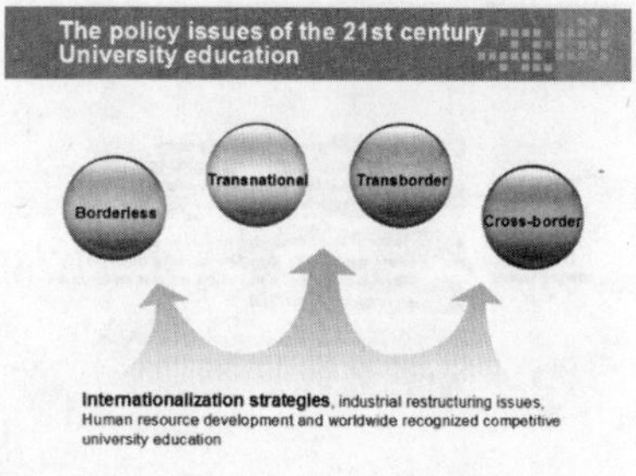

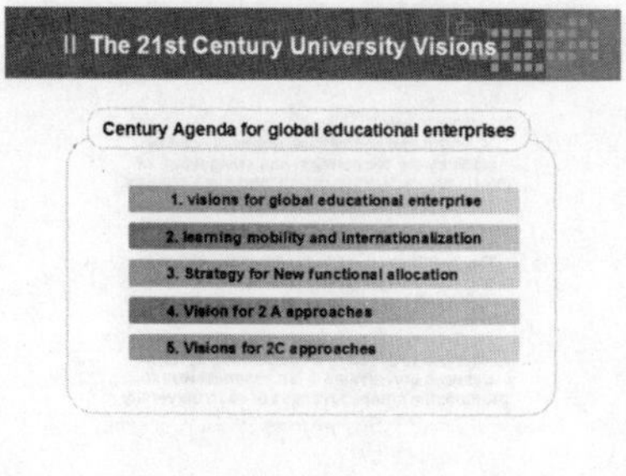

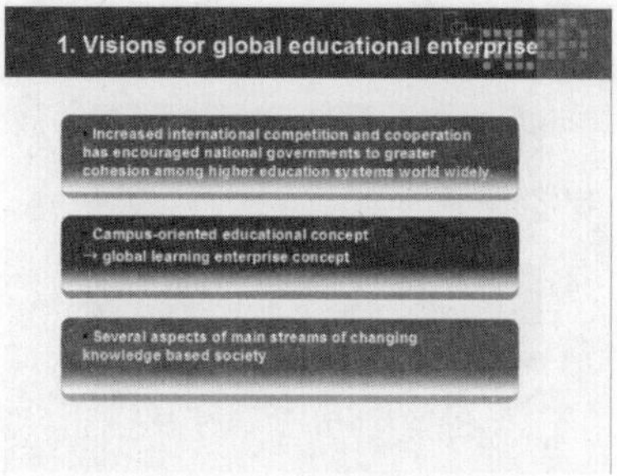

2. Learning mobility and internationalization-1

Labors mobility and brain drain of human capital mobility

The scientific and technological exploitation

Equal partnership between the developed and underdeveloped countries

2. Learning mobility and internationalization-2

The expansion of borderless education and transnational Education should be first priority positioned as a major trend.

The international link system to make knowledge distribution efficient as its problems

2. Learning mobility and internationalization-3

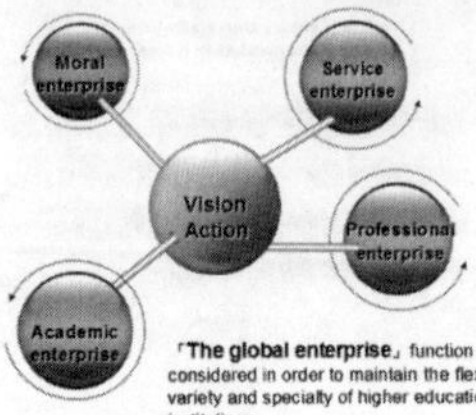

「The global enterprise」 function should be considered in order to maintain the flexibility, variety and specialty of higher education institutions

3. Strategy for New functional allocation : Issues of conformity vs diversity-1

- The appearance it presents is me-too-ism syndrome or conformity of academic institutions following certain university developmental strategies in spite of widely different types and sizes, and educational goals.
- In the national perspectives, strategy for new functional allocations among different universities is essential in terms of their history, location, size, educational missions and timely strategies for new century.
- These strategies are centered around the concept of specialization and classification of university's mission and educational functions.

3. Strategy for New functional allocation : Issues of conformity vs diversity-2

The major driving forces

- ·Expansion of university autonomy
  ·Reinforcement of lifelong higher education
  ·Conversion to the consumer oriented educational system
- ·Expansion of the international education
  ·Increase of self－directed learning function
  ·Reinforcement of just-in-time education function on required in the field
- ·Expansion of quality management system
  ·The mobility of college population

4. Vision for 2 A approaches: balance between autonomy and accountability-1

· A nation's development strategy aiming to build a knowledge- based society would obviously have to incorporate the country as a whole

· Details of this task would include designing a new paradigm on the requirements for becoming a knowledge power and on the maximum use of relevant tools to this end, as well as an integrated system allowing for the efficient communication of knowledge.

4. Vision for 2 A approaches: balance between autonomy and accountability-1

· A nation's development strategy aiming to build a knowledge- based society would obviously have to incorporate the country as a whole

· Details of this task would include designing a new paradigm on the requirements for becoming a knowledge power and on the maximum use of relevant tools to this end, as well as an integrated system allowing for the efficient communication of knowledge.

5. Visions for 2C approaches: Cooperation and competitiveness

A useful and competitive university can be made by the cooperation and competition of inter- university, inter-region, and inter- country.

The 'two C strategy' is fundamental vision to university reform.

The construction of a cooperating system between universities is an essential way to promote the competitiveness of each university

Ⅲ Policy issues in Korea

1. Quality issues of higher education
2. Demographic shifts of higher education
3. High priority issues

Ⅲ Policy issues in Korea

❖ In response to concerns of policy issues and changes of higher education environments, some institutions are reallocating their resources and re-examining their approach to providing higher education.

Ⅲ Policy issues in Korea

Two routes for learns
· academic
· retraining

Two functions
· research oriented
· learning oriented

Two modes
· full-time
· part time

Two clienteles
· elite
· man education

Two sets of destinations
· regular higher education
· work-related continuing higher learning

Two approaches
· national
· international
(Korean and foreign languages)

Two types of learning
· blended learning
· on-line or off-line learning

Major policy issues are linked to major reform activities and the socio-economic needs and the characteristics of the students.

1. Quality issues of higher education

• Bk21 (Brain Korea 21) project
→ a good example of quality maintaining policy of higher education.

The project is geared towards regaining the overall higher education system in Korea to successfully coping with the challenges generally speaking

University accreditation issues such as ranking, standard, classification and incentive are key issue related to quality of higher education

2. Demographic shifts of higher education

❖ A key issue of higher education in Korea should be selection processes for higher education institutions such as admission standard, admission criteria, and admission policies.

3. High priority issues

❖ High priorities of higher education policy in Korea are the reduction of the student/teacher ratio, government funding allocation, the admission policy and specialization.

❖ The reduction of the student/ teacher ratio

❖ Specialization policy

❖ However, there have been consequences.

❖ The government bring "reform monopoly syndrome"

Ⅳ. Conclusion-1

❖ One of these changes is the decreasing pool of student population. The decreasing pool of high school students is already beginning to have long-term demographic impacts.

❖ In particular, the 21st century university visions will be reexamined according to restructuring of overall university in term of socio-economic changes system in Korea.

❖ These policy issues are controversial in terms of comprehensive reform agenda.

Ⅳ. Conclusion-2

❖ **The following core issues for Korea's future must be considered to achieve century visions of higher education**

- quality and access in a lifelong perspective
- education 'for all' implies priority for the educationally under served
- Enhancing the international dimension of higher education and training policies.
- financing high quality education and training for all (OECD, 1992)
- setting Korea as and 「educational welfare society」 on track for sustainable development
- Renewing the structures of higher education system and production in a knowledge – intensive direction
- Implementing institutional reform aimed at strengthening public confidence both nationally and globally in institutions

Thank You !

李铉清简历

韩国祥明大学校长。

工作经历：

1975—1978 年，韩国汉阳大学教育学院系主任助理，讲师。

1979 年，韩国教育部高等教育研究会。

1982 年，美国密歇根大学药学院助理研究员。

1982—1983 年，美国南伊利诺伊大学技术学院教育学助教。

1985—1989 年，美国南卡罗莱纳大学教育学教授。

1983—1991 年，韩国釜山国立大学教育学教授。

1991—1993 年，美国加州大学伯克利分校访问学者。

1993—1998 年，韩国大学教育委员高等教育研究所执行主任。

1998—2006 年，韩国大学教育委员会秘书长。

2006—2008 年，韩国湖南大学校长。

2008 年至今，韩国祥明大学校长。

开拓高等教育交流，打造坚实合作基础

韩国高丽大学副校长 南尚九

尊敬的各位大学校长、政府官员，以及所有为本次论坛付出辛勤劳动的论坛主办方人员，能够在本次论坛上就如何加强东亚峰会框架下的高等教育合作这一主题发言，我感到非常荣幸。

发言之前，我想借此良机向大家简要介绍高丽大学。1905 年，当时的朝鲜王朝的财务大臣建立了普成大学，即为高丽大学的前身。一百多年来，韩国高丽大学为其引领国内思想的发展和民主自由运动的传统深感自豪。现在大家看到的幻灯片就向大家展示了高丽大学自成立以来历史上的重要日期，其中包括早期学校扩建到 2005 年的建校百年纪念，还有我们最近提出的“愿景宣言”，它阐述了高丽大学截至 2030 年的发展目标。

这里展示的是高丽大学的一些基本数据，包括学生和教职员工的人数。在学校国际化方面，我们也取得了引人注目的成就：目前 40% 的本科课程为英文授课，而且我们加入了两个著名的国际大学联盟，即环太平洋大学联盟（APRU）和 21 世纪大学协会（U21）。在 2010 年的 QS 世界大学排名中，高丽大学名列 191 位。

进入主题之前，我认为我们非常有必要了解未来世界高等教育发展的趋势。我在这方面的分析，有赖于马力克 · 凡 · 得温德（Marijk van der Wende）教授 2007 在《国际教育杂志》上发表的《经济合作与发展组织（OECD）国家高等教育的国际化——未来十年内的挑战和机遇》一文。该文预见了四种可能性，即开放性网联、全球化、新型公共管理和高等教育公司的出现。这些可能性意味着大学正在不断加强与国内、国外的交流与合作，欧盟启动“伊拉姆斯·蒙杜斯（Erasmus Mundus）”计划就是我们有目共睹的一个例证。

鉴于此，我坚信，高丽大学能够与各参会高校携手为加强东亚峰会框架下诸多方面的学术交流作出贡献。就学生流动而言，目前高丽大学正在开展联合培养项目，例如中国复旦大学、新加坡国立大学和高丽大学合办的“S立方”三校工商管理硕士项目。之外，我校工程学院与佐治亚理工学院，商学院与格里菲斯大学都合作开展了双学位项目。

同时，我校还划拨大量资金用于设立奖学金，资助来自各国的优秀留学生——如蒙古留学生——到高丽大学攻读学士学位。

东亚各国高等教育体系及其国际合作项目依旧具有广阔的前景。因此，东亚峰会框架下的合作是一项长期的、远大的工程，要求大学、政府和社区利益相关方之间结成创新性的合作关系。

我诚挚地希望本次会议能够为东亚高校之间的成功合作奠定更加坚实的基础。

谢谢大家。

（刘静　译）

南尚九英文发言稿

Promote Higher Education Exchanges and Lay Solid Foundations for Cooperation

Sang-Koo Nam

Provost and Executive Vice President, Korea University

Dear University Presidents, government officials, and all the staff members who have devoted their time and effort to host this event, I feel very much honored to be here and to be able to deliver a speech on the theme of how to strengthen the educational cooperation and exchanges under the 10 + 6 framework.

Before I make comments and suggestions on the theme, I would like to give a brief introduction of Korea University to you. Having been founded as Bosung College by the treasurer of the Royal Household under the Chosun Dynasty in 1905, Korea University is proud of its century-long tradition of leading the nation in intellectual thought, and the movements for democracy and freedom. This slide indicates important dates in the history of the university from its foundation, early expansion up to our Centennial celebrations in 2005 and our recent "Declaration of Vision" proposing goals for the future development of Korea University up to 2030.

This slide shows general statistics about Korea University including number of students, faculty, and staff members. In terms of internationalization, it is noticeable that we currently deliver over 40 percent of all its undergraduate courses in English, and also belong to two prestigious international associations of universities—APRU (Association of Pacific Rim Universities) and U21

(Universitas 21). For 2010 QS World University Rankings, we are ranked at 191.

Before we move on to the main subject, I believe it is essential for us to comprehend the future trends in global higher education. For this analysis I am relying on the work of Professor Marijk van der Wende in an article entitled "Internationalization of Higher Education in the OECD Countries, Challenges and Opportunities for the Coming Decade", published in 2007, in the *Journal of International Education*. In the article, four possible scenarios such as open networking, globalization, new public management, emergence of higher education Inc., are being described. What these scenarios imply is that universities are intensifying exchanges and cooperation locally and globally, as we witnessed it from European Union launching "the Erasmus Mundus Program".

In this regard, to strengthen the educational cooperation and exchanges under the East Asia Summit Framework, I strongly believe Korea University is able to contribute to academic exchanges on various aspects among participating universities. In terms of student mobility, Korea University currently offer a number of joint educational programs such as our "S-cubed" trio MBA program with Fudan, NUS and KU. We also have dual degrees established with the Georgia Institute of Technology and our College of Engineering as well as between Griffith University and the Korea University Business School.

Also regarding scholarship program, we also have allocated significant financial resources to providing talented and deserving international students from countries like Mongolia for example, with the finances they need to become an international degree seeking undergraduate student at Korea University.

The future horizons of the higher education systems in the East Asian countries and their international cooperation programs are still wide open. The mapping of such a program under the East Asia Summit Framework is thus a long-term and very ambitious project that will involve forging innovative partnerships among universities, government and community stakeholders.

I truly hope that this event will bring a more solid base for East Asian universities to build upon a successful collaborative relationship.

Thank you.

南尚九简历

韩国高丽大学教务长，执行副校长，博士，教授。

研究领域：

金融学。

教育背景：

1970 年，韩国首尔国际大学工程院理学学士。

1972 年，韩国首尔国际大学工商管理研究生院 MBA。

1975 年，美国宾夕法尼亚大学金融学 MBA。

1981 年，美国宾夕法尼亚大学金融学博士。

工作经历：

1979—1983 年，美国休斯敦大学金融学助教。

1983 年至今，韩国高丽大学金融学教授。

1994—1996 年，韩国高丽大学工商管理学院副院长。

1996—1998 年，韩国高丽大学科研和国际事务部主任。

2001—2003 年，韩国高丽大学工商管理学院院长。

2010 年起，韩国高丽大学教务长、执行副校长。

加强东亚峰会框架下高等教育的合作与交流，注重高学历人才的培养

新西兰坎特伯雷大学副校长　斯蒂夫·维伍尔

首先我要感谢中国教育部张秀琴司长邀请坎特伯雷大学作为新西兰高校的代表参加此次论坛。对此我深感荣幸。

坎特伯雷大学位于新西兰基督城。相信在场的许多来宾都知道，9月4日新西兰遭受了7.1级大地震，震中仅距我校40公里。我本人是一名地质学家，我非常高兴地告诉各位，坎特伯雷大学在震后两周内即恢复了正常的运行，而且地震并未造成我校任何人员伤亡，校内设计精良的现代建筑无重大损毁。正是这样一场地震，让我们更加确信我们拥有一个非常安全的工作环境。我们愿意将本次经验与东亚的“邻居们”一起分享，这样在应对下一次地震或者自然灾害时就有值得借鉴的经验。

新西兰充分意识到与东亚“邻居们”的经济合作与伙伴关系的重要性。新西兰是与中国签署《自由贸易协定》的首个经合组织（OECD）成员国。

新西兰的高校在与东亚国家在研究和教学合作上扮演着重要的角色，并且已经与中国的高校建立了领域广泛的交流与合作，其中就包括与中国高校签署了超过120多份合作协议。

在参加本次论坛后，我还将与坎特伯雷大学访问代表团——其中包括我校两位副校长——一起访问北京、西安 、武汉、上海的十余所院校，以加强双方之间的合作并与有志于继续攻读博士学位的学生进行座谈。

新西兰希望与所有东亚国家加强和扩大联系。目前，约有10000名

来自东亚国家的学生在新西兰高校就读。

新西兰的8所高校共有博士生7000多名，其中35%为国际学生，除此之外，新西兰还可接纳3000名博士生，其中多数学生将来自东亚峰会成员国。我所在的坎特伯雷大学，拟在未来的几年将本校的博士生人数在现有的基础上，再增加500人左右，同时我们刚启动了一项5亿美元基建项目，以改善学校设施。

博士生教育非常重要，因为这往往涉及国家间的联合培养、教师互换与合作研究。我本人就指导过来自中国、印度尼西亚和菲律宾的博士生，而且每指导一名学生都形成了牢固、持续的合作科研关系。

坎特伯雷大学意识到与东亚高校合作的重要性，东亚峰会框架下16个国家构成的网络则为此提供了一个有效的平台。

作为合作的实例，在2009年，坎特伯雷大学与武汉华中科技大学合作建设了孔子学院。该孔子学院的院长是我的同事林勇博士，他也参加了本次论坛。

在新西兰，我们致力于与东亚国家开展更加密切的高等教育与研究合作，以此来建立相互的经济优势，促进对彼此文化的认识和了解。

谢谢大家。

（刘静　译）

斯蒂夫·维伍尔英文发言稿

Promote Higher Education Cooperation within the East Asia Summit Framework and Prioritize Training for Highly Qualified University Students

Steve Weaver

Assistant Vice-Chancellor, University of Canterbury, New Zealand

I wish to thank Ms. Zhang Xiuqin, Director-General of the Chinese Ministry of Education, for inviting the University of Canterbury as the leading representative of New Zealand's universities at this Forum. It is an honour to attend.

The University of Canterbury is in the City of Christchurch, and many of you will know that on September the 4th we were rocked by a Magnitude 7.1 earthquake centred only 40 km away. Being a geologist myself, I am pleased to report that the university resumed full operations within 2 weeks of the earthquake. There were no injuries to staff or students and there was no significant damage to our modern, well-engineered buildings. The earthquake confirmed that we have a very safe working environment. We share this experience with many of our neighbours in East Asia who will be familiar with earthquakes and other natural hazards.

New Zealand recognises the economic importance of collaboration and partnership with its neighbours in East Asia. This is reflected by New Zealand being the first OECD country to sign a Free Trade Agreement with China.

Our universities have a key role to play through research and teaching connections with East Asia countries. NZ universities already have a wide range of exchanges and collaborations in place including more than 120 agreements with Chinese universities.

After I attend this forum, I will join a team of colleagues from the University of Canterbury, including two Vice-Presidents, that will visit more than 10 universities and institutes in Beijing, Xian, Wuhan and Shanghai to strengthen our collaborations with them and to talk to prospective PhD students.

New Zealand wishes to strengthen and extend its relationships with all East Asia countries. At present, 10,000 students from EAS countries are studying in NZ universities.

New Zealand's 8 universities have at present about 7,000 PhD students-about 35% of these are international students. New Zealand has a capacity to take an additional 3,000 PhD students-most of these will be international students from East Asia Summit countries. My own institution, the University of Canterbury, has a policy to increase the number of PhD students by 500 over the next few years and we have just started a $500M building programme to improve university facilities.

PhD students are particularly important because they often involve joint supervision and lead to staff exchange and collaborative research between countries. I have supervised PhD students from China, Indonesia and the Philippines and in each case strong and continuing research ties resulted.

The University of Canterbury recognises the importance of cooperation with its counterparts in East Asia and the network of the 16 countries of the East Asia Summit provides a very effective platform.

As an example of our commitment, in 2009 we opened at the University of Canterbury, a Confucius Institute, in partnership with Huazhong University of Science & Technology, Wuhan. (Slide 5 Confucius Institute opening). My colleague, Dr Adam Lam, the Director of the Confucius Institute, is here at this Forum.

In New Zealand we are committed to closer cooperation in Higher Education and Research with the countries of East Asia for mutual economic advantage and increased cultural awareness and understanding.

Thank you!

斯蒂夫·维伍尔简历

新西兰坎特伯雷大学副校长，分管研究，并当选为该校理事会成员，博士，教授。曾任地质科学系主任及研究生院院长。获英国伦敦大学哲学博士学位以及伯明翰大学理学博士学位。现任新西兰皇家学会研究员、新西兰化学研究所研究员以及英国伦敦地质学会会员，并出版了大量专著。主要研究新西兰、南极洲和东非地质。

开设暑期东亚研究英语课程，大力支持学生交流

泰国朱拉隆功大学副校长　M.R. 卡拉雅·汀萨巴

“东亚峰会高等教育合作论坛”是一项盛举。我认为学生的互换交流是东亚峰会框架下高等教育合作的一个关键要素。东亚的竞争力很大程度上取决于成员国相互之间的密切合作。这种合作在各个方面都得到了加强，高等教育就是其中之一。而学生互换交流为这方面取得的成功起到了很大的作用。究其原因，高校学生是我们社会未来的领导者，如果我们推进学生交流，开阔视野，我们未来的领导者才能成为国际化人才。如果可以为东亚高校学生提供这样的机会，他们会获益匪浅，并为实现东亚梦想作出贡献。容我再次强调，学生互换交流至关重要。

当前存在的问题和解决的方法：到目前为止，东亚地区的学生交流互动大多是单向的，并且愿意接收的学校为数不多。我们需要为学生寻求一个交换流动的平台。那么要如何才能做到呢？我们如何构建这种更为和谐的互换交流平台？我认为，可以在每个国家每年至少有一所大学开展为期 1 ~ 2 个月的关于东亚研究的项目。

这些项目应当用英语进行教学，这样才能吸引整个东亚地区的各国学生参与。各国大学之间应当定期组织会议。各成员国政府应当对其参与这些项目的学生给予经济支持。当然，面向各国学生的招收名额控制在每个国家 2 名以内，这样才能扩大招生的覆盖面，使我们的互换交流真正成为跨东亚的交流。

我认为课程开设的内容应该包括历史、经济、商务、行政管理、国

际关系，并涉及东亚的文化。普遍必修的核心课程应当包括关于东亚的介绍，东亚的人文，等等。至于选修课程，可以是关于东亚区域一些独特的问题。我们为此作好了充分的准备。2017 年朱拉隆功大学将迎来她的百年校庆，朱拉隆功大学所有外国项目课程都采用英语授课。总计 540 门课程，其中 85 门是国际课程。学校有东南亚研究硕士学位授予权，泰语研究硕士学位及博士学位授予权，韩语研究硕士学位授予权，国际发展研究硕士学位授予权。其中很多都是与泰国其他高校联合开设的。

在东亚峰会框架下，高等教育的合作与发展有赖于学生互换交流这一关键环节。我们应当促进这一地区各国高校间的密切合作，进一步提高学生交流工作的质量。各院校需要来自公共和私营部门的有力的经济支持，这样才能促成这个专门为学生交流而设的项目的开展。

谢谢!

（付蕾　译）

M. R. 卡拉雅·汀萨巴英文发言 PPT

Provide English-based Short Summer Courses on East Asia studies to Support Student Mobility

M. R. Kalaya Tingsabadh

Vice President, Chulalongkorn University Thailand

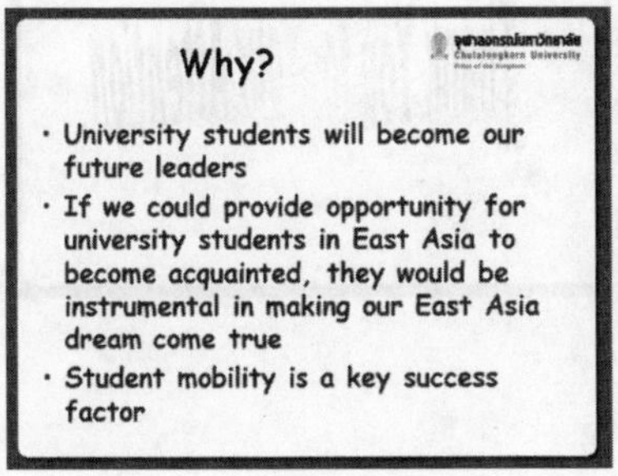

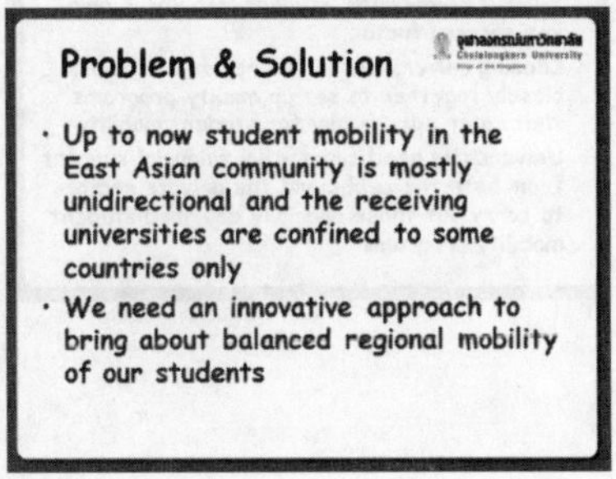

How?

- Establishment of regional 1-2 month programs on East Asian Studies in at least one university per country within the East Asia region
- Such programs should use English as the medium of instruction to allow full participation from students of all countries in this network
- The programs should be organized regularly and can rotate among universities in each country

How? (contd.)

- The government of every member country should be encouraged to provide financial support to their own university students to participate in such programs in as many countries as possible
- Each program at each university should enroll not more than two students per country to make it truly East Asian

Program content

- History, economy, business, politics and government, international relations, arts and culture, for examples.
- Common core courses in every program e.g. Introduction to East Asia, East Asian People and Culture, etc.
- Electives dealing with relevant issues on each particular sub-region of East Asia

Full Participation of Chulalongkorn University

- Chulalongkorn University is fully prepared to participate in this project
- At C.U. we already have the following programs all taught in English: M.A. in Southeast Asian Studies, and M.A. and Ph.D. in Thai Studies (as well as M.A. in Korean Studies and M.A. in International Development Studies)

Conclusion

- To bring about cooperation and development of Higher Education under the East Asian Summit Framework, student mobility is one key success factor
- Leading universities in the region must work closely together to set up quality programs that cater specifically for student mobility
- Universities need substantial financial support from both the public and the private sectors to carry out those specially designed student mobility programs

Thank You for Your Attention

M. R. 卡拉雅·汀萨巴简历

泰国朱拉隆功大学副校长，博士。

教育背景：

1971 年，英国约克大学语言/教育学学士。

1972 年，英国伦敦大学学院现代英语硕士。

1980 年，英国伦敦大学学院语音学与语言学博士。

工作经历：

1971 年，泰国清迈大学人文学院英语系讲师。

1975 年，泰国清迈大学校务部英语中心学院行政人员。

1980 年，泰国朱拉隆功大学文学院语言学系讲师。

1984 年，泰国朱拉隆功大学文学院语言学系助教。

1996—2004 年，泰国朱拉隆功大学文学院院长。

2000 年至今，泰国朱拉隆功大学董事会成员。

2004—2008 年，泰国朱拉隆功大学研究生院院长。

2008 年至今，泰国朱拉隆功大学副校长。

第四部分　专题论文

Section IV: Papers

开启区域合作大门，拓展学校发展空间

——论云南大学国际化发展的区域性定位与区域化战略

云南大学　于欣力　郑　蔚

一、引　言

在不同的历史发展阶段，每个大学都会根据自身的建设和发展需要，如学科建设、人才培养、科研、服务地方、国际合作等，而对学校的总体发展目标作出适当的调整。从国际一流大学到一般高校，都是如此，所不同的是，一些高校能够遵循高等教育“大众化、综合化、多样化、国际化”的发展趋势，本着“实事求是，用力可得”的原则制定出科学、合理的发展目标和战略。

近十年来，云南大学的发展定位和目标进行了一些战略性的调整。21世纪初，我校的发展定位是“立足边疆、服务云南、提升水平、办出特色”。2008年，我校建设发展的总目标是：“经过五年的努力，主要发展指标进入全国高校50强，再经过五年的努力，综合实力进入全国高校50强，把云大办成西部一流、国内先进、国际知名的高水平研究教学型综合大学。”2010年初，学校又重新确立了近期的发展目标：“建设区域性高水平研究型综合大学，挺进全国高校50强。”

从以上办学理念和发展目标的内容可以看出，国际化发展的维度正日益成为我校总体发展战略的一个重要组成部分，这主要体现在两个方面。其一，学校的国际化视野不断拓展，不断融入其办学的定位和目标当中。“立足边疆”是依据我校所处的地理位置而确立的办学定位，与此相应，学校发展的目标是服务本地的政治、经济和文化建设，即“服务云南”。然而，全球化趋势下的高校国际化发展是大势所趋，因此学校的国际化发展不断提上日程。为了提升自身的国际化水平和层次，学校的办学目标从本地走向全国，从国内走向国际，即不仅要成为国内先进高校也要在国际高等教育领域争取一席之地。随着学校国际化发展的不断深入，我们逐步认识到自身的优势所在，一方面要力争跻身全国高水平大学之列，另一方面要在一定地理区域之内发挥重要的作用。与“国际知名”的目标相比较而言，“区域性高水平研究型综合大学”的概念是我校国际化发展战略的具体表述，即要在云南作为东南亚“桥头堡”的背景下，以我校面对周边国家高校的相对优势为基础，充分利用我们的地缘优势，使我校发展成为东南亚地区高等教育领域内的领军高校之一。

本文拟对云南大学的“区域性”加以探讨，重新定位其内涵和外延，以便开启区域合作大门，拓展学校发展空间，并以此为基础，明确我校在未来一段时间内需要重点开展的几项工作。

二、云南大学发展目标中的“区域性”范畴定位

一般而言，对云南大学的“区域性”的理解指的是其地处中国西南部的现实。这一点反映在我校早先提出的发展目标之中，即“西部一流、国内先进、国际知名”。而就更广泛的意义上来说，特别是在新一轮西部大开发战略和“桥头堡”建设的背景下的“区域性”的范畴和定位。

作为一所地处边疆的大学，云南大学在制定发展目标的时候，必须分析其区域性定位，而对区域性定位的分析又离不开对云南的地理、区域文化、经济政治等各方面的分析。众所周知，云南与越南、缅甸、老挝三国接壤，陆地边界线很长；云南又处于中华文化圈与东南亚文化圈、南亚文化圈最前沿的地方，与西亚和非洲文化圈邻近，有相似的文化底蕴，云南自古就与东南亚、南亚、西亚、东非的国家有着较为密切的经

济、文化联系。

回顾历史，我们不难发现，由于各自利益不同，中国及周边国家所关注的问题也不尽相同。例如，大湄公河沿岸各国对水资源环境的诉求，下游国家倾向于对上游国家提出相应的环保要求，这与某些欧洲国家的情况类似。进一步看，由于政治主张的差别，领土争议、边界摩擦及其导致的军事冲突，大湄公河次区域各国之间并非始终保持着睦邻友好的双边和多边关系。在全球化的背景之下，各国的政治、经济、社会发展均有赖于其国际关系的发展，尤其有赖于与周边国家的互利共赢关系的建立。然而，在这种复杂的形势下，高等教育合作却是各国均不会反对，而且容易推动的一项合作项目，这是各国不断发展高等教育合作的重要基础。

教育合作是增进理解、提升认同、合作共赢的重要基础，是区域人力资源开发计划的重要内容，是各国真正具有优势互补、合作条件比较成熟、发展空间巨大的合作领域之一。加快高等教育合作是中国与相关各国共同推进东亚合作的重要方面。中国作为区域内的一个大国，是推动地区合作发展的中坚力量，推动合作符合中国的经济、政治利益，有利于地区稳定和发展。

云南大学的“区域性”定位以我校所具备的地缘优势为基础，即学校的发展必须立足于一定的现实条件，以便在我们所处的地理范围之内发挥我校作为一所区域性的高等学府所应当发挥的作用。但是，我校的区域化发展战略却不能局限于我们所处的地理区域。就我校的国际化发展战略而言，“区域化”应当包含两个层次：其一，在本校所处地理区域内实施广泛而富有实际成效的国际交流与合作，充分利用区域性的地缘优势提升自身水平，带动周边地区的高等教育发展，乃至为整个地区的社会经济发展和区域和平作出贡献。其二，在大力实施国际化发展战略的过程中，广泛开展多层次、全方位的国际学术交流与合作，按地理范畴和地域文化的区域性，与我校的战略合作伙伴开展不同层次的合作。因此，我校区域性战略发展的目标应当以中国的西南部地区和东南亚十国为核心，以南亚次大陆的印度和孟加拉为重要支撑，辐射西亚和东部非洲等地区。

三、关于“区域性”教育交流带来的机遇和国际化战略的再思考

（一）相对于国内高水平大学的比较优势

当前云南大学与国内高水平大学相比的现实情况是，云南大学受地域、历史、体制及资源条件等方面的制约，以及学校自身存在的诸多问题，我校的综合实力与国内高水平大学相比还有很大差距。

但是，如果综合考虑和充分运用国内和国际两个平台的特点，发挥我校的特色和优势，我们也并非完全没有机会。

当我们充分发挥毗邻南亚、东南亚、西亚和东非的优势，以全球化的视野去思索、谋划，输出我们优势的教育资源（如孔子学院等），进而就可以在国际教育市场上占有一席之地，进而让世界更多的人了解我校的优秀学科。充分利用我校拥有一些独特的优势，如地理优势：云南地形地貌复杂、气候多样、物产丰富，素有“植物王国”、“动物王国”、“有色金属王国”之美誉，使我校学科发展占据得天独厚的优势条件，我校的生物多样性研究在全国名列前茅。地缘优势：云南省与东南亚、南亚各国地域上山水相连，文化宗教传承相通，便利的交通和人文环境使我们与南亚和东南亚各国进行合作与交流具有其他地区无法比拟的区位优势。人文优势：云南有25个少数民族在这里世代栖居、繁衍，形成了具有丰富、独特的少数民族文化，借助云南省制定的“民族文化大省”战略与我校的民族学研究在全国首屈一指的地位相结合。以上三个方面的优势不仅是我校实施区域化发展战略的重要支撑，同时也是我们与国内高水平大学的相对优势。

（二）相对于周边国家高校的比较优势

同周边国家的高校相比，我们也具备了一定的比较优势。

第一，就自身而言，作为云南省最早建立的高校之一，云南大学经过了近90年的发展。历史上，我们曾经有过位列全国高校前15位的辉

煌（1946 年《大英简明百科全书》）。改革开放后，特别是 20 世纪 90 年代以来，云南大学获得了长足的发展。1996 年列入国家首批“211 工程”重点建设大学，2001 年成为西部大开发重点建设院校，2004 年成为教育部和云南省政府重点共建高校。近几年来，云南大学紧紧抓住“211 工程”建设和省部共建的机遇，通过深化改革，加快发展，学校的综合实力和整体水平上了新的台阶。云南大学已成为一所以民族学、生态学为特色，文、史、哲、经、管、工、理、法、教育、医、农等学科内容较为齐全，人才密集的全国重点综合性大学。随着我国高等教育改革的纵深发展，我国高校获得了前所未有的发展机遇。我校自 20 世纪 90 年代以来获得了长足的发展，成为西南地区乃至大湄公河次区域的一所重要的高等学府。在“东亚峰会高等教育论坛”期间，我校通过与东盟十国和日本、韩国、印度等高校代表的交流，我们发现周边国家高校具有与我校拓展纵深合作和交流关系的强烈愿望。例如，老挝苏冯那翁大学校长坎姆菲·斯萨旺教授在发言中提道：“琅勃拉邦是世界文化遗产城市，我们希望和亚洲国家的高等教育机构开展旅游管理、国际贸易和世界遗产保护方面的学术交流。”斯萨旺教授在与我校的单独会晤中表示，云南大学在旅游管理方面的教学、科研成果在整个东南亚地区都备受瞩目，希望与我校开展这方面的合作。此外，从近年来我校招收来华留学生的情况看，周边国家学生都希望到我校留学深造，尤其是越南、缅甸、老挝、柬埔寨、泰国和韩国的学生。

第二，中国经济近年来的迅猛发展，以及在教育部的指导下与国内高水平高校的全方位合作也是我们同周边国家高校的比较优势。

（1）中国大环境良好。

（2）教育部的指导。

（3）复旦大学对我校的对口支援。

（4）与国内各层次高校分享国际合作与交流的经验。

第三，国际关系研究，尤其是针对东南亚、南亚、西亚和非洲的研究使我们知己知彼。近日，中缅油气管道在昆明正式开工，这是我校东南亚研究的学者近年来研究成果上升为国家战略的一个显著例证。就云南大学自身而言，民族学、高原山地生态学是我们传统的优势学科，近年来上述学科对外交流非常活跃。特别是我校成为教育部教育援外基地后，针对东南亚和非洲积极开展了生态保护的援外培训项目，为上述国家培训了一批专家和高级官员。

四、“区域性”合作框架下的重点工作

以我校的区域化定位为基础，从我校的区域化战略为导向，这就需要我们在未来 3 ~ 5 年内实现纵深发展方向和做好重点工作。我们认为学生的交流与互动，深入推进以孔子学院为龙头的海外教育和在周边国家的联合办学，以及努力争取将“东亚峰会框架下的高等教育合作与发展”发展成为一个长效机制是一段时间内区域合作的重中之重。

(一) 学生交流

来华留学生教育管理历来是学校国际教育交流工作中的一项重点。我校来华留学生工作发展大致经历了三个阶段。从 20 世纪 80 年代中期年至 20 世纪末，我校留学生工作在省内处于领军地位，由国际学术教育交流中心负责留学生教育管理，长年招收各类长短期语言生到校学习，年招生量为 350 ~ 500 人，时国际交流处负责接待外国访问学者，年接待量 20 人左右。同时承担教育部、教育厅委派的留学生夏令营接待工作，以良好的教学质量和优质的服务赢得各界好评。

2000 年至 2006 年，由于各种原因，我校留学生工作相对滞后，甚至落后于省内部分高校，招生量基本维持在 20 世纪末期水平，学生类别单一，大部分为语言进修生，只有少量学位学历生就读。虽然 2005 年 12 月在原国际学术教育交流中心的基础上成立了留学生院，但由于之前多年的工作滞后，积重难返，并未使我校留学生教育管理的局面获得较大改观。

自 2007 年 1 月我校被列为接受中国政府奖学金留学生的院校后，我校留学生工作出现了突飞猛进的势头，一方面招生人数逐年增加，另一

方面生源结构得到极大优化。截至2009年10月，已累计招收各类奖学金留学生440余名，多数为本科生和研究生层次；学校招收留学生人数由2006年的不足800人次上升到2009年的1700多人次（其中，学历生224人次，含本科生、硕士生、博士生三个层次，约占总数的14%）。我校与泰国宋卡王子大学“2+2”合作办学进入实质合作阶段，2005年在泰国宋卡王子大学入学的本科生于2007年开始陆续到我校进行第三、四学年的学习，首期项目学生已经于2009年毕业，第二批项目学生也于今年7月顺利毕业。这个项目填补了我校留学生教育管理史上的一项空白。2009年，随着国家汉办孔子学院奖学金的设立，300余名学生向我校提出申请，由于名额有限，最终录取四周至一年期的语言进修生和各专业本科生、硕士生、博士生150人。同时，省教育厅设立的云南省政府奖学金的授予力度也逐年加强，极大地鼓励了周边国家留学生到我校学习的热情。2009年，我校留学生教育各项工作开展卓有成效，因此被教育部授予“来华留学生教育先进集体”称号（全国仅58所院校获此殊荣）。

在未来一个时期内，我校来华留学生教育管理的重点，是继续扩大招生规模，不断优化学生结构，逐步规范管理体制，使我校留学生工作尽快步入正常轨道，实现又好又快的发展。

（二）孔子学院建设

我校自2005年开始筹备第一所孔子学院以来，目前共在伊朗、孟加拉、缅甸开设了三所孔子学院（课堂）。这三所孔子学院分别位于西亚、南亚和东南亚，是我们区域合作的重点区域，也是我们今后对外联合办学的重点，我们走出去办学的支点。经过5年的发展，已经取得了令人欣慰的成果，我们也在不断努力，争取用几年的时间将我校孔子学院的总数增加到五所。

1. 伊朗德黑兰大学孔子学院

我校与伊朗德黑兰大学共建孔子学院的工作于2008年启动，2009年1月，我校何天淳校长率团出访伊朗，出席伊朗德黑兰大学孔子学院揭牌仪式。此前，双方就孔子学院的开办做了大量准备工作，尤其是得到了国家汉办和中国驻伊朗大使馆的大力支持与协助。揭牌仪式当天，中国驻伊朗大使馆解晓岩大使、伊朗驻中国大使馆曼苏尔大使亲临现场并作重要发言。新华社、中国国际广播电台、《文汇报》、香港凤凰卫视等媒体驻德黑兰的记者，伊朗国家电视台、《德黑兰时报》、《消息报》和《市民报》等主流媒体记者应邀出席了孔子学院的揭牌仪式，并及时进行了全方位的现场报道。翌日，国内众多官方和民间网站及时转载了该孔子学院挂牌成立的报道。

伊朗德黑兰大学孔子学院正式挂牌，不仅标志着该学院教学、管理和文化活动的全面启动，同时也为我校与德黑兰大学的学术教育交流搭建了良好的平台。借孔子学院理事会召开之际，我校何天淳校长与德黑兰大学拉赫巴尔校长就两校友好交流进行磋商，并签订了学术交流备忘录，为两校学术合作与交流的可持续发展奠定了良好的基础。

该孔子学院正式运作以来，我校共有一名中方院长和两名青年教师在学院任教。首任中方院长姚继德教授卸任回国之际，德黑兰大学副校长穆萨维教授致函我校何天淳校长，对姚教授为该孔子学院和两校交流所作的贡献表示感谢。第二任中方院长仇学琴教授到任之后，一方面全力开展教学工作；另一方面积极筹办各项文化活动，例如成立了“李白诗会”，举办中秋晚会，并首开“武术汉语”之先河，将汉语教学与中华武术融为一体，使孔子学院的教学活动更加丰富多彩。

2. 孟加拉南北大学孔子学院

我校与孟加拉南北大学共建的孟加拉南北大学孔子学院成立于2006年2月。2009年，该校搬迁至新校区，虽然给孔子学院的教学活动带来一定影响，但是在合作双方的共同努力下，使校区搬迁工作对教学工作的影响降至最低。同时，校区环境的改善也为孔子学院的发展带来新的契机。在中方院长蒋印莲教授的努力下，南北大学为孔子学院划拨了60平方米的办公用地，使学院办公环境得到极大改善。

2009年9月，我校派资深对外汉语教师周铭东副教授接任孟加拉南北大学孔子学院中方院长。目前学院有院长一人，教师一人，志愿者两人，招生人数仍维持在200人以上，共开设5个教学班。该孔子学院一向注重汉语教学以外的各类文化活动。

3. 缅甸曼德勒福庆语言电脑学校孔子课堂

缅甸曼德勒福庆语言电脑学校（简称“福庆学校”）是当地侨领集资筹办的一所华文学校。我校于2008年年底开始与该校筹建孔子课堂，缅方对此表示出极大的诚意，该校董事会积极捐资为孔子课堂建盖了四层教学楼。今年5月，我校肖宪副校长率团出访缅甸，出席缅甸曼德勒福庆语言电脑学校孔子课堂挂牌仪式。仪式上，中国驻曼德勒总领馆唐英总领事和福庆学校董事长高景山先生分别发表了热情洋溢的讲话，缅甸唯一的华文报纸《金凤凰》（双周刊）对此次活动作了长篇报道。

自正式运作以来，该孔子课堂开展了大量教学工作，目前招收正规班17个，学员287人；速成班11个，学员123人；会话班4个，学员58人；中级班7个，学员112人，学生总人数达到580人。孔子课堂招生人数多，教学任务重，但是由于我校此前为福庆学校培养了一些本土教师，因此不但有效地缓解了师资不足的矛盾，而且摸索出一条师资本土化培养的路子。除此之外，该孔子课堂还开展了大量文化活动，并及时编写活动简报上报学校和汉办，迄今共编写简报12期。由于该孔子课堂业绩显著，其中方院长史芳副教授已被评为2009年度“孔子学院先进个人”。

在未来一段时期内，我校孔子学院发展的目标是，继续稳定现有规模，在国家汉办和学校人事等相关部门的支持下，扩大教师外派力度；进一步提升办学水平，争取在3年内以开办下属于现有孔子学院的“孔子课堂”的形式逐步扩大各孔子学院（课堂）规模；在国家汉办的领导下，在各合作单位的协助下，编写1~2部当地化的汉语教材；充分利用孔子学院奖学金的支持，进一步加强汉语教师本土化的发展进程，在未来5年内实现至少每一所孔子学院（课堂）具有一名本土教师的目标；以孔子学院建设为寄托，进一步拓展与孔子学院（课堂）周边高校的合作关系，以汉语国际推广为龙头，协助条件成熟和合作意愿较强的1~2所高校建立中国文化中心或中国汉语中心，帮助1~2所学校筹建中文系。

（三）争取把“东亚峰会框架下的高等教育合作与发展”发展成为一个长效机制

在2010年10月13~15日举办的“东亚峰会高等教育论坛”上，东盟十国与南亚的印度，东北亚的日本、韩国和大洋洲的澳大利亚、新西兰的教育官员和大学校长就“东亚峰会框架下的高等教育合作与发展”这一主题展开了热烈而富有成效的讨论。与会代表就“东亚峰会框架下的高等教育合作”展开了热烈的讨论。我校何天淳校长在发言中倡议将“东亚峰会高等教育论坛”确立为一个长效机制，为东盟+N框架内的各国高校提供长期交流与合作的平台。何校长的倡议得到了与会代表的热烈响应，很多代表认为这是一个积极而富有建设性的建议，希望各国教育主管部门共同协作，为这一目标的实现提供制度保障。

举办此次会议使我们有了跟上述国家的一流高校进一步合作的机会，同时这也与我们提出区域性的概念基本吻合。

在这一前提和背景之下，我校将积极配合各国教育部和国内外各相关高校、驻华使领馆通力合作，共襄盛举，及早实现这一目标。同时，我校也将尽力争取担任“东亚峰会高等教育论坛”秘书处单位，为该论坛的长期举办贡献一份力量。

总之，从我校的区域性定位出发，大力实施我校的区域性发展战略是推进我校国际化发展的一条重要途径。众所周知，教育国际交流合作是中外人文交流、公共外交的重要领域，在国家总体外交中具有重要战略作用。在“区域性”高水平研究型大学的建设过程中，如何紧紧围绕“大国是关键，周边是首要，发展中国家是基础，多边是重要舞台”的战略部署，积极开展全方位、多层次、宽领域的教育交流与合作。通过来华留学生工作的大力开展，和以孔子学院建设为龙头的汉语国际的推广，尽力把“东亚峰会高等教育论坛”发展成一个区域性各国高校对话的高端平台，将是我们未来一段时期内的重要奋斗目标。

东亚高等教育合作现状与前瞻
——以中韩两国高等教育合作为例

浙江大学　徐小洲　朴钟鹤

随着东亚经济贸易往来的日益紧密，各国在高等教育合作上也不断走向更深、更广、更高。中韩两国于1992年实现了邦交正常化，并由此翻开了中韩两国教育交流合作的新的一页。当年两国教育主管部门通过派遣代表团，实现互访，迈出了教育交流合作的第一步。二十多年来，两国在高等教育领域不断谋求合作和共同发展，业已取得了丰硕的成果。本文拟就中韩两国高等教育合作的政策保障，交流合作现状，浙江大学在中韩两国高等教育合作方面所做的努力等问题进行简要阐释，并在此基础上对中韩两国高等教育合作的前景进行前瞻。

一、日渐完善的政策保障

中韩两国在高等教育领域的合作，首先得益于两国政府在政策上给予充分的保障。二十多年来，两国为确保各项教育交流合作能够稳步推进，签署了多项教育交流协议，并建构了多项磋商机制。

首部协议签署于1995年7月。两国教育部经多次协商于北京签署了《中华人民共和国教育部与大韩民国教育部教育交流与合作协议》。该协议的签订不仅标志着双方教育交流合作走向制度化，同时也为日后其他协议的制定，奠定了坚实的基础。

1998年11月，两国签署了《中韩两国政府青年交流谅解备忘录》；2001年与2004年，教育部与韩国教育部续签了《2001—2003教育交流与合作协议》与《2004—2006 教育交流与合作协议》；2008 年 5 月和 8 月，双方又分别签署了《中韩两国高等教育学历学位互认备忘录》和《2008—2010 中韩教育交流协议》等两份重要文件。《中韩两国高等教育学历学位互认备忘录》的签署为推动留学生交流的持续良性发展提供了坚实的基础。《2008—2010 中韩教育交流协议》则提出从 2009 年开始将两国政府交换奖学金生规模扩大至每年 60 人的目标。①

在上述政府间合作框架之外，从 2005 年起，两国又建立了一年一次的教育部司局级磋商机制和不定期的两国教育部长会晤机制。上述机制的确立不仅丰富了中韩两国教育交流的对话平台，还为两国教育交流与合作走向纵深提供了可能。

二、丰富多样的高等教育合作平台

在上述政策保障之基础上，两国在高等教育领域的合作上不断谋求机制创新。两国高校及政府通过创建各类论坛、互派留学生、加强教师交流、合作办学等方式将现有的合作推向更高、更深。

（一）多元化的论坛

为加强中韩两国在高层次人才培养，推动两国高校校际交流与合作，教育部于 2006 年 7 月在长春举办了首届中韩“15 + 15”大学强强合作研讨会。2007 年 10 月，在中韩两国教育部的共同主持下，首届“中韩大学校长论坛”得以成行。该论坛旨在构建两国大学之间合作与交流的平台。清华大学等 20 所中国大学和高丽大学等 23 所韩国大学参加了在首尔举行的该届论坛，并联合发表了《首尔宣言》。② 该宣言的签署，为中韩两国高校间的交流构建了更为通畅的沟通渠道。2010 年 6 月，第二届“中韩大学校长论坛”在中国吉林召开。教育部、国家留学基金管理委

① 驻韩使馆教育处．中韩教育交流简介［EB/OL］．中华人民共和国驻大韩民国大使馆教育处网站，2010 - 10 - 14，http：//www. cscse. edu. cn.

② 首届中韩大学校长论坛在首尔举行［EB/OL］．韩国留学网，2007 - 11 - 01，http：//www. hanguoliuxue. org. cn.

员会、国家汉办、孔子学院总部和韩国教育科技部以及中国22所、韩国19所高校参与了该届论坛。[①] 与会嘉宾就中韩大学在高等教育国际化中所面临的机遇和挑战等议题进行了研讨。

除上述中韩大学校长论坛之外，韩国高等教育财团及有关高校还与我国一批重点院校联合举办了各种论坛及学术研究活动。例如，2007年，浙江大学与高丽大学举办了“中韩公共治理研究生学术论坛”；2009年，人民大学与韩国高丽大学共同举办了“2009中韩公共管理博士论坛”等。该类论坛为有学术潜力的研究生搭建了交流对话的平台。这种青年学生之间的直接对话，不仅有利于开阔学生的视野，更为彼此加深了解，增进友谊创造了难得的机会。此外，“北京论坛”、“上海论坛”、“世界儒学论坛”等诸多论坛在中韩两国乃至东亚学术界也产生较大影响，形成一定的辐射效应，并为整个东亚地区的学术交流提供了一种参考模式。

（二）学者交换奖学金项目

高校教师作为教书育人和推动科研发展的中坚力量，在高等教育发展上起到了引领学术发展和开创国家未来的重要作用。中韩两国高等教育合作，亦是两国师生间的一种交融。为此，韩国高等教育财团和中国国家留学基金管理委员会，通过设立学者交换奖学金项目，为两国学者之间的交流与合作搭建了广阔的平台。

1. 中国国家留学基金管理委员会——“亚洲留学奖学金”

“亚洲留学奖学金”是教育部面向亚洲学生、学者设立的全额奖学金项目。目前，由国家留学基金委员会负责此项目的招生及日常管理工作。该项奖学金为亚洲学生、学者在亚洲各国之间的流动提供了经费支持，并在教育交流合作空间的拓展以及亚洲高等教育质量的提升上发挥了助推器的作用。

---

① 晓蔚．第二届中韩大学校长论坛在我校举行［N］．吉林大学报，2010－06－18.

韩国学者可通过申请高级进修生的方式来获取该项奖学金。所谓高级进修生须具有硕士学位以上的学历或副教授以上职称，年龄不超过50岁。中方为来华学者提供每月2000元人民币的奖学金生活费；首次来华一次性安置补助费；门诊医疗服务和留学生综合医疗保险；一次性城市间交通费等优惠政策。此外，还可享受免交注册费、学费、实验费等杂费，免费校内住宿等优厚待遇。①

2. 韩国高等教育财团——“国际交换学者奖学金项目”

成立于1974年的韩国高等教育财团是由韩国教育部许可并登记注册的非赢利性公益法人。该财团秉承促进学术发展的理念，对优秀人才给予资助和培养。国际交换学者奖学金项目作为该集团下设一子项目，主要面向亚洲学者，为申请成功者提供在韩开展研究的机会。该项目亦是中韩两国学者进行学术交流的一种有效途径。

近年来，中国学者申请该项目的人数呈现逐年增加的态势。申请者主要来自“211”院校。申请人首先要有两年以上的工作经历，持有博士学位，年龄在50岁以下。并且具备较高的学术水平和科研以及英语交流能力。学者研究领域涉及人文社会科学、石油化工、信息科学与技术、生命科学等诸多学科。

作为游学的保障，韩国高等教育财团为申请成功者提供每月220万韩币奖学金，一次性初始安置费100万韩币，以及往返国际机票、医疗保险和100万韩币的完成论文撰写奖励。

（三）留学生交流

早在唐朝，韩国便通过派遣遣唐使来中国学习古代优秀文化。近年来，随着中国经济实力的迅速提升，中韩两国经贸合作的日益紧密，韩国来华留学的留学生数量也呈现逐年递增的态势。目前在华留学生人数已达64000余人，位居在华外国留学生总数之首。在华毕业的博士总数

① 亚洲留学奖学金申请办法［EB/OL］. 国家留学网，2009-11-29，http://www.csc.edu.cn.

业已超过600人。[1] 中国已成为继美国之后韩国留学人员最为信赖的留学目的地国家。

与此同时，中国赴韩留学人数也有较快增长。2005年，我国赴韩留学人员仅为9378人。2008年，这一数字被迅速刷新，共有44746人选择赴韩留学，占在韩外国留学生总数的2/3。其中博士生1372人、硕士生4038人、本科生19914人，大专生9007人。[2] 2010年，赴韩留学人数更是创纪录地达到了63000余人，占在韩外国留学生总数的84%。[3] 单就数量而言，两国均已成为对方最大的外来留学生输入国。

两国高校间留学生的交流与培养，对于双方友好合作关系的延续及发展有着重要意义。但面对日益增加的留学生数量，如何构建高效的留学渠道和保证生源质量，已然成为摆在两国之间的重要课题。不过，现实告诉我们，随着两国留学生数量的不断增加，中韩两国在高等教育领域的合作将变得更加紧密。

（四）孔子学院与合作办学

改革开放不仅促进了中国经济的发展，同时也为汉语的推广提供了前所未有的机遇。随着整个华文世界活力的不断增强，汉语的实用价值逐步得到认同，初步获取了国际性语言的地位。作为中国的友好邻邦，韩国自古以来便深受中国文化的影响。其语言文字中仍保留有大量的汉字词汇。这种天时地利为韩国人学习汉语奠定了一定优势。2004年，我国为满足中韩经贸对汉语人才的需求以及来自韩国国内的汉语热，在首尔成立了全球第一家孔子学院。孔子学院主要采用中外合作办学的方式。中国国内的大学作为孔子学院的支持单位，主要为其提供教学资源。目前，我国在韩开设有12所孔子学院。

---

① 驻韩使馆教育处．中韩教育交流简介［EB/OL］．中华人民共和国驻大韩民国大使馆教育处网站，2010－10－14，http：//www. cscse. edu. cn.

② 驻韩使馆教育处．中韩教育交流简介［EB/OL］．中华人民共和国驻大韩民国大使馆教育处网站，2010－10－14，http：//www. cscse. edu. cn.

③ 金小彤．韩国吸引力持续增加，中国留学生超6万人［EB/OL］．求实潮教育网，2010－5－11，http：//www. qsc. zju. edu. cn.

除了创办孔子学院，中韩合作办学也日益增多。中韩两国的合作办学主要采取如下两种方式：一是独立设置的中韩合作办学机构；二是非独立设置的中韩合作办学机构。前者由中韩双方共同出资，具有法人资格和办学条件，独立承担办学责任。后者主要采取学校领导下的二级学院制，由高校与外方合作者共同创办，但不具有法人资格，具体由二级学院管理运作。①

孔子学院的建立和合作办学的蓬勃发展，都昭示着中韩两国高等教育的合作，已由初始时的简单交流访问，走向纵深发展阶段。

三、浙江大学实践纪要

浙江大学始终以创办世界一流大学为己任，一贯坚持走国际化发展的路线。近年来，浙江大学为推进东亚高等教育的交流合作，积极参与并组织各类论坛。如 2002 年 4 月，时任浙江大学校长的潘云鹤教授率中国大学校长代表团出席了中韩大学校长会议。来自中韩两国的 20 余所著名大学的校长和韩国教育部部长李相周、中国驻韩大使李滨等中韩教育界最高领导出席该届大会，并作了重要发言。潘云鹤校长关于《中国高水平大学面临 21 世纪的挑战与中韩合作》的发言在与会者中引起热烈反响。②

此外，浙江大学与韩国多所高校签订了校际合作协议。例如，1995 年，原浙江大学与高丽大学签订了校际协议，并于 2008 年重新签署了校际协议和学生交流备忘录。2007 年，浙江大学行政管理研究所与高丽大学政府研究所签署两所合作备忘录，就教师互换项目、研究生交换项目、合办国际会议等达成协议。2007—2008 年，两校联合主办了两届“中韩公共治理研究生学术论坛”。2009 年，浙江大学选派了 5 名本科生赴高

---

① 侯彦弘．关于中韩合作办学的几点思考［J］．华章，2007（5）：2.

② 浙江大学外事处．潘云鹤校长率中国大学校长代表团出席中韩大学校长会议［EB/OL］．浙江大学办公网，2002 - 5 - 2，http：//www.ir.zju.edu.cn.

丽大学留学一年。①

另外，浙江大学管理学院与延世大学商学院于2005年签订了两院合作协议，开展学生互换培养等工作。2006年，浙江大学与韩国庆熙大学合作，定期举行“韩中未来指导者”韩国留学生培训活动。截止到2009年12月，该项培训共举行了四届。参与该项活动的韩国留学生通过为期一个月的汉语强化学习，不仅提升了汉语水平，还增进了对中国的了解。

据浙江大学外事处统计，截止到2010年10月25日，浙江大学韩国留学生总数为1019人。其中学位生710人（博士生18人，硕士生41人，本科生651人），汉语语言生235人，专业进修生26人。对韩留学生教育正呈现蒸蒸日上的趋势。

四、中韩两国高等教育合作的未来发展趋势

科学技术的迅猛发展和经济往来的日益紧密为中韩两国高等教育的合作带来了前所未有的机遇。两国在高等教育领域的合作可以充分借助信息技术的发达，以及经济合作中的模式，不断尝试构建新的模式，以便将现有的成果推向更高的阶段。

（一）以信息技术为依托，实现资源共享

信息技术的快速发展，拉近了人与人之间的距离，地球俨然成为一个小村庄。便捷和高效的网络系统为中韩两国高等教育合作搭建了更为广泛的平台。中韩两国可依托网络实现远程教育，建立网上虚拟学校，通过网络组织教学，将更多的学生吸纳到国际教育之中。

另外，两国学者可以通过网络不定期地举行学术论坛，实现资源共享。具体可以建立网络资源库，将研究成果以论文的形式呈献给相关领域的学者，通过沟通，不断完善已有成果，并为进一步的合作建立良好的基础。

---

① 浙江大学外事处．杨卫校长访问日、韩高校并出席“浙江大学—富士电机创新中心”理事会年会［EB/OL］．浙江大学办公网，2010－4－23，http：//www.ir.zju.edu.cn.

（二）在“校园亚洲”构想下，实现深层次的合作

1999年6月，欧洲29个国家为消除区域内学生流动的障碍，提高欧洲高等教育的国际竞争力，在意大利博洛尼亚共同签署了《博洛尼亚宣言》。该宣言旨在到2010年时建立“欧洲高等教育区”，进而实现欧洲高等教育一体化的目标。

在欧洲高等教育改革的启示下，2010年4月16日，第一届中日韩大学间交流合作促进会议在日本东京举行。会议提出一个名为“校园亚洲”的构想，以推进中日韩大学间的交流与合作，并决定设置两个工作组就如何推进三国大学间的交流合作展开深入讨论。①

“校园亚洲”的愿景虽处于萌芽阶段，但该模式一旦确立，势必将大大推动中韩乃至整个东亚高等教育的合作。

① 王洋．中日韩三国提出“校园亚洲”构想推进大学交流［EB/OL］．大连天健网，2010－4－17，http：//news. runsky. com.

南开大学与东亚高校国际合作浅议

南开大学　关乃佳　李　莉

南开大学创建于1919年。在九十多年的发展历程中，学校始终坚持国际化、开放式办学方针，目前已与39个国家和地区的270多所高校和科研机构建立了学术交流与合作关系，涉及教师交流、学生交换、合作办学、合作科研项目等多个方面。其中，南开大学非常重视与东盟"10+6"框架下的各国高校及教育机构间的合作与交流，尤其因坐落于中国东部港口城市——天津——这一独特的地缘优势，东亚各国高校均成为我校的重要战略合作伙伴，往来合作十分密切。据统计，截至2009年12月，南开大学共与东亚和大洋洲的8个国家的98所高校（机构）签订交流协议112份，占学校全部交流协议的38%。

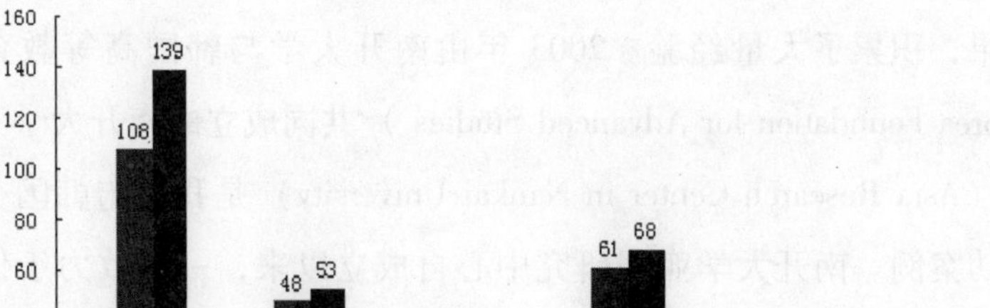

交流国家（地区）协议分布图

南开大学非常重视与日本高校的合作与交流，早在1980年就与日本爱知大学签订了交流协议，是中国最早与日本大学交流的单位之一。以

“全方位、多层次”为特点的南开—爱大合作模式，已成功进展多年，得到了教育部的肯定和兄弟院校及社会各界的广泛好评。目前，南开大学已经与日本包括早稻田大学、京都大学在内的37所知名高校和教育机构建立友好关系并签订了合作协议。

2006年2月，南开大学与日本爱知大学合作建立了爱知大学孔子学院，成为中日文化交流的又一良好平台。2009年10月，由中国教育部主办、南开大学承办的第六届中日大学校长论坛在南开大学举办，中日两国包括北京大学、清华大学、东京大学、早稻田大学等35所著名高校参加。在教育部有关领导和主管部门的有力指导下，在参加论坛各校的大力支持、配合下，论坛获得了圆满成功，取得了一系列重要成果，并有力推进了南开大学与日本一流大学的合作迈上新的台阶。

南开大学与韩国高校的交流历史久远，有着深厚的友谊基础与合作经验。迄今为止，南开大学已与韩国首尔大学、高丽大学、西江大学、庆北大学等30多所高校签订了合作交流协议，交流内容包括互换学者及留学生、合作研究、举办国际会议等多种形式。2009年在国家汉办的批准和支持下，南开大学与韩国济州汉拿大学签约共建了孔子学院，进一步发挥了我校作为汉语国际教育与传播基地的积极作用。

南开大学还注重与韩国企业以及科研机构的合作与交流，并取得了丰硕成果，积累了大量经验。2003年由南开大学与韩国高等教育财团（The Korea Foundation for Advanced Studies）共同成立的南开大学亚洲研究中心（Asia Research Center in Nankai University）是我校与韩国交流的一项成功案例。南开大学亚洲研究中心自成立以来，一直致力于促进学校在相关领域的学术研究及与兄弟院校的交流与合作，并为南开大学、为亚洲国家和地区的学术繁荣作出了重要贡献。

当然，除日本、韩国以外，南开大学重要的战略合作伙伴还涉及新加坡、澳大利亚、新西兰等国。其中我校与新加坡国立大学、南洋理工大学及新加坡管理大学均建立了良好的学术交流合作关系。今年3月，根据《中新优秀大学生交流项目谅解备忘录》中的中新大学生互换与交流计划，我校 11 名学生与国内其他 3 所高校学生组成第七届优秀大学生赴新加坡访问团，由教育部带队赴新加坡出访上述 3 所高校，不仅加强了我校学生与新加坡 3 所高校学生的交流，而且增进了中新两国青年的友谊，特别是加深了他们彼此的相互了解，密切了两国青年学生的友好往来。

澳大利亚也是我校交流的一个重点国家，我校与墨尔本大学自 1985 年就签订了交流协议，除了校际的学术合作，墨尔本的排球队 2009 年还应邀到南开参加比赛。澳大利亚国立大学 1981 年便与南开大学签订了学术交流协议，这些年双方互访交流也是非常密切，2009 年南开大学经济学院与澳大利亚国立大学克劳福德经济与政府学院签署了联合培养硕士的项目。南开大学还与悉尼大学、拉筹伯大学、莫纳什大学、弗林德斯大学建立了实质性的合作关系。

南开大学以她独特的魅力吸引了大批国外学生来此留学。2009 年南开大学累计接收长、短期留学生约 2400 人，其中由于南开大学与东亚高校、教育机构之间频繁的学术交流更是吸引了大量本地区的留学生。以 2010—2011 学年度我校来华留学生数目为例，来自东盟“10 + 6”国家的留学生人数就占据总数的 76% 之多，充分显示了我校与东亚地区高等教育机构交流与合作的广泛程度。

在看到我校与东亚地区高校国际交流与合作取得丰硕成果的同时，还应该清醒地看到所存在的问题：一是发展不平衡。我校与日本、韩国、新加坡、澳大利亚等国家交往频繁，但与菲律宾、越南等多数东南亚国家交往较少。二是一些国家来华留学人数偏少。中国赴澳大利亚、新西兰留学人数众多，而这两个国家来我校留学人数较少。

针对以上问题，我们认为，应该借助“东亚峰会高等教育合作论坛”这个平台，共同探讨东亚峰会框架下在高等教育领域的合作前景和有效途径，进一步增进东亚各国相互了解和友谊，推动区域间的教育交流与合作。为此，我们建议：

（1）要密切关注东亚高等教育的发展，树立真正的国际化意识。

现代大学只有加强同世界所有优秀大学的交流合作，才能真正拓宽师生的国际视野、提升办学的整体水平、扩大学校的世界影响，这是高校国际化发展的一个基本立足点。但是，当前一些人每说起高等教育的国际化，就倾向于只同欧美的大学进行交流合作，自觉不自觉地发生一种情感和选择上的偏向。

针对这种“西方中心主义”倾向，我们认为，国际化并不等于欧美化，国际化应该是全面的、多元的。从学科建设和师资队伍建设的角度来看，应该关注东亚、东南亚地区的高等教育，关注这一地区的高校发展，积极汲取经验、开展合作。对一所立志成为世界一流大学的高校而言，应该有一定数量的研究这些欧美之外的国家和地区的经济、历史、文化的学者，否则其国际学术交流和国际化就是不完整的。正因如此，南开大学在推进国际化过程中，强调既要学习欧美前沿的东西，还要全面了解世界，拥有真正国际化的视野和胸怀，与世界上包括东亚、东南亚等绝大多数国家和地区的名校建立实质性的联系。

（2）要使中国成为东亚最大留学目的地国。

落实温家宝总理在2009年第四届东亚峰会上提出“在未来5年内向东亚发展中国家成员新增2000个中国政府奖学金名额和200个公共管理硕士（MPA）奖学金名额”的承诺，积极实施好2020年东盟来华留学生和中国到东盟的留学生都达到10万人左右的“双十万计划”。我们要以更加开放、更加积极的姿态推动来华留学工作的快速发展。我们应该进一步完善来华留学管理制度，用英语讲授专业和相关课程，尽可能地吸引东亚地区的学生来华留学，使来华留学工作逐步成为中国对外开放的一面旗帜。

（3）开展学校间实质性的交流与合作。

第一，利用东盟“10+6”这一良好沟通框架在地理、传统得天独厚的优势条件下，共同开展形式多样、多层次的交流以及学者互访活动。第二，积极开展专业和科研领域的合作，如共建研究中心、合作举办国际会议等。第三，依托学校优势学科，共同展开合作项目，如共建孔子学院、开展语言培训项目等。第四，开展学生互换、学分互认、学生“2+2”、“3+2”项目。

第五部分　论坛成果

Section V: Achievements of the Forum

“东亚峰会高等教育合作论坛”会议纪要

2010年10月14～15日，由中国教育部和云南省政府主办，云南省教育厅和云南大学承办的“东亚峰会高等教育合作论坛”在昆明顺利召开并取得了圆满成功。本次论坛是落实2009年10月温家宝总理在“第四届东亚峰会”提出的倡议的具体行动，是首次在东亚峰会框架下搭建多边教育交流合作平台的新尝试。包括中国、文莱、柬埔寨、印度尼西亚、老挝、马来西亚、缅甸、菲律宾、新加坡、泰国、澳大利亚、印度、日本、韩国、新西兰在内的15个东亚峰会成员国的教育官员、大学校长、驻华使节等与会代表共150余人出席了论坛，共签署20份校际合作协议。

本次论坛旨在通过东亚峰会框架下各国政府部门和高等教育机构的参与，探索开展高等教育合作的重点领域和有效途径，推进东亚区域内高等教育合作行动框架与合作机制的构建。东亚峰会各成员国教育部官员和大学校长共同围绕“东亚峰会框架下的高等教育合作与发展”进行了专题发言和深入探讨，达成了六点共识：

（1）倡议搭建东亚峰会框架下教育交流与合作的稳定平台，完善交流与合作机制，加强教育高层对话，促进和推动东亚峰会各成员国在教育领域的合作。

（2）倡议建立东亚峰会框架下的大学校长机制化交流平台，加强高校间交流与互访，提高教育质量和现代化水平，联合培养硕士和博士，推动高校间实质性的人才培养和科研合作。

（3）倡议扩大开放，深化合作，相互增设奖学金，增加教育资源和受教育机会，加强区域经济发展和创新型人才培养，促进国际学生流动和高水平留学生教育的发展。

（4）倡议进一步推进东亚峰会各成员国之间的学历学位互认，高校间的学分转移和互认。尽力降低区域内国家之间学生流动的障碍，提高区域内高等教育在全世界范围内的吸引力。

（5）倡议各国政府加强在人力资源培训方面的合作，充分发挥各自比较优势，设置相应培训项目，促进人力资源素质的共同提高。

（6）倡议加强各成员国之间青年的人文交流活动，促进相互了解，深化传统友谊，夯实民意基础。

所有与会代表对中国政府首倡召开“东亚峰会高等教育合作论坛”表示赞赏，对主办方与承办方为组织和召开本次论坛所作的努力表示感谢。

2010 年 10 月　昆明

附件一："东亚峰会高等教育合作论坛"会议纪要（英文）

Co-hosted by the Ministry of Education of the People's Republic of China and the People's Government of Yunnan Province, the East Asia Summit Higher Education Cooperation Forum was jointly organized by Yunnan Provincial Department of Education and Yunnan University and held successfully from October 14 to 15, 2010 in Kunming. The Forum was a follow-up action to the proposal by Chinese Premier Wen Jiabao at the 4th East Asia Summit in 2009, as well as the first attempt on multilateral education exchanges and cooperation within the EAS framework. The Forum was attended by more than 150 participants from China, Brunei, Cambodia, Indonesia, Laos, Malaysia, Myanmar, the Philippines, Singapore, Thailand, Australia, India, Japan, Korea, and New Zealand. The participants included education officials, university presidents as well as diplomatic envoys to China from 15 member states of the EAS. During the Forum, 20 intercollegiate agreements have been inked.

With the participation of authorities and higher education institutions from the member states of the EAS, the Forum made an attempt to find priority areas and effective approaches to higher education cooperation and facilitate the establishment of a higher education action framework and cooperative mechanism in the region within the EAS framework. Education officials and university presidents from the member states of the EAS, focusing on the topic of "Higher Education Cooperation and Development within the East Asia Summit Framework", had intense discussions and finally agreed on six points of consensus as follows:

1. Establish a regular platform for education exchanges and cooperation within the EAS framework, better the mechanism for education exchanges and cooperation, strengthen high-ranking contacts of education and facilitate

education cooperation among the EAS members.

2. Establish an institutionalized platform within the EAS framework for dialogue and communication among university presidents so as to intensify exchanges and visits among colleges and universities. Improve and modernize quality education, and substantively facilitate personnel training and scientific research cooperation among higher education institutions by jointly cultivating masters and doctors.

3. Widen opening up and deepen cooperation by increasing scholarships and education resources and improving access to education. Strengthen regional economic development and the cultivation of creative talents, and facilitate the mobility of international students and the development of high-level international education.

4. Further the mutual recognition of academic degrees and qualifications, and credit transfer and mutual recognition of credits among higher education institutions within the member states of the EAS. Strive to reduce the barriers against the mobility of students among these countries and boost the appeal of the higher education of this region to the whole world.

5. Strengthen cooperation among relevant governments in human resources training for common progress in human resources quality improvement by complementing each other and establishing various training programs.

6. Enhance cultural exchanges among the youth within the member states of the EAS for a better mutual understanding, closer traditional friendship and stronger people-to-people communication.

All participants appreciated the ground-breaking initiative made by the Chinese government to hold this "East Asia Summit Higher Education Cooperation Forum" and thanked the hosts and organizers for their efforts in organizing and holding this forum.

Kunming, October 2010

附件二：各相关高校签署协议情况

中方大学	外方大学
北京师范大学	文莱大学（文莱）
哈尔滨工业大学	印度尼西亚大学（印度尼西亚）
	哈山诺丁大学（印度尼西亚）
扬州大学	文莱大学（文莱）
	印度尼西亚大学（印度尼西亚）
	旁遮普大学（印度）
内蒙古大学	文莱大学（文莱）
	旁遮普大学（印度）
昆明学院	印度尼西亚大学（印度尼西亚）
云南中医学院	宣素南塔皇家大学（泰国）
昆明理工大学	苏冯那翁大学（老挝）
	宣素南塔皇家大学（泰国）
云南师范大学	旁遮普大学（印度）
	苏冯那翁大学（老挝）
云南大学	文莱大学（文莱）
	清迈大学（泰国）
	南洋理工大学（新加坡）
	高丽大学（韩国）
	祥明大学（韩国）
	坎特伯雷大学（新西兰）

附件三：各相关高校签署协议情况（英文）

Chinese Universities	Foreign Universities
Beijing Normal University	Universiti Brunei Darussalam (Brunei)
Harbin Institute of Technology	Universitas Indonesia (Indonesia)
	Hasanuddin University (Indonesia)
Yangzhou University	Universiti Brunei Darussalam (Brunei)
	Universitas Indonesia (Indonesia)
	Panjab University, Chandigarh (India)
Inner Mongolia University	Universiti Brunei Darussalam (Brunei)
	Panjab University, Chandigarh (India)
Kunming College	Universitas Indonesia (Indonesia)
Yunnan College of Traditional Chinese Medicine	Suan Sunandha Rajabhat University (Thailand)
Kunming University of Science and Technology	Souphanouvong University (Laos)
	Suan Sunandha Rajabhat University (Thailand)
Yunnan Normal University	Panjab University, Chandigarh (India)
	Souphanouvong University (Laos)
Yunnan University	Universiti Brunei Darussalam (Brunei)
	Chiang Mai University (Thailand)
	Nanyang Technological University (Singapore)
	Korea University (South Korea)
	Sangmyung University (South Korea)
	University of Canterbury (New Zealand)

中国教育部国际合作与交流司副司长刘宝利宣读会议纪要

Mr. Liu Baoli, Deputy Director General, Department of International Cooperation and Exchanges, Ministry of Education of PRC, reading Minutes of the East Asia Summit Higher Education Cooperation Forum

“东亚峰会高等教育合作论坛”会场

Plenary Venue

“东亚峰会高等教育合作论坛”会场
Plenary Venue

参会代表
Participants at the forum

参会代表一对一交流
One-to-one Exchange Session

参会代表一对一交流
One-to-one Exchange Session

参会代表一对一交流
One-to-one Exchange Session

参会代表一对一交流
One-to-one Exchange Session

北京师范大学与文莱大学签署合作协议

Cooperation agreement signed between Beijing Normal University and Universiti Brunei Darussalam

哈尔滨工业大学与印度尼西亚大学签署合作协议

Cooperation agreement signed between Harbin Institute of Technology and Universitas Indonesia

哈尔滨工业大学与印度尼西亚哈山诺丁大学签署合作协议
Cooperation agreement signed between Harbin Institute of Technology and Hasanuddin University, Indonesia

内蒙古大学与印度旁遮普大学签署合作协议
Cooperation agreement signed between Inner Mongolia University and Panjab University, Chandigarh, India

内蒙古大学与文莱大学签署合作协议
Cooperation agreement signed between Inner Mongolia University and Universiti Brunei Darussalam

扬州大学与印度旁遮普大学签署合作协议
Cooperation agreement signed between Yangzhou University and Panjab University, Chandigarh, India

扬州大学与文莱大学签署合作协议
Cooperation agreement signed between Yangzhou University and Universiti Brunei Darussalam

云南大学与新加坡南洋理工大学签署合作协议
Cooperation agreement signed between Yunnan University and Nanyang Technological University, Singapore

云南大学与韩国高丽大学签署合作协议

Cooperation agreement signed between Yunnan University and Korea University

云南大学与韩国祥明大学签署合作协议

Cooperation agreement signed between Yunnan University and Sangmyung University, South Korea

云南大学与泰国清迈大学签署合作协议
Cooperation agreement signed between Yunnan University and Chiang Mai University, Thailand

云南大学与文莱大学签署合作协议
Cooperation agreement signed between Yunnan University and Universiti Brunei Darussalam

云南大学与新西兰坎特伯雷大学签署合作协议
Cooperation agreement signed between Yunnan University and University of Canterbury, New Zealand

云南师范大学与印度旁遮普大学签署合作协议
Cooperation agreement signed between Yunnan Normal University and Panjab University, Chandigarh, India

云南师范大学与老挝苏冯那翁大学签署合作协议
Cooperation agreement signed between Yunnan Normal University and Souphanouvong University, Laos

昆明学院与印度尼西亚大学签署合作协议
Cooperation agreement signed between Kunming College and Universitas Indonesia

昆明理工大学与老挝苏冯那翁大学签署合作协议
Cooperation agreement signed between Kunming University of Science and Technology and Souphanouvong University, Laos

昆明理工大学与泰国宣素南塔大学签署合作协议
Cooperation agreement signed between Kunming University of Science and Technology and Suan Sunandha Rajabhat University, Thailand

新加坡教育部高等教育司副司长林国伟接受媒体采访

Interview with Mr. Peter Lam Kok Wai, Deputy Director, Higher Education, Ministry of Education, Singapore

云南省教育厅厅长罗崇敏接受媒体采访

Interview with Mr. Luo Chongmin, Director-General, Yunnan Provincial Department of Education

云南大学校长何天淳接受媒体采访

Interview with Prof. He Tianchun, President, Yunnan University

"东亚峰会高等教育合作论坛"筹备组部分成员
Some Members of the Organizing Committee of the East Asia Summit Higher Education Forum

"东亚峰会高等教育合作论坛"部分工作人员合影
Some Organizing Committee Staff Members

第六部分　媒体报道

Seciont VI: Media Coverage of the Forum

云南举办“东亚峰会高等教育合作论坛”

“东亚峰会高等教育合作论坛”开幕

与会各国教育官员

10月14日上午，由中国教育部和云南省政府主办的“东亚峰会高等教育合作论坛”在昆明举行。

来自中国和文莱、柬埔寨、印度尼西亚、老挝、马来西亚、缅甸、菲律宾、新加坡、泰国、日本、韩国、澳大利亚、新西兰、印度的教育官员、大学校长、驻华使节以及云南省政府的有关领导等近一百五十人出席了论坛的开幕仪式。中央政治局委员、国务委员刘延东向论坛发来了贺信。

2009年10月，温家宝总理在“第四届东亚峰会”上倡议：召开“东亚峰会高等教育合作论坛”，促进各成员国在东亚峰会框架下，开展高等教育领域合作，推动各国的文化、教育交流，增进各国的友谊和团结。据云南省教育厅厅长罗崇敏介绍，本次论坛的主题是“东亚峰会框架下的高等教育合作”，与会的东亚各国政府教育官员及国内外40余所高校的代表，将探索开展高等教育合作的重点领域和有效途径，推进东亚区域内高等教育合作行动框架与合作机制的构建，开展务实合作，使高等教育合作真正成为推进东亚区域全面发展的重要动力。

罗崇敏说，云南省现已经有了东盟及澳大利亚多国的留学生，但是数量仍然有限，例如云南仅有300人在澳大利亚留学，而澳大利亚只有70多人在滇留学。他呼吁：各与会国加大互派留学生的数量。他承诺：云南将进一步提高到云南学习的留学生的奖学金金额，鼓励各国留学生赴滇学习。

云南与东盟各国地缘相近，文化多元，颇具相互交流的优势。罗崇敏倡议：今后每年定期在云南举办这样的论坛，建立中国与东盟、澳洲及其他亚洲国家大学教育交流合作的平台。

记者：吴家春，编辑：冯媛，《中国日报》2010年10月15日

“东亚峰会高等教育合作论坛”开幕

刘延东发来贺信

本报昆明10月14日讯　由教育部和云南省政府主办，云南省教育厅和云南大学承办的“东亚峰会高等教育合作论坛”今天在昆明隆重开幕，中共中央政治局委员、国务委员刘延东发来贺信。教育部副部长王立英，云南省委常委、副省长李江出席论坛开幕式并致辞。

“东亚峰会高等教育合作论坛”是由温家宝总理2009年10月在“第四届东亚峰会”上倡议召开的，是各成员国在东亚峰会框架下开展高等教育领域合作的首次尝试。主要目的是沟通交流各国在东亚峰会框架下开展教育交流与合作的政策性倾向与计划。本次论坛的主题是“东亚峰会框架下的高等教育合作”，与会代表将围绕这一主题深入讨论，通过东亚各国政府部门和大学的参与，论坛探索开展高等教育合作的重点领域和有效途径，推进东亚区域内高等教育合作行动框架和合作机制的构建。开展务实合作，使高等教育合作真正成为推进东亚区域全面发展的重要动力。

来自中国和文莱、柬埔寨、印度尼西亚、老挝、马来西亚、缅甸、菲律宾、新加坡、泰国、日本、韩国、澳大利亚、新西兰、印度的教育官员、大学校长、驻华使节以及云南省政府的有关领导150余人出席了开幕式。

记者：焦新，《中国教育报》2010年10月14日

“东亚峰会高等教育合作论坛”闭幕

通过《会议纪要》 签署20份校际合作协议

本报昆明10月15日讯　由教育部和云南省政府主办的“东亚峰会高等教育合作论坛”今天圆满闭幕。经过认真讨论和协商，论坛通过了《东亚峰会高等教育合作论坛会议纪要》，记录与会代表所达成的共识；与会院校代表共签署20份校际合作协议。

在为期两天的会议过程中，东亚峰会框架下的各国与会代表就“东亚峰会框架下的高等教育合作”展开广泛、热烈的讨论，就一系列实质性问题提出了创新性的建议。闭幕式当天，全体与会代表通过了本次论坛的会议纪要，并在完善交流与合作机制、联合培养硕士和博士、增设奖学金、推动学历学位互认、高校间的学分转移和互认等方面达成了六点重要共识。会议纪要纪要指出，作为东亚峰会的一项重要后续行动，本次论坛的任务是在东亚峰会的框架下，通过各国政府部门和高等教育机构的参与，探索开展高等教育合作的重要领域和有效途径，推进东亚区域内高等教育合作行动框架与合作机制的构建。

本次论坛系东亚峰会框架下高等教育领域合作的首次尝试，充分显示了东亚峰会各成员国希望在此领域开展全面合作的强烈愿望。

记者：焦新，《中国教育报》2010年10月16日

东亚峰会成员国
20 所高校签署合作备忘录

中新社昆明（2010 年）10 月 15 日电　正在此间举行的“东亚峰会高等教育合作论坛”上，来自中国、文莱、印尼、泰国、印度、新加坡、韩国、新西兰等 15 个东亚峰会成员国的 20 所高校签署了 20 份合作备忘录，以便更加务实地推动区域内各成员国间的高等教育合作。

据了解，此次签署的 20 份校际合作备忘录均为框架性协议，内容主要涉及互派留学生、教师交流与培训、组织学术研讨、共享教育资源和办学经验、加强学生体育和文化交流等方面，具体合作项目将由签署协议高校的相关院系进行商谈。

中国北京师范大学校长钟秉林表示，东亚各国地域相连、文化相异、诉求相近，高等教育合作不但可以推动教育的共同发展，还将提升整个区域的竞争力。东亚峰会各成员国对此也已经达成共识。目前，教育交流已成为东亚峰会成员国之间最活跃的合作领域之一。

据中国教育部国际合作与交流司司长张秀琴介绍，近年来，中国十分重视与东亚各国的高等教育合作：建立东盟教育委员会；与菲律宾、泰国、越南、韩国、日本等国签署互认学历学位协议；在东亚峰会成员国中建立 81 所孔子学院和孔子课堂；互派留学生数量急剧增加；举办中国—东盟青少年夏令营等活动，为增进青少年友谊创造条件。

“东亚峰会高等教育合作论坛”期间，各国的政府官员及大学校长纷纷提出具体建议，希望加强教育高层的对话，建立东亚峰会框架下的大学校长机制化交流平台，加强高校间交流与互访，联合培养硕士和博士，相互增设奖学金，学历学位互认等，减少教育合作交流过程中的障碍。

记者：张丹，编辑：杨晶，中新云南新闻网 2010 年 10 月 15 日

印度学者称中印高等教育合作将惠及整个亚洲

中新网昆明（2010 年）10 月 14 日电　印度旁遮普大学校长琅勃·钱德尔·索博蒂 14 日在此间召开的“东亚峰会高等教育合作论坛”上表示，中国与印度高等教育互补性强，两国应加强合作，造福整个亚洲地区。

琅勃指出，中印高等教育有许多共同点。例如中印两国同属人口大国，都需要高等教育来创造更多的教育机会，促进国家的发展；高校都已以公立为主，有多部门监管确保教育质量；两国都十分重视对女性的教育，许多政府重要职务都由女性担任；目前两国高校都致力于进一步提高入学率和教育质量，教育投入不断增加。这些共识都为两国的高等教育合作奠定了基础。

“中印两国的经济和科技水平处于同一阶段，但产业结构却各具特色。”琅勃说，中国制造业占国民经济的 54%，且工业制成品大量出口，被誉为“世界工厂”。而印度则靠服务业撑起了整个经济的半壁江山，特别是在信息技术服务领域，因此被称为“世界办公室”。“这种产业差异恰好反映了双方在教育方面的互补性。”琅勃建议，中印两国应面对本国的现代化需要，利用双方的地缘优势，加强高等教育合作。

“作为当今世界发展最快的两个新兴经济体和人口大国，中印两国的高等教育合作已经超越了双边范畴。”琅勃用一加一大于二来形容中印两国教育合作的深远影响，“不仅造福两国 24 亿人口，还将惠及亚洲和世界”。

“今年是中印建交60周年，两国的教育合作迎来了更好的发展时机。”云南省教育厅厅长罗崇敏表示，云南作为中国通往印度的门户，下一步，云南省将会加大与印度互派留学生、科研技术合作、教师交流培训、汉语推广的力度，以进一步推进教育合作。

记者：张丹，中国新闻网2010年10月14日

“东亚峰会高等教育合作论坛”在云南昆明开幕

国际在线消息　由中国教育部和云南省政府主办的“东亚峰会高等教育合作论坛”14日在昆明开幕。

来自中国、文莱、柬埔寨等10多个国家的教育官员、大学校长、驻华使节出席大会，论坛期间，与会代表将围绕“东亚峰会框架下的高等教育合作”这一主题进行深入讨论。

“东亚峰会高等教育合作论坛”是由中国总理温家宝2009年10月在“第四届东亚峰会”上倡议召开的。主要目的是沟通交流各国在东亚峰会框架下开展教育交流与合作的政策性倾向与计划。

据介绍，通过东亚各国政府部门和大学的参与，论坛将探索开展高等教育合作的重点领域和有效途径，推进东亚区域内高等教育合作行动框架与合作机制的构建，开展务实合作，使高等教育合作真正成为推进东亚区域全面发展的重要动力。

驻云南记者：贾宜超，编辑：沈湜，国际在线专稿2010年10月14日

东亚 15 国在昆明探讨国际高等教育合作

【解说】14 日，在云南昆明召开的“东亚峰会高等教育合作论坛”上，来自中国、澳大利亚、马来西亚、韩国等 15 个国家的教育官员共同探讨区域内国际高等教育合作的前景和途径。

14 日下午，“东亚峰会高等教育合作论坛”进入各国教育官员交流发言单元，15 国教育部门高层官员依次围绕本国的高等教育现状和国际合作展望发表讲话。新加坡教育部高等教育司副司长林国伟在会议上带来了新加坡高等教育管理和海外学术交流经验，他同时希望能再借鉴别国更多的先进教育管理经验。

【同期】新加坡教育部高等教育司副司长林国伟：

“我认为非常有必要建立一个（教育）网络系统，这能让东亚区域里的其他政府也能参与进来。”

【解说】论坛上，各国官员围绕“增加教育经费”、“全球化教学”、“全球流动性学校”等主题进行了深入探讨发言，并在互派留学生规模、高端人才交流培养、学术交流、科研合作、语言、文化和体育交流等具体问题上发表了观点。

据了解，本次论坛旨在东亚峰会框架下拓展各成员国之间开展多边合作对话的有效平台，加强教育高层对话，共同研究积极推动中国与东亚峰会成员国教育的战略性合作。

新华社记者何春好、王姗（实习）昆明报道。

新华网云南频道（http：//www. yn. xinhua. net. com）2010 年 10 月 15 日

东亚峰会成员国共商高等教育合作与发展之路

新华网云南频道10月15日电 “东亚峰会高等教育合作论坛”14日在昆明举行，在东亚峰会框架下各成员国共商高等教育合作与发展之路。

“东亚峰会高等教育合作论坛”是由中国总理温家宝于2009年10月在“第四届东亚峰会”上倡议召开的，其主要目的是沟通交流各国在东亚峰会框架下开展教育交流与合作的政策性倾向与计划。

此次论坛由中国教育部和云南省人民政府主办，东亚峰会成员国的政府教育部门官员和60多所大学负责人参加论坛。

教育部副部长王立英在论坛上说，中国政府愿意与东亚峰会各成员国在高等教育领域共同开创新理念，迎接新挑战，共同探索合作共赢之路。她倡议，完善交流合作机制，加强教育高层对话，共同研究积极推动中国与东亚峰会各成员国教育领域的战略性合作；进一步扩大东亚峰会各成员国之间互派留学生规模，大力推动重点实施高端人才的交流培养；进一步推进东亚峰会各成员国高校间的学分转移和互认，增进学术交流与科研合作，鼓励中国与东亚峰会各成员国大学建立全面、务实的教育合作关系；进一步加强青年学生之间的语言、文化和体育交流。

澳大利亚教育、就业和劳资关系部副部长凯瑟琳·坎贝尔说，最近20年东亚峰会成员国高等教育发展迅速，规模不断扩大，相互间加强高等教育的交流合作，有利于增强各国人民的相互了解，对于共同迎接全球化挑战非常重要。

印度旁遮普大学琅勃·钱德尔·索博蒂校长说，高等教育在各国经济社会发展中的作用显著，各国加强高等教育交流合作需满足不同文化背景的人的教育需求，树立全球教育观，提升受教育者的竞争力。

记者：杨跃萍，李怀岩，新华网云南省频道（http：//www. yn. xinhua. net. com）

“东亚峰会高等教育合作论坛”将在昆举行

本报讯　由中国教育部和云南省政府主办、云南省教育厅和云南大学承办的“东亚峰会高等教育合作论坛”将于10月14日在昆明隆重开幕。

论坛是由温家宝总理2009年10月在“第四届东亚峰会”上倡议召开的，是各成员国在东亚峰会框架下开展高等教育领域合作的首次尝试，主要目的是沟通交流各国在东亚峰会框架下开展教育交流与合作的政策性倾向与计划。本次论坛的主题是“东亚峰会框架下的高等教育合作”，与会代表将围绕这一主题分两个单元进行讨论。通过东亚各国政府部门和高等教育机构的参与，探索开展高等教育合作的重点领域和有效途径，推进东亚区域内高等教育合作行动框架与合作机制的构建，开展务实合作，使高等教育合作真正成为推进东亚区域全面发展的重要动力。

中国和文莱、柬埔寨、印度尼西亚、老挝、马来西亚、菲律宾、新加坡、泰国、日本、韩国、澳大利亚、新西兰、印度的教育官员、大学校长、驻华使节以及云南省政府的有关领导等150人将出席论坛。

记者：罗霞，杨凡，《云南日报》2010年10月13日

推进东亚区域高等教育合作

“东亚峰会高等教育合作论坛”在昆开幕 刘延东致信祝贺

本报讯　昨日，一曲由云南艺术学院文华学院师生演奏的中国经典民乐《喜洋洋》，拉开了“东亚峰会高等教育合作论坛”的序幕。论坛由教育部和云南省政府主办，云南省教育厅和云南大学承办，将探索东亚峰会成员国之间开展高等教育合作的重点领域和有效途径，推进东亚区域内高等教育合作行动框架和合作机制的构建。中共中央政治局委员、国务委员刘延东发来贺信。贺信说，东亚是世界经济发展最具活力和潜力的地区之一，随着东亚地区经济一体化进程的加快，东亚各国的联系进一步得到加强，教育交流已经成为成员国之间最活跃的合作领域之一。借助“东亚峰会高等教育合作论坛”这一平台，共同探讨东亚峰会框架下在高等教育领域的合作前景和有效途径，必将增进东亚各国的相互了解和友谊，推动区域间的教育交流与合作。希望充分利用本次论坛，广泛沟通交流，深化合作内涵，努力开创携手共进、互利共赢的新局面。

教育部副部长王立英，云南省委常委、副省长李江，省政协副主席罗黎辉出席论坛。

王立英对论坛提出四点倡议，一是希望论坛成为开展多边合作对话的有效平台，共同研究、积极推动中国与东亚峰会各成员国教育的战略性合作；二是进一步扩大互派留学生规模，大力推动、重点实施高端人才的交流培养；三是进一步推进高校间的学分转移和互认，增进学术交流与科研合作；四是进一步加强青年学生之间的语言、文化和体育交流，以增进相互理解，为本地区乃至全世界的和平与发展作出积极贡献。

李江在致辞中指出，目前，云南高校已与50个国家、地区和国际组织建立了教育合作关系，在滇留学生达到1.5万人，其中60%来自东盟国家，云南已成为中国吸纳东盟国家留学生最多的地区。同时，云南在国外已建立7所孔子学院（课堂），省内高校普遍开设有东南亚语种专业课程，在学人数超过1万人。此次“东亚峰会高等教育合作论坛”在云南成功举办，既是落实东亚领导人峰会倡议的一项重要举措，也是促进东亚峰会成员国之间教育合作交流的重要途径，必将在更加广阔的区域范围内促进教育互补协作、资源共享，推动教育事业不断向前发展。

“东亚峰会高等教育合作论坛”是由温家宝总理2009年10月在“第四届东亚峰会”上倡议召开的，是各成员国在东亚峰会框架下开展高等教育领域合作的首次尝试。论坛通过东亚各国政府部门和高等教育机构的参与，推进务实合作，使高等教育合作真正成为推进东亚区域全面发展的重要动力。国内外有关高校将在本次论坛充分交流的基础上，签署校际合作协议。

来自中国和文莱、柬埔寨、印度尼西亚、老挝、马来西亚、缅甸、菲律宾、新加坡、泰国、日本、韩国、澳大利亚、新西兰、印度等15个东亚峰会成员国的教育官员、驻华使馆代表，国内外60余所大学校长出席开幕式。

记者：罗霞，陈云芬，罗容婵，《云南日报》2010年10月15日

“东亚峰会高等教育合作论坛”闭幕

达成6项共识
签署20份校际合作协议

本报讯　昨日，为期两天的“东亚峰会高等教育合作论坛”在昆明闭幕。论坛围绕东亚峰会框架下的高等教育合作与发展达成6项共识，与会高校签署了20份校际合作协议。

论坛期间，与会10余个国家的教育部官员和驻华使节相继发言，对在东亚峰会框架下加强高等教育合作表达了强烈的愿望。与会高校的校长分别介绍了各校办学情况，并就高等教育如何适应经济全球化发展、如何提高办学水平等进行了广泛交流。论坛通过了《东亚峰会高等教育合作论坛会议纪要》，达成6点共识：搭建东亚峰会框架下教育交流与合作的稳定平台，完善交流与合作机制，加强教育高层对话，推动东亚峰会各成员国在教育领域进一步开展合作，建立东亚峰会框架下的大学校长机制化交流平台，加强高校间的交流与互访，提高教育质量和现代化水平，联合培养硕士和博士，推动高校间实质性的人才培养和科研合作，深化合作，相互增设奖学金，增加教育资源和受教育机会，加强区域经济发展和创新型人才培养，促进国际学生流动和高水平留学生教育发展；进一步推进东亚峰会各成员国之间的学历学位互认、高校间的学分转移和互认，提高区域内高等教育在全世界范围内的吸引力；各国政府加强在人力资源培训方面的合作，促进人力资源素质共同提高；加强各成员国青年之间的人文交流活动，深化传统友谊，夯实民意基础。

论坛期间，经过协商，与会高校签署了20份校际合作协议，涵盖教学、科研、师生互换交流等方面。其中，云南大学与文莱、韩国等国院校签订了6份校际合作协议。

省政协副主席罗黎辉出席论坛闭幕式。

记者：罗霞，罗蓉婵，陈云芬，《云南日报》2010年10月16日

“东亚峰会高等教育合作论坛”昨闭幕

韩国校长想与云南校长互换

本报讯　为期两天的“东亚峰会高等教育合作论坛”昨日在昆闭幕，与会代表就各国的教育交流合作达成一致共识，充分显示出在高等教育领域展开全面合作的强烈愿望。其中，仅云南大学，就与新加坡南洋理工大学、新西兰坎特伯雷大学等6所国外高校签署校际合作协议。

新形势：建议校长互取经验

“我们第一次是和北京的大学校长进行了互换，大家希望的话即刻跟我的大学进行互换，我们在各自的大学待上两三天，我们可以进行这样的互换。”

在东亚峰会高等教育合作论坛大学校长的自由发言中，韩国高丽大学副校长南尚九介绍，除了留学生互派、加强科研合作之外，高丽大学还有一个大学校长互换的交流项目，他也希望有更多高校校长可以参与到这个项目中来，相互学习各自先进的教学管理经验。

新问题：留学生就业成本较高

北京师范大学校长钟秉林认为，高等教育为推动各国教育发展作出了巨大的贡献，提高留学生就业的机会，在留学生求职的过程中还存在着信息量小、成本较高、工作量大等方面的问题。钟秉林提议，社会、政府、用人单位应该为留学生就业搭建平台。在给留学生带来巨大就业挑战的基础上，创造大量的就业机会。设立创业竞赛、政策法规、求职策略等栏目，满足留学生用人单位的个性化发展。鼓励各国政府通过倡导等方式，在留学生留学各国专设秘书处协调好留学生就业工作。

新成果：滇高校签署12份协议

论坛上，来自各个国家的大学校长纷纷忙着推介各自学校，意图寻求更多的合作机会。最终，他们也换来了20份校际合作协议的签署。

其中，涉及我省高校的合作协议共有12份。云南大学与新加坡南洋理工大学、新西兰坎特伯雷大学、韩国高丽大学、韩国祥明大学、泰国清迈大学、文莱大学6所国外高校签署了校际合作协议，数量居全省高校之首。此外，云南师范大学、昆明理工大学、昆明学院、云南中医学院也分别与1至2所海外高校达成合作协议。

记者：刘超，实习生：孙琴霞，《春城晚报》2010年10月16日

后记

“东亚峰会高等教育合作论坛”是温家宝总理在2009年10月召开的“第四届东亚峰会”上倡议召开的，目的是沟通交流各国在东亚峰会框架下开展高等教育交流与合作的政策性倾向与计划。本论坛于2010年10月14～15日在美丽的春城——昆明召开，有来自15个东亚峰会成员国的教育官员、大学校长和驻华使领馆官员等共150余人出席论坛。参加论坛的高校总数达40余所。中华人民共和国国务委员刘延东专门为本次论坛发来了贺信。

在“东亚峰会高等教育合作论坛”的筹备阶段，主办方教育部及承办方云南大学就酝酿出版一本关于开展东亚峰会框架下的高等教育交流与合作的论文集，同时将此次论坛打造成为一个精品并使之机制化。为了让沟通与交流真正落到实处，并且让东亚地区高等教育界的各位有识之士共享论坛参会代表的百家之言，我们特意收集了参会代表的发言稿和部分参会代表专门为本次论坛撰写的学术论文。

教育部对本次论坛的成功举办给予了充分肯定，并对本书的出版给予了大力支持，郝平副部长亲自为本书撰写了序言。全书共分为六个部分，即开幕式领导致辞、教育官员发言、大学校长发言、专题论文、论坛成果和媒体报道。编者根据每位参会代表发言的内容和所要表达的主旨思想，为每篇发言稿加上了标题以飨读者。

在此，谨向参会代表及社会各界人士为本次论坛的成功举办和本书的出版给予的支持表示衷心的感谢。同时对本书的每位编译人员致以诚挚的谢意，感谢他们在承担各自的本职工作之余为本书倾注的大量心血。谢谢！

Afterword

The East Asia Higher Education Cooperation Forum was a follow-up action to the proposal by Chinese Premier Wen Jiabao at the 4th East Asia Summit in October, 2009, which aimed to communicate and exchange the policy of educational potential and planning among the East Asian countries within the East Asia Summit framework. The Forum was held from October 14 – 15th, 2010 in Kunming, the Spring City of China. In total, over 150 participants from 15 East Asia Summit members, including educational officials, university rectors from 40 higher education institutions as well as diplomatic envoys attended this forum. Moreover, the State Councilor of PRC, Madam Liu Yandong particularly sent a congratulation letter to this forum.

The Ministry of Education of China and Yunnan University had planned to compile a symposium on higher education cooperation and exchange within the East Asia Summit framework in order to hold a regularly competitive and mechanized forum during the preparation phase. With the purposes of carrying out the communication and exchanges in practice, sharing points of view from the participants with readers with foresight among the higher education field in East Asia, we collected some speeches, academic theses written for this forum from the participants.

The Ministry of Education of China not only highly appreciated conduction of this forum, but also strongly supported this symposium, Vice Minister Hao Ping has written the preface for it. The book consists of six parts as follows:

remarks from high-ranking officials & university rectors on the opening ceremony, speeches of educational officials, speeches of some university rectors, theses, minutes of the forum and reports from the media. To facilitate understanding, the editors concluded titles for some speeches to correspond to the expressed contents and main idea.

Hereby, we take this opportunity to thank all the participants for attending the Forum and contributing to the publication of this book. Meanwhile, we must thank our editors and translators for their hard work and efforts.

